C. S. LEWIS

LATTER-DAY TRUTHS IN NARNIA

C. S. LEWIS

LATTER-DAY TRUTHS IN NARNIA

Marianna Edwards Richardson
and
Christine Edwards Thackeray

CFI
Springville, Utah

ISBN 13: 978-1-59955-193-7

Published by CFI, an imprint of Cedar Fort, Inc., 2373 W. 700 S., Springville, UT 84663
Distributed by Cedar Fort, Inc., www.cedarfort.com

LIBRARY OF CONGRESS CATALOGING-IN-PUBLICATION DATA
Richardson, Marianna Edwards.
  Latter-day truths in Narnia Dr. Marianna Edwards Richardson and Christine Edwards Thackeray.
    p. cm.
  Includes bibliographical references.
  ISBN 978-1-59955-193-7 (acid-free paper)
  1. Lewis, C. S. (Clive Staples), 1898-1963. 2. Christianity and literature. I. Thackeray, Christine. II. Title.

  PR6023.E926Z857 2008
  823'.912--dc22
  [B]

                    2008022881

Cover design by Angela Olsen
Cover design © 2008 by Lyle Mortimer
Edited and typeset by Melissa J. Caldwell

Printed in the United States of America

10 9 8 7 6 5 4 3 2 1

Printed on acid-free paper

To our sweet and patient husbands, Greg and Steve, who have supported us through this journey to Narnia and back again. We appreciate their love and understanding for our never-ending projects and ideas. They inspire us and keep us going in the right direction. Love you more!

Other books in Spiritual Context—LDS Perspectives

Alfred Edersheim—A Jewish Scholar for the Mormon Prophets

Contents

Contents

PREFACE

y love story for C. S. Lewis is an oft-told tale of a mother reading *The Lion, the Witch and the Wardrobe* to her child as she drifts off to sleep. More recently, I remember having the Narnia books read out loud during lunchtime at the university where I work. It was endearing to hear professors laugh at the same lines I had enjoyed so many years earlier. Lewis's children's books have a forever quality to them that encourage their reading at any age.

While reading his fiction and nonfiction works, I have been amazed at his glad-hearted views of deep and soul-wrenching concepts. Lewis did have experiences with grief, pain, and failure. He understood the frustrations of this world, yet he was not marred by them. Instead, he sought deeper spiritual insights from such hard-won battles. He realized that life is more than what we see and deeper than what we feel. There is another dimension to life that is, in some ways, inexpressible. So Lewis chose to express them, using creatures not of this world, such as talking lions, apprenticing devils, and ethereal Martians.

One aspect of his writings that has touched me deeply is his concept of joy. For young Lewis, this feeling of joy took on different forms. He found joy in the green hills of Castlereagh, a flowering currant bush, the presence of autumn in a children's book, and his brother's toy garden. Later, he would find joy in literature, Norse myths, friendship, his Christian beliefs, and finally, marriage to Joy Davidman.

Unfortunately, this joy was short-lived time and time again during his mortal life. At the young age of eight, his mother died of cancer. His wife was also taken by cancer quickly after their short, but happy marriage. He definitely knew the bitter side of life, but never forgot the sweet desire to feel joy. This consistent underlying theme in Lewis's writings, his undeviating desire to return to the eternal joy and love and beauty found only in and through our Lord, Jesus Christ, awakens in my own heart a similar desire. It is one of the reasons I believe he is loved by so many. Because his writings awaken in the reader this same sweet desire to feel eternal joy, I have personally felt a sweet joy while undertaking this project as I have read and reread his words.

I also want to thank my sister, Christine Thackeray, for becoming my writing partner on this book and future projects. It has been especially enjoyable to create this book with her. Our relationship has reminded me of the loving and caring relationship Lewis had with his brother, Warren. Christine has a fresh and vivid perception of things. I feel like I am racing to keep up with her. I have intensely treasured our discussions on Lewis and his works. It has sharpened my thoughts and writing. Life is always more fun when we share it with others, and this part of my life has been made particularly pleasant with my sister as my writing companion.

Marianna Richardson

CHAPTER ONE

The Joy of C. S. Lewis

nce there was a four-year-old boy who had a dog named Jacksie that he loved with all his heart. One day Jacksie was struck by a car and killed. The young boy was devastated. After thinking about it, he stomped out of his bedroom and announced to his family that he had decided to change his name to Jacksie and would answer to nothing else. No matter how his parents protested, the child held fast to his conviction and, sure enough, his parents started calling him Jacksie. Over time it was shortened to Jacks and finally Jack, which was the name his friends called him for the rest of his life.[1]

That boy was C. S. Lewis, who grew up to be an accomplished scholar, writer, and Christian apologist.[2] Jack's incredible insight and wonderful stories have long been a favorite of the LDS community and have been referenced thousands of times throughout LDS writing. Even Shakespeare pales in comparison to the number of times C. S. Lewis has been quoted by Mormon authors, scholars, and General Authorities to illustrate or emphasize doctrinal truths.[3]

The diabolical techniques of the devil as portrayed in *Screwtape Letters* have graced our pulpits and lessons. The concept of being a "living house" in need of serious and painful renovation reappears at consistent intervals in Church instruction. Most recently, the wonderfully allegorical *Chronicles of Narnia* have been remade for our children to enjoy in brilliant color and advanced technology on the silver screen, giving parents a forum to discuss such topics as repentance, the Atonement, and true love through the metaphor of a lion named Aslan.

In addition to his stories, Lewis has a knack for using common situations that we can relate to and apply in our lives. He speaks of making math errors, being busy, falling down, and making room in our overstuffed lives for the gospel. Some of these familiar nuggets include:

- "A sum can be put right: but only by going back till you find the error and working it afresh from that point, never by simply going on."[4]

- "Christ says, 'Give me All. I don't want so much of your time and so much of your money and so much of your work: I want You.' "[5]

- "No amount of falls will really undo us if we keep picking ourselves up each time."[6]

- "The more often he feels without acting, the less he will be able ever to act, and, in the long run, the less he will be able to feel."[7]

- "God wants to give us something, but cannot, because our hands are full—there's nowhere for Him to put it."[8]

- "The love of our neighbor is the only door out of the dungeon of self."[9]

- "The great thing, if one can, is to stop regarding all the unpleasant things as interruptions of one's 'own,' or 'real' life. The truth is of course that what one calls the interruptions are precisely one's real life—the life God is sending one day by day."[10]

YOUR TEACHING MUST WEAR A MODERN DRESS

C. S. Lewis has a unique way of touching our hearts and opening our eyes. He is able to take complex ideas and illustrate them through simple and direct means. He explained that in order to have the greatest impact, "your teaching must be timeless and wear a modern dress."[11] It is precisely this type of physical metaphor that makes Lewis so easy to use in conjunction with other instruction; his words are like an illustration or written visual aid, clarifying difficult doctrinal concepts.

Other metaphors used by Lewis include:

- "This world is a great sculptor's shop. We are the statues and there is a rumour going round the shop that some of us are some day going to come to life."[12]

- "Indeed, the safest road to Hell is the gradual one—the gentle slope, soft underfoot, without sudden turnings, without milestones, without signposts."[13]

- "A silly idea is current that good people do not know what temptation means. This is an obvious lie. Only those who try to resist temptation know how strong it is. . . . You find out the strength of a wind by trying to walk against it, not by lying down."[14]

- "Our Father [in Heaven] refreshes us on the journey [through life] with some pleasant inns, but [he] will not encourage us to mistake them for home."[15]

During World War II, the British people were struggling with the ravages of war. The BBC decided to produce a series of lectures on Christianity to attempt to lift their nation. C. S. Lewis was invited to host these lectures because he was not of the clergy. The small audience grew with every broadcast and these lectures were later compiled into what became the book *Mere Christianity*. It was Lewis's concerted effort to speak to the common man, in terms he could understand, that greatly increased his following. He often used examples from his own life and conversion to Christianity or personal discoveries as he strived to live what he knew to be true.

LEWIS'S CONVERSION AND BEING SURPRISED BY JOY

Although raised in the Church of Ireland, C. S. Lewis stopped attending as a youth and by the time he entered Oxford decided he did not believe in God at all. But the Lord would not leave him alone. J. R. R. Tolkien, Charles Williams, Owen Barfield, the writings of George MacDonald, and so many others touched him deeply until he was ready to open a door and let in the truth. Lewis titled the book detailing his conversion *Surprised by Joy*. From that time forward, joy became a consistent quest in his life while continuing to search for truth. What Lewis finally realized was "God cannot give us a happiness and peace apart from Himself, because it is not there."[16]

After his conversion to Christianity, Lewis felt a great responsibility to share what he believed. When *Screwtape Letters* became an international bestseller, Lewis was flooded with correspondence from people with personal problems or who were working out their own faith. For hours each day, he painstakingly answered each letter personally for almost twenty years. Many of those letters have been published after his death.

It is in one of these letters that we find a clue to Lewis's feelings about The Church of Jesus Christ of Latter-day Saints. Officially, there is no record that Lewis had any contact with the Church but he did correspond regularly with a woman who lived in Salt Lake City. Although we do not have the original letter, Lewis's reply to her inquiry was as follows, "I am afraid I am not going to be much help about all the religious bodies mentioned in your letter of March 2nd. I have always in my books been concerned simply to put forward 'mere' Christianity, and am no guide on these (most regrettable) 'interdenominational' questions. I do however strongly object to the tyrannic and unscriptural insolence of anything that calls itself a Church and makes teetotalism a condition of membership."[17]

In all fairness, we do not have Lewis's complete thoughts on the subject. He was far more concerned with an individual's faith in Christ than in any specific denomination. But in the original preface to *Screwtape Letters,* Lewis shows his humility and willingness to learn. When he was speculating on the doctrine of angels and devils, he wrote, "I believe this not in the sense that it is part of my creed, but in the sense that it is one of my opinions. My religion would not be in ruins if this opinion were shown to be false."[18]

Lewis did not have the fulness of the gospel in this life. Yet, he did understand great truths and had an incredible ability to clearly convey the principles which he knew to be true. Our common ground includes (1) our shared belief in Christ, (2) our individual challenge to achieve the best within us despite our weaknesses, and (3) our hope for eternal joy in the world to come, in which we revel in his brilliance.

LEWIS AMONG THE SAINTS

As mentioned before, C. S. Lewis has been quoted extensively throughout Church writings. Specifically he has been referenced about one hundred times in Church-sponsored publications, one-third of those being in general conference addresses. It is important to note the use of C. S. Lewis's words by General Authorities does not mean that his faith has in any way dictated or determined LDS belief. These references from Lewis's works have been used to underscore eternal truths, not to determine them.

As Moroni taught: "Wherefore, every thing which inviteth and enticeth to do good, and to love God, and to serve him, is inspired of God" (Moroni 7:13). Latter-day Saint prophets and scholars give additional knowledge and understanding to Lewis's insights in order to fully express the restored view of the gospel of Jesus Christ, which C. S. Lewis did not have.

William Clayton Kimball has written a most thoughtful article about Lewis and Mormonism in which he commented, "A critical reader can find many points of doctrine wherein he differs from us. But we must not hold Lewis guilty for not having the insights that come from modern Revelation, and these differences in doctrine do not diminish his power as an articulate ally in the cause of Christian decency. We sometimes forget that there are pearls of great price not produced in our own oyster beds."[19]

Two Great Pearls

Two examples come immediately to mind of pearls given to us by Lewis. The first is Lewis's thoughts on discipleship. Neal A. Maxwell was a clear admirer of the Christian apologist, frequently quoting him in his private publications. He was the first to reference Lewis's words in a church publication. On the one hundredth anniversary of Lewis's birth, Elder Maxwell spoke at a C. S. Lewis symposium at BYU where he noted Lewis's insights into the journey of Christian discipleship and publicly thanked him, adding that he hoped to do so personally one day.[20] Interestingly, although Elder Maxwell did quote Lewis more than any other apostle, he was followed closely by Jeffrey R. Holland, James E. Faust, and Dallin H. Oaks.

Another pearl from C. S. Lewis is his definition of pride. When President Ezra Taft Benson stood before the Church and spoke about pride he referred to Lewis's definition: "Pride gets no pleasure out of having something, only out of having more of it than the next man. . . . It is the comparison that makes you proud: the pleasure of being above the rest."[21]

President Benson begins with this idea, but steadily moves forward. Using scriptural examples and modern revelation, he expands on it, bringing specific suggestions to assist us in recognizing and changing this common weakness among the Saints and in our own lives.

It is this marriage of ideas that we want to explore, the heart and expressions of C. S. Lewis coupled with the added light of modern revelation. To do this, we have broken down the following study into three major areas:

PART ONE is titled "Surprised by Joy" and includes a biography of Lewis's life. Along this journey, there are many clues to the man he would become. Trials become gifts as his imagination grows due to grief and parental neglect. His questioning mind, which initially pulls him away from truth, brings him back with an eyes-wide-open clarity. Finally, as a confirmed bachelor, Lewis finds love near the end of his life just to have it snatched away again. While coping with the pain of loss, he shares his grief and healing with his readers.

Lewis took the title of the book detailing his conversion, *Surprised by Joy,* from a sonnet by William Wordsworth describing his grief over the death of his beloved daughter. Wordsworth bemoans "the silent Tomb, That spot which no vicissitude can find?"[22] Similarly, the early death of Lewis's mother left him to look at her silent tomb with sadness.

Lewis spends the beginning of his life pursuing joy but finds it to be fleeting and difficult to maintain. Finally, his search takes him to a different tomb—the tomb of Christ. There, he finds something greater than the elusive joy he had been seeking.

PART TWO is "Defining Joy." In 2006 a woman named Anne Jenkins donated a letter written by Lewis to Queen's University that divulged something most of us had already guessed for quite a while. In this letter written to Jenkins when she was ten, Lewis states, "The whole Narnian story is about Christ." He goes on to explain that *The Lion, The Witch and The Wardrobe* is about "the Crucifixion of Christ and the resurrection." He also explains that Prince Caspian "tells the restoration of true religion after corruption."[23]

Through his fiction works, Lewis goes into great detail using symbols to illustrate the gospel of Jesus Christ. In his nonfiction works he describes these same themes head on. In this section, the seven books of *The Chronicles of Narnia* series are used as a basis for discussing these themes, coordinating his other works and modern revelation. It is a clear look at what Lewis really believes theologically compared to the fulness of the gospel.

PART THREE is "Living Joyfully" which examines some of the most notable references to C. S. Lewis by modern apostles and prophets. Starting with Neal A. Maxwell's quotes on discipleship and continuing with the topic of sin and temptation often mentioned in *Screwtape Letters,* the words of apostles and prophets are presented as they converge on a variety of topics using Lewis's quotes.

Each chapter holds stories and treasures shared in conjunction with the Lewis quotations, all of which are presented to provide a more comprehensive LDS perspective of the addressed topic. This is not a complete list, but is meant to be indicative of the way C. S. Lewis has been used to emphasize LDS doctrine and to remind each of us of the joy available through real truth.[24]

NOTES

1. Gormley, *C. S. Lewis, The Man Behind Narnia,* 1.
2. The term "apologist" refers to "a person who argues in defense or justification of

something, such as a doctrine, policy, or institution." See *The American Heritage Dictionary,* 2003.

3. The term *C. S. Lewis* generates 2,046 hits when you search on Gospelink.com (a Deseret Book computer info-base program), including both 1,581 from the primary source and 465 from other LDS websites. Shakespeare only has 1,339 total (273 primary source and 1,066 from other LDS websites).

4. Lewis, *The Great Divorce,* viii.

5. Lewis, *Mere Christianity,* 196.

6. *Collected Letters, vol. II,* Hooper, ed., 507.

7. Lewis, *Screwtape Letters,* 67.

8. Lewis, *The Problem of Pain,* 94.

9. Lewis, *George MacDonald: An Anthology,* 27.

10. Lewis, *They Stand Together,* 499.

11. Lewis, *God in the Dock,* 94.

12. Lewis, *Mere Christianity,* 159.

13. Lewis, *Screwtape Letters,* 61.

14. Lewis, *Mere Christianity,* 143.

15. Lewis, *The Problem of Pain,* 116.

16. Lewis, *Mere Christianity,* 50.

17. Lewis, *Collected Letters,* vol. III, 184.

18. From original Preface to *Screwtape Letters,* no longer in print.

19. Kimball, "The Christian Commitment: C. S. Lewis and the Defense of Doctrine," 197.

20. Maxwell, "Insights on Discipleship," *The Man and His Message* (Salt Lake City, UT: Bookcraft, 1999), 8.

21. Lewis, *Mere Christianity,* 122.

22. Wordsworth, "Desideria," *The Oxford Book of Verse,* 537.

23. From a letter to Anne Jenkins. See BBC News, 14 June 2006. www.news.bbc.co.uk

24. See Appendix A, "A List of C. S. Lewis Quotes and their LDS References."

PART ONE

"SURPRISED BY JOY"

Surprised by joy—impatient as the Wind
I wished to share the transport—Oh! With whom
But Thee, long buried in the silent tomb,
That spot which no vicissitude can find?

WILLIAM WORDSWORTH

This section is a glance at the life of C. S. Lewis and his
life-long search for joy.

CHAPTER TWO

A Joyless Beginning

n 1953 "Jack" Lewis wrote an Italian priest, asking for his prayers as he tried to write a book on prayer. He wanted to help those that were new to the faith to understand how to pray, but he couldn't write it. He confessed that he wondered if God even wanted him to do it and eventually abandoned the forty-five page manuscript. A decade later, Lewis completed his book on prayer just before his death, but it was written in a whole different format than his original concept.

Instead of a thoughtful, intellectual discussion of the subject as in *The Problem of Pain* or *Miracles*, Lewis invented an imaginary friend named Malcolm with whom he discusses the various aspects of prayer. At times, he veers off topic but then he returns, arriving at fascinating new insights. With Joy's death still fresh in his mind and in constant pain due to serious health conditions, Lewis's last few letters in this book are the most touching. Here, he speaks of life as merely a foretaste of the real joy that is to come, concluding that "joy is the serious business of Heaven."[1]

There seems to be a continual theme of searching for joy throughout his life. Lewis's definition of joy was similar to the German term *sehnsucht*, which means a wistful longing or slavish desire for something unattainable and out of reach. According to this definition, joy can only be found in small moments during this earth life. Yet Lewis sought and hoped for a joy that would be forever. Although it seemed to Lewis that joy was elusive throughout his life, his urgency to continually feel joy never slackened.[2]

A LIFE SHATTERED

C. S. Lewis's life began in a happy home with loving parents who were on the rise socially and financially. His father, Albert Lewis, was a solicitor in Belfast, Ireland. His mother, Florence Hamilton, was witty, well-read, and the daughter of an Anglican priest. Lewis had an older brother, Warren, and their youthful sibling relationship would develop into a strong bond lasting throughout their lives together.

In *Surprised by Joy,* Lewis described this early time with his family by quoting Milton's *Paradise Lost,* "Happy, but for so happy ill secured."[3] Lewis's contented life was soon shattered with the early death of his mother. On August 23, 1908, Flora Lewis died of stomach cancer. His young life was truly "ill fenced for Heaven to keep out such a foe."[4]

Although his grandfather was a minister, Lewis does not remember his upbringing as being strongly religious. Their family did attend church sometimes and he did know how to pray. He prayed very hard for his mother to get better, but it did not do any good. His angel mother was gone. Reflecting back on this experience later in life, Lewis did not see his prayerful pleadings as a religious experience. These youthful prayers were too irreligious for their failure to bring about a spiritual awakening or reformation.[5]

Perhaps the clearest insight into the heart of young Lewis can be found in a fictional character he created, grappling with the same issue. In the *Magician's Nephew,* young Digory is sent with his dying mother to live with a crazy uncle and spinster aunt in England. Digory wants to see his mother well again. He will do anything to save her, even ride a flying horse, pick a magic apple, and battle an evil witch. Lewis's own feelings are expressed by Digory as he describes the feeling of hoping so desperately for something that you almost fight against the hope because of previous disappointments.[6] Digory is able to save his mother, but young Lewis could not. The happiness of the Lewis's home and family life disappeared with the death of his mother. The discovery or rediscovery of his faith would not happen until he was well into adulthood.

His father suffered a great deal after the death of his beloved wife. He became emotionally distraught and his temper would flare with the least provocation. Warren and Jack were alone during much of this tender time. Warren was four years older than Jack and was sent to a boarding school in England. Jack was still too young to go (which was probably a great blessing) and had private tutors that came to their home. He spent a lot of time by himself upstairs enduring indoor silences.

FINDING JOY IN IMAGINATION AND NATURE
Jack tried to find solace in the depths of his imagination and the splendor he found in nature. He found momentary joy in pondering works

of literature that took him to places far away from his hard young life. One of his favorite books at this time was Beatrix Potter's *Squirrel Nutkin*.

In this story Potter tells of Nutkin, a mischievous squirrel, and his brother Twinkleberry. These two young brother squirrels to journey to Owl Island together to find nuts and acorns for winter. Its rich descriptions of the colors of autumn with the golden and green leaves of the hazel bush, the blue smoke from a wood fire, yellow and scarlet oak apples, and multi-hued crooked chestnut trees painted a wonderful escape. Jack's affinity for the book was obviously based on his own wish to run away with his brother from their pitiful situation. In the end, they did get free through books, nature, and their sustenance and support for each other.

In the tradition of Potter, Lewis began humanizing animals, giving them unusual names and intense feelings. Warren and Jack wrote a series of stories in an imaginary world named Boxen where animals talked and ruled the world. They drew maps of Boxen and even wrote histories of it. While Warren was away at boarding school, Jack would send Warren letters about the happenings of their imaginary world. For example, King Bunny became a prisoner of a political uprising. General Quicksteppe tried to rescue his bunny king while the common citizenry were rioting in the streets over the political upheaval. The plots were very complex and extensive.[7] Young Lewis even sketched drawings of animals with clothes, smoking, and chatting outside of an art gallery. His humanizing of animals, trying to understand their thoughts and feelings, would help later in his imaginative creation of Narnia.

Another source of joy for young Jack was Henry Wadsworth Longfellow's series of poems titled *Norse Ballads*. These were stories of longing, love, death, hate, excitement, battles, forgiveness, and seeking the unattainable. Young Lewis became obsessed with Norse myths and legends. There is a sense of anguish for that which is lost, similar to young Lewis's heartfelt feelings for his mother. The richness of the language of these poems affected young Lewis and his love for the written word. In Longfellow's poem, "Tegnér's Drapa," some of the imagery of Balder the Beautiful, the Norse sun god, is very similar to Lewis's later descriptions of Narnia and Aslan:[8]

Balder the Beautiful,
God of the summer sun,
Fairest of all the Gods!
Light from his forehead beamed,

Runes were upon his tongue,
As on the warrior's sword.

All things in earth and air
Bound were by magic spell
Never to do him harm;
Even the plants and stones.[9]

At age fifteen, Jack was home on holiday from school when he went to visit a neighbor, Arthur, who was a few years older than himself. He saw him reading a book, *Myths of the Norsemen*. From that point on, Jack and Arthur developed a close friendship that lasted their entire lives. Arthur Greeves became the first person with whom Jack could really share his most secret interests and delights. They had a similar love for books, music, and nature. Jack wrote extensive letters to Arthur during his youth and continued corresponding with Arthur throughout his life. Eventually, Jack's interest in mythology and poetry would shape his adult career as a professor in Medieval literature.

Experiencing the beauties of nature also brought him glimpses of joy. One of his earliest remembered experiences with nature was when he was three and his older brother, Warren (nicknamed Warnie), brought into the nursery a toy garden on a biscuit tin. It was a child-like miniature of the garden the boys had played in all summer. This small garden allowed Lewis to see nature in a new way. He began to be aware of nature as an art form. He was amazed at the power of nature to fill his soul. He could see in this miniature garden shapes and colors and an exuberance that filled him with delight.[10] Little things in nature could strike Jack with great power. A flowering currant bush on a summer day brought joy to Jack with such force that he remembered it throughout his life.

As a young boy between the ages of two and seven, Jack spent many summers in lovely Northern Ireland with Warren and his mother. Castlerock and the North Antrium coast were considered by Lewis as some of the most beautiful places he would ever know.[11] He would keep these images in his mind. The green Castlereagh Hills would become the standard for the creation of the world of Narnia later in life.

The transitory nature of these childhood experiences left a longing or hope in Lewis that these joyous experiences could continue. The more mature Lewis realized the fleeting nature of joy does not mean there is no eternal joy to be found. Instead, this insatiable yearning for lasting joy meant that earthly pleasure was not meant to satisfy our joyful longings.

These yearnings arouse in each of us the suggestion that we should strive for the "real Desire."[12] This longing for the real thing or everlasting joy is a theme in many of Lewis's works and becomes a lifelong personal quest.

JOYLESS SCHOOLING AND INSIGHTFUL TUTORING

Jack was soon considered old enough to join Warren at the Wynyard School in Hertfordshire. Poor Warren had been at the boarding school for three years before Jack came to join him. The school was a joyless and mind-numbing place with a headmaster on the verge of insanity; he was admitted into an insane asylum shortly after the school was closed. Mr. Capron would beat the boys mercilessly while teaching them very little. Lewis described the only stimulating elements in the headmaster's teaching were the well-used canes hanging over the fireplace. The school finally dissolved in 1910 because of the small enrollment of students.[13]

After being liberated from this educational nightmare, Warren and Jack started going to Campbell College, which was very close to their home. Because of health problems, the boys were sent to another school in the English midlands to help their ailing lungs.[14] It was during this time as a young adolescent that Lewis gave up religion. He became increasingly involved in his books and received a classical scholarship to Wyvern College. His classical books and educational training became the focus of his time and study.

Jack still had difficulty with the educational system at Wyvern. There was a ruling "clique" at the school called the Bloods. These older boys who were the prefects and student monitors at the school were given the upper hand to order the younger boys around. In order to be accepted by this group of boys, one needed to be good in sports and willing to do these other boys' chores whenever ordered to do so. Jack was not good at sports, nor did he appreciate the extra chores. The only way he could retaliate was using his wit and gift of mimicking behind the backs of these senior boys.

In *The Silver Chair,* Eustace and Jill attend a private co-educational school called Experiment House. The school has a similar group of bullies whom Jill calls "Them." In the first scene of the book, Jill is crying because "they" have been bullying her. Eustace and Jill are trying to escape "Them" when they open the door and find themselves in Narnia. Though Lewis did not escape as quickly and easily as Jill and Eustace, he was rescued by a professor who finally gave him the education his eager mind had been waiting for through his previous years of difficult schooling.

In 1914, Lewis began studying with William T. Kirkpatrick (1848–1921) or "the Great Knock." Lewis studied with him for three years.

Kirkpatrick had been the headmaster of Lurgan College, which was the school Lewis's father, Albert, had attended as a young man. Albert paid Kirkpatrick to privately tutor his boys to prepare them for higher education. Kirkpatrick successfully prepared Warren so he could attend Royal Military College. He also rigorously trained Lewis to prepare him for entrance exams to Oxford University.[15]

Lewis gave Kirkpatrick the credit for teaching him how to think by stressing logical thought and searching for truth.[16] In *The Lion, The Witch and the Wardrobe,* the professor's name, Digory Kirke, seems to reflect the influence Kirkpatrick had upon Lewis. After the children return from Narnia in this book, it is the remarkable Professor Kirke who reminds them to keep their eyes open for others who have been to Narnia. He also gives them the hope of other adventures. Kirkpatrick opened Lewis's eyes educationally and paved the way for Lewis's adventures at Oxford.

NOTES

1. Lewis, *Letters from Malcolm,* 93.
2. For further information, see Schultz and West, *The C. S. Lewis Readers' Encyclopedia,* 224–25.
3. Milton, *Paradise Lost, IV,* line 370.
4. Ibid., line 372.
5. For more information written by Lewis about this spiritual time of his young life, see Lewis, *Surprised by Joy,* 20.
6. See Lewis, *The Chronicles of Narnia,* 54. Additional citations will reference this book as *Narnia.*
7. For more information, read Hooper, *Boxen: The Imaginary World of C. S. Lewis,* and Lewis, *Surprised by Joy,* 13–16.
8. Compare this to the first time that Digory and Polly see Aslan creating Narnia through a magical song. As the new sun begins to lighten the sky, the children turn to see the source of this marvelous creation. Lewis describes the lion as being huge and bright, as the sun. See Lewis, *Narnia,* 119–20.
9. Longfellow, *Tegnér's Drapa,* lines 19–28.
10. For further information, read Lewis, *Surprised by Joy,* 5.
11. For further information, read Duriez, *A Field Guide to Narnia,* 4–5.
12. For a more in depth discussion on Lewis's feelings on joy, read *Surprised by Joy,* preface, 18–19, and "Joy" on 203–205.
13. For further reading on Wynyard School, see *Surprised by Joy,* 26–39.
14. Lewis's ailing lungs came from smoking from a very young age.
15. For further reading about Lewis's education, see *Surprised by Joy,* 95–175.
16. See Lewis, *Narnia,* 196.

CHAPTER THREE

Glimpses of Joy

t the young age of twenty-one, Lewis published his first work under the pseudonym Clive Hamilton. He titled it *Spirits in Bondage: A Cycle of Lyrics* (1919). It is a cynical collection of poems written while he was a military trainee at Oxford and a soldier in the trenches of World War I. In a letter to his childhood friend, Arthur Greeves, Lewis described these poems as centering on the idea that nature is completely diabolical and malevolent against man. If God exists, he is outside of and in opposition to the cosmic arrangement of the happenings on earth. In his verses, Lewis writes about a Lord who is pitiless and "mocks the broken people praying round his iron throne."[1]

Lewis definitely struggled with many concerns about life. The world around him was in upheaval going into the Great War. In general, society entered a stage of lost innocence. C. S. Lewis would not be sheltered from the difficulties of war. The death of loved ones continued to be a part of his life. Yet through all of life's difficulties, there seemed to be glimpses of joy that he continued to find through his friends, his studies, and the beauties of nature.

GOING TO OXFORD

Because of the intense tutoring of the Great Knock, Jack was offered a scholarship to Oxford. His acceptance to the university was dependent upon his passing the Oxford entrance exams. These preliminary exams, called Responsions, were to test competencies in all the basic areas of academics. Lewis was brilliant in modern languages and literature, but he had little skill in mathematics. He flunked the exam because of his math scores. He spent the rest of the spring cramming for a retake.

Jack would spend the spring and fall of 1917 at Oxford. Initially, he spent his time studying and enjoying student life. Oxford had very few students at this time, and Jack enjoyed his relative freedom.

Before he could take the tests again, Jack became a soldier in the Royal British Army. He accepted a commission as a cadet in an army battalion. He continued being housed at Oxford, but his life now included the regimen of army life.

Jack's roommate was also from Ireland, Paddy Moore. His mother, Janie Moore, and sister, Maureen, lived in Bristol, England. Paddy's mother was attached to her son since she had been estranged from her husband for many years. She moved to Oxford to be near her son. Jack became a welcome visitor and enjoyed the companionship of this family.

As the time drew closer for their departure to the French battlefront, Paddy and Jack discussed the possibility of their deaths. Paddy and Jack made a pact that if Jack died, Paddy would look after Albert, Jack's father; if Paddy died, Jack would look after Janie and Maureen. This promise would make a lasting impression on Jack's life.

THE GREAT WAR

Paddy went to war first, but Jack soon followed. The war accelerated quickly, and Jack found himself leaving for the front much sooner than he had anticipated. He sent an urgent telegram to his father asking him to come and say goodbye before he left. He only had a few days before he left for France. His father wrote back that he could not understand the telegram, asking him to please write back to explain the situation.

This was a difficult response for Jack. He could not comprehend his father's reticence to see him or his misunderstanding of such a clear message of his own personal need. When Albert finally realized Jack was gone to war, he later wrote to his son that he was truly shaken up about his leaving.[2] This experience strained their relationship for years to come. It would take some time for Jack to forgive his father. Even though his feelings had been hurt, Lewis continued to write his father letters about his experiences on the front lines. It is through these letters that we gain a glimpse of what his war experience was like.

After being in the trenches for a few months, Jack contracted trench fever. He wrote to his father during his convalescence about the cliffs and a grey sea. From his window, he contemplated the natural scenes around him, looking beyond the hospital yard to the wooded countryside.[3] During this time of physical healing, he continued to seek the solace of nature to help him heal.

He returned to fight just in time for a large offensive strike by the German army in March 1918. He described his life in the trenches as being confining and depressing. The trenches were dug deep into the ground. Soldiers had to walk down a shaft of about twenty steps to get to the bottom. Bunks lined the trenches where the soldiers tried to sleep in snug, tight-fitting quarters. Braziers were used to keep the men warm and to cook meager, simple meals.[4]

Ironically, Lewis was hit by an English shell meant for the German lines. The explosion killed some of Lewis's friends, and then the exploding shrapnel hit him three times—once in the hand, once in the upper leg, and finally, under his arm which punctured his lung. Luckily, he was able to crawl out of danger and medics found him quickly.

Warren was a British officer also fighting in France at the time. Albert, their father, wrote Warnie that Jack was severely wounded and he should go visit him right away. Warren borrowed a bicycle and found Jack in good spirits and his wounds healing up nicely.[5] Because of this injury, Lewis came home and did not fight again in the war. He was allowed entrance into Oxford without having to retake the Responsions because of his service record.

It is during these war experiences that he wrote the poetry for his book *Spirits in Bondage*. There are many bitter phrases in these poems reflecting Jack's emotional responses to the war. He repeatedly expresses the useless nature of praying to a God who does not hear.[6]

Later in life, Lewis wrote very little about his personal experiences in the Great War. There are battles in his books, but they are treated without extreme or gross detail. In his autobiography, he does make statements illustrating the magnitude of his repulsive memories. He describes the smashed men, the corpses, and the barren landscape. He allowed these memories to fade, coming to the realization that these memories are in many ways unimportant.[7] Lewis's faith seems to have completely washed away the fears of war, but not the memory.

A MATTER OF FRIENDSHIP

During his convalescence, Jack received word from Janie Moore that Paddy, her son, had been killed in action. Jack transferred to a hospital in London, and Mrs. Moore came to visit him regularly. Jack asked his father to come visit too, but Albert refused to come. Warren even wrote to his father trying to get him to visit his little brother, but Albert would not budge. Since the death of his wife, Albert had been plagued by depression and alcoholism, and he had a difficult time leaving his home. Jack was deeply hurt by what he considered an inexcusable neglect now that he was back in England.

Jack kept his promise to his friend, Paddy. He would take care of Mrs. Moore all of her life. He also enjoyed her company and especially appreciated their relationship during this difficult time of healing. There has been much written about (and speculation concerning) the relationship between Mrs. Moore and C. S. Lewis. Owen Barfield, Jack's friend who was acquainted with Mrs. Moore, made the comment years later about the speculation of many people concerning their relationship. He did not feel that their relationship was more than platonic. Mrs. Moore was a great deal older than Jack and Owen Barfield, at least, did not think she was particularly attractive.[8]

Whether their relationship was platonic or not, their connection was one of loyalty, friendship, and trust. Janie Moore experienced many years of ill health near the end of her life, yet Lewis always visited her and cared for her until her death in 1951 at the age of seventy-eight. Another friend, Walter Hooper, discussed the relationship of Mrs. Moore and Jack and pointed out that their association ended as a lasting example of Christian charity. Jack had made a vow to a friend and he kept it well.

Together, Mrs. Moore and Jack set up a household in Oxford so he could continue his studies and scholarly career. Jack kept an extensive diary between the years of 1922 to 1927. He wrote about the day to day dealings of his life during this time. The diary is now published with the title taken from an epic poem Lewis wrote during this period of time called *Dymer*. He wrote, "With all my road before me—yet to-day / Here, if at all, we meet."[9] At age twenty-five, he did have all his life's road before him.

Lewis wrote detailed entries. He wrote about his household chores, his academic studies, his writing of letters and poetry, his difficulties trying to find a job, and his concerns over money. Through this detail, the reader is able to get inside his thoughts and mind and gain a greater understanding of the running of his household, his relationship with Mrs. Moore, Warren, and his friends.[10]

Like most of us, Lewis did have lapses in keeping his journal. In his diary entry dated June 20, 1923, he recommitted to start writing daily again in his journal no matter the cost of labor and time. He had let his entries slip because of school pressures. Lewis observed that writing a daily journal allowed people to watch the larger movements in their lives and pay less attention to the frustration of individual days.[11]

Jack was very involved in the daily lives of Mrs. Moore and Maureen, her teenage daughter. He did the dishes, peeled potatoes, and walked the dog. He attended Maureen's school plays and Mrs. Moore's parties, and enjoyed playing cards with them and their guests. Rather than becoming a sequestered scholar, Lewis chose to live with Mrs. Moore and Maureen. Jack finally had a home and family.

JACK'S RELATIONSHIP WITH HIS FATHER

Even though Jack did have a surrogate family, his father still lived in Ireland. Initially, Lewis kept the arrangement of living with Mrs. Moore and Maureen a secret from his father. Eventually, his father found out and never understood why Lewis continued with these living arrangements.

Albert still tried to be a part of Jack's life. They wrote newsy letters to each other, but their relationship remained strained because of Jack's disappointments when he had asked his father to visit him and Albert had not come. Jack visited his father yearly in Ireland. During the Christmas break of 1922, Lewis wrote about their time together in his diary. These visits were often excruciatingly uncomfortable. Albert would try hard to be accommodating by going on walks with Lewis, but Lewis often felt like a prisoner in Albert's company. Lewis had conflicting feelings for his father. On one hand, he thought his father was pathetic; yet, he felt sympathy for him as well. Even with these emotions, Lewis continued to write and visit him. Lewis tried to develop a better relationship with his father, struggling to rise above years of childhood neglect.

Albert also tried to be generous with his son during Jack's days as a student at Oxford. Lewis had a small scholarship that covered much of his tuition, but not his living expenses. Albert worked hard to get his son an additional gratuity for having been injured during the war. He also sent him a small allowance, calculated for a single bachelor living alone. Since Jack was establishing a household with other people dependent upon him for financial support, he found himself constantly in need of additional funds.

In the spring of 1925, Jack was elected a fellow at Magdalen College at Oxford University. He sent a telegram to his father. His father was so moved that he knelt and offered thanksgiving for this great blessing in his son's life. A few days later, Jack wrote his father a long letter of gratitude for his father's generous support over the past six years of his schooling. He thanked his father for waiting without complaint but full of encouragement. He acknowledged that it was his father's patient help that enabled him to hang on financially during those difficult school years. From this time on, their relationship seemed to heal.

Albert Lewis died on September 25, 1929, at age sixty-six. In April

1935, Lewis wrote a letter to Leo Baker, a university pal. He talked about his father's death, regretting the strained connection with his father but grateful the relationship was at its best at the end of his father's life.[12]

THE KILNS

In contrast to his father, Warren became a part of Jack's household with Mrs. Moore and Maureen. Together, Mrs. Moore, Jack, and Warren jointly bought a home in 1930 called "the Kilns." The title for the property was in Mrs. Moore's name with the brothers holding life tenancy. This was the home Jack and Warren would have as their main residence for the rest of their lives. After Mrs. Moore's death, the two brothers lived in this home together until Jack's death. Jack's bond with Warren was a constant source of family love and connection throughout his life. (Warren would live nine and a half years longer than his brother Jack.)

The home was old and simply constructed with two brick kilns still next to the home where bricks had originally been made; hence, the reason for the house's name. The grounds around the home were eight acres of woods with a view from a cliff, which Warren described as "simply glorious." There was also a lovely pond for pondering and reflecting. A local tradition was that the poet Shelly, a favorite of Jack's, had often meditated there.

Nature continued to have a profound effect on Jack's spiritual life. He found great solace and inspiration from walking in the woods, sitting by the pond, or enjoying a view. In his diary on March 27, 1924, he described walking up to the ruined Walton Castle on top of a wooded hill. After a peaceful climb, he reached the castle. Its appearance to him was like a young boy's dream. He ran down to the rocks of the ruined structure and sat down in the wet grass. Lewis felt he had seldom had a better moment. He found glimpses of joy in these nature reveries as he saw a fir grove or looked at a leaf. He could feel joy just within his grasp, but it would never quite arrive.[13]

BECOMING A WRITER AND A SCHOLAR

While at Oxford, Lewis continued to study hard trying to become a published author and a scholar in Old English literature. A typical day in the life of Lewis during this time included an astounding amount of studying and reading. Many friends have commented on the breadth of his knowledge on a variety of subjects. His entry on October 16, 1922, illustrates the amount and scope of his studies at Oxford. He bicycled after breakfast to a 10 o'clock lecture given by Henry Cecil Kennedy Wyld on the history of the English language. After the hour-long lecture, Lewis commented he heard nothing that he had not known for five years. After lunch, he bicycled again to the library to check out W. M. Rossetti's compilation of the poem of *Troilus* and *Il Filostrato* and then came home. After reading this work, he remarked that other than *Macbeth* and some other old ballads, he did not think any poetry had affected him more.[14] His diary includes some wonderful literary commentary, too. He found humor in Milton's prose. He also tried to find out what John Dryden meant by wit, but characterized his wit as meaning something different each time.

Lewis had an amusing way of characterizing his teachers. In his diary, he would write brutally candid descriptions of them. He described Miss Wardale, a teacher and tutor in Old English grammar, as an elderly, pallid woman that had a monstrous lower lip, which hung loose to expose an irregular gum line. He portrayed Charles Talbut Onions, a lexicographer and grammarian, as a good lecturer who stammered, unless he was quoting verses, which he did very well.[15]

Walter Hooper, the editor of Lewis's diary, mentions the fact that both of the Lewis brothers were not good spellers. Hooper points out the most characteristic mistake Lewis made was with contractions, such as *can't* being written as *ca'nt*. In the published diaries, Hooper kept some of the original spellings as found in Jack's notebook.[16]

At the age of twenty-eight, Lewis published another poem entitled, *Dymer* (1926). This poem is of epic proportions, based on the tale of a man, Dymer, who begets a monster. The monster becomes a god, only after tragically killing his father. Lewis enjoyed these grand mythical stories because he felt their themes were applicable to modern life. He believed the essence of myth enabled man to understand the supernatural and man's relationship to God.

In *Dymer*, Lewis portrays feelings of pessimism and antagonism toward God. The myth, or story, of Christianity had been lumped together in his mind with all other forms of supernaturalism and religious beliefs. These musings caused Lewis to write in *Dymer* that joy can only flash for a moment in the present; then, it is gone. For Lewis, joy was only a wish and a flicker. At this time in Lewis's life, he experienced joy as a hopeless longing for something better.

NOTES

1. Lewis, *Spirits in Bondage,* line 17. For more information, read the Prologue to *Spirits in Bondage.* The entire text of *Spirits in Bondage* can be downloaded from www. gutenberg.org.

2. For a more in-depth discussion, read Wilson, *C. S. Lewis: A Biography,* 54.

3. Read Hooper, *Collected Letters of C. S. Lewis,* vol. 1, 356.

4. Ibid., 351.

5. Ibid., 366 and Jacobs, *The Narnian,* 71–72.

6. See Lewis, *Spirits in Bondage,* poem XI, "In Prison."

7. For a further understanding, read *Surprised by Joy,* 222–30.

8. For further information, read Owen Barfield's short introduction to the book, *All My Road Before Me.*

9. Lewis, *Dymer,* 1.

10. For further information about this time of Lewis's life, read, *All My Road Before Me,* Walter Hooper, ed. This book is C. S. Lewis's diary that he kept during his early years at Oxford.

11. *All My Road Before Me,* Hooper, ed., 246.

12. This is more fully discussed in Duriez, *Tolkien and C. S. Lewis,* 39.

13. *All My Road Before Me,* Hooper, ed., xi, 307.

14. Ibid., 120.

15. Ibid., 122.

16. With the diary entries after April 1926, Walter Hooper did not change any of the spelling mistakes in *All My Road Before Me.*

CHAPTER FOUR

Joyful Discoveries

n Lewis's work *A Pilgrim's Regress,* the main character, John, has a vision of a sweet and beautiful island that fills him with such strong desire that he searches for it for the rest of his life. He becomes obsessed with this vision. He yearns for it. Nothing else he sees or thinks about is as desirable as the incessant longing he feels. His vision has given him something to hope for, a purpose to his life. The very act of wanting it makes his life worth living.[1]

As Lewis grew older, he began to realize that he was missing something in his life. Lewis went through a spiritual changing process. He was never a bad person, and evil had never been a significant part of his character. But, as Lewis turned thirty, his thoughts went through a metamorphosis. He moved from a complete rejection of God to a realization that there was a greater power in heaven to an eventual acknowledgement of the need for a Savior.

HIS SPIRITUAL STATE

Jack wanted to protect himself from experiencing the heartaches he suffered after the death of his mother and the death of his friends during the Great War. He entered another great battle, a spiritual battle for his soul. At first, he had tried to keep his soul to himself. He tried to call his soul his own. He wanted to avoid suffering, rather than search for or find delight. By choosing to reject God, he could not hear the voice of God and had nothing to obey. He felt he had nothing to fear, in terms of hurt or sorrow, since he did not believe in anything.[2]

In 1926, Lewis started his first job. He was a don (a teacher who lectured and tutored students, often on a one-on-one basis) at Magdalen

College. He had three rooms to call his own at Oxford. In the afternoons and weekends, he still spent time with Mrs. Moore and Maureen. Lewis gave tutorials to students studying English, philosophy, politics, and economics. He became a well-respected professor.

On April 26, another teacher, Thomas Dewar Weldon, visited Lewis for a late-night chat. They started discussing the historical truth of the Gospels. During the course of their friendly discussion, Lewis admitted there was a lot that could not be explained away. He got to bed late that night with a headache and regretting his wasted evening, even though he admitted it had been interesting.[3]

Lewis continued to have similar discussions with others and within his own mind about the truth. He referred to this as the "great war," which he fought within his own soul. He pondered about truth and tried to achieve a right or good feeling about it. Instead, he found himself going nearer and nearer to the asylum.[4] He experienced severe headaches during this time as well.

Owen Barfield was a fellow graduate student who caused Lewis to deliberate over his beliefs. In 1922, Barfield became an adherent of anthroposophism, which was a spiritual science developed by Rudolf Steiner (1861–1925).[5] Anthroposophists encourage investigations of the spiritual world with the same precision and clarity as natural scientists. Imagination, inspiration, and intuition are used to determine human wisdom.

Lewis argued strongly against Barfield's views on spirituality. He was hostile to this modern movement. Their discussions caused Lewis to question what his beliefs really were. Through these discussions, Lewis began to see the necessity of having the proper perspective on the strengths and weaknesses of any given age or period of human development. He began to question his uncritical acceptance of the intellectual climate common to his particular time and age. He characterized it as chronological snobbery and realized that it caused skepticism for other ways of looking at the world. It was at this time he rethought the supposition that modern thought was always the best.

Although Lewis did not agree with Barfield, he admired him and appreciated the discussions they had. Barfield helped Lewis think more imaginatively and spiritually, combining inspiration with his already formidable intellect.

BECOMING A THEIST
During this time of spiritual upheaval, Lewis would seek the solace of nature to help clear his head. On one of his walks, he described his state of

mind as being muddled, full of undigested scraps of various philosophies pushing and shoving in his mind. Even with his difficult state of mind, he was still aware of the sun above him and the valley below. The silence enabled him to think. He tried using Kirkian rationalism, but found his mind was a mess. While thinking about these different ways of viewing truth, Lewis found himself in danger of slipping back into his most childish superstitions, that of a belief in God.[6]

In an early summer day in 1929, Lewis went on a bus ride crossing Headington Hill Park and thought about the question of human freedom. He began to feel uncomfortable, like he was wearing constrained clothing or a suit of armor. Suddenly, a door appeared in front of him, and Lewis realized that he had the opportunity to open it or leave it closed. He realized that if he was willing to believe in God, he could open the door. As he opened the door, he felt freer than he had ever felt before.

After this bus ride, Lewis could not deny the spiritual heartfelt experience he had. His mind would reflect back on those feelings even when he was studying or thinking about other things. He sensed the insistent approach of him whom he so earnestly had tried not to meet. The Lord himself declared that "the voice of the Lord is unto all men, and there is none to escape; and there is no eye that shall not see, neither ear that shall not hear, neither heart that shall not be penetrated" (D&C 1:2). Finally, Lewis did surrender himself to God. He admitted that God was God and knelt and prayed. Lewis described himself as the "most dejected and reluctant convert in all England."[7]

Receiving Christ

Jack's spiritual bus ride changed him forever. He now believed there was a God, but he still was not converted to any specific religion or dogma. Later, Lewis wrote about another heavenly bus ride in *The Great Divorce*. Lewis commented that any man "who reaches Heaven will find that what he abandoned (even in plucking out his right eye) was precisely nothing."[8] On Jack's journey toward understanding truth, he could not take all his baggage with him. There were previous things he believed and taught that he could not retain, but had to reject and leave behind. Lewis continued to change as he moved along his path of testimony.

Lewis began to read daily passages from the Bible. He started with John's Gospel in Greek. The works of George MacDonald also became a favorite of his. Even though he had read MacDonald's works previously in his childhood, he was now able to discern the spirit of the books. He would later put MacDonald on a singular pedestal as being a writer who was continually close to the Spirit of Christ. In the preface to an anthology of George MacDonald's works, Lewis wrote that the qualities of MacDonald's words in describing imaginative and magical experiences had the quality of a real universe in which we live. MacDonald mingled magic with the divine, still maintaining the authenticity of truth in his stories and words.[9]

Others helped Lewis along his spiritual way. Another friend who influenced his faith was J. R. R. Tolkien, who taught at Oxford during this time. Tolkien was a faithful member of the Catholic Church. He taught ancient languages and texts, and his area of expertise was determining common origins of modern written and spoken languages. Lewis remarked that his friendship with Tolkien actually broke down two prejudices. The first was to never trust a Papist; the second was to never trust a philologist. Tolkien was both.

Hugo Dyson (1869–1975) was a friend to both Tolkien and Lewis, and he was a devout Christian. One night, the three friends discussed at length their belief in Christ and the veracity of the Gospels. This discussion profoundly affected all three of them and caused both Tolkien and Lewis to write about this experience later.

Tolkien wrote a poem, *Mythopoeia* (or "mythmaking") with the subtitle "Philomythus to Misomythus" (or "myth-lover to myth-hater"). In this long poem, he describes their night-long discussion through the words of the two characters in the poem (the myth-lover and the myth-hater). Tolkien tried to reach the heart of Lewis to stir his knowledge of truth to the forefront of his mind.[10]

In response, Lewis wrote a pointed essay on the power of story and fact in the Gospels. He saw the union of perfect myth and perfect fact created in the story of Jesus Christ, which claimed only our love and obedience in order to believe in its truth. The wonder and delight of the story is addressed to the savage, the child, and the poet inside each of us.

The Gospel accounts of the life of Jesus Christ demand both imagination and reason to understand them. There are the facts about the Savior's life which are true. There are also parts of the story, such as the Atonement and the Resurrection, that must be taken on faith that engender a quality of wonder, awe, or "myth" (as Tolkien and Lewis would define it) in order to spiritually understand them. These spiritual discussions about the New Testament enabled Lewis to think and ponder about his need for a savior.

The event that would determine his final conversion to Christianity was another journey in nature. One morning in 1931, Lewis went for a ride to the zoo in the sidecar of Warren's motorcycle. He described his experience simply as beginning the journey without believing that Jesus Christ was the Son of God and upon reaching the zoo, he did believe.

Lewis was now faith-filled. His quest for joy had become a journey that was full of hope, not hopelessness. Rather than rejecting God, God became the center of his existence. He would continue to dedicate his life to learning and teaching about Christ.

NOTES

1. See Lewis, *The Pilgrim's Regress,* 16.
2. Additional insights can be found in Lewis, *Surprised by Joy,* 210, 238.
3. For more information, read Lewis, *All My Road Before Me,* 380.
4. Ibid., 449.
5. The word *anthroposophism* comes from two Greek words—*anthropos* (human) and *sophia* (wisdom).
6. For additional understanding about his thoughts during this time, read Lewis, *All My Road Before Me,* 431–32.
7. Read Lewis's own account of his conversion to God in Lewis, *Surprised by Joy,* 238.
8. For further understanding of the bus ride to heaven, read Lewis, *The Great Divorce,* Preface, 10.
9. For further information, see *George Macdonald: An Anthology,* preface by C. S. Lewis.
10. To read the entire poem, read J. R. R. Tolkien, *Tree and Leaf* [1964], (Boston: Houghton Mifflin, 1989). Jacobs, *Narnian,* 145, and Duriez, *Tolkien and Lewis,* 54, are other great discussions of this conversation.

CHAPTER FIVE

Sharing Joy

ack's life did not become instantly easier after converting to Christianity. Mrs. Moore, who was a confirmed atheist throughout her life, was not supportive of Lewis's newfound faith. After Mrs. Moore's death, Lewis wrote an interesting comment in *The Four Loves* that may have come from personal experience. He observed that a family member who becomes a Christian may experience great resentment, bitterness, and rancor from the unbelieving members of his family.[1]

Yet, Lewis enjoyed sharing his faith with others. He began to write books that expressed his testimony. His first book after becoming a Christian was *The Pilgrim's Regress* (1933), which was also his first book of prose, not poetry. In this story, Lewis tried to explain his own spiritual journey of becoming a Christian. It is written as an allegory with the main character, John, searching for joy and truth and finding them through faith. Lewis would continue to write books that would promote faith in Christ through both story and allegory.

Lewis felt a great responsibility as a writer to answer letters from his readers. He especially felt the need to shore up those in need of extra support in their Christian faith. Lewis wrote to one woman 138 times over a period of ten years. He told a friend that she was a "silly, tiresome old woman," but he also knew that she was poor, sick, and lonely, too.[2]

He would answer letters about his books and about Christianity in general. In 1955, an American mother of a nine-year-old boy wrote Lewis fearing that her son was sinning. She was afraid her son loved Aslan more than Jesus. Lewis wrote her back with some words of encouragement to

tell her son and possible words for a prayer her son could say. At the end
of the prayer, Lewis added supplementary words, asking that he would
be forgiven for worrying any other children and doing them any harm
because of the books he had written.[3]

FRIENDSHIP AND WRITING

Lewis saw friendship as one of the four loves: affection, friendship,
eros, and charity (or agape). According to Lewis, friendship was shared
between people with a common interest. Friends are best imagined side-
by-side looking at a common goal. There are no gender requirements for
a friend, and the friendship relationship amplifies the good or evil in
people.

Lewis was a great friend. During his lifetime, Lewis spent a lot of
time alone. But he was not a loner. He enjoyed people and was a loyal and
true friend. Even if he was not physically near a friend, he enjoyed corresponding with them through letters. Owen Barfield described reading
a letter from Jack as "opening the envelope and hearing his voice."[4] There
are volumes and volumes of his letters that have now been published.
They give wonderful insights into Lewis and his love of people, especially
his friends. Many of them had a variety of interests. In 1929, Tolkien
described his friendship with Lewis as "compensating for much."[5] Lewis
tended to seek out friends who would help him learn things or understand
other points of view.

Lewis especially enjoyed discussing his writing projects with his
friends. Writing can be a lonely process, but Lewis tried to get his writing friends to get together and discuss their projects or ideas for books or
articles. Many of his friends would later become famous for their literary
accomplishments.

THE INKLINGS

As early as the spring of 1926, Lewis was invited by Tolkien to join an
informal reading group called The Coalbiters. The name referred to people
during the wintertime who got so close to the fire they seemed to bite the
coal. This group was exploring Old Icelandic literature. Through these
gatherings, Tolkien and Lewis would meet regularly, discussing their love
of reading and writing. Lewis wrote in a letter to Arthur Greeves that
Tolkien would return to his rooms after their meeting and continue to talk
for hours of the gods and giants of Asgard.

In the early 1930s, Lewis and Tolkien decided to start a group of like-
minded literary minds. They decided to name it "the Inklings" as a play

on words because it could mean an idea and also someone who dabbles in ink. Initially, the original group did not continue for very long; but Lewis wanted to start the group again a few years later, using the same name. This time the group continued until it was disbanded in 1949.[6] Once a week the group would meet at a local pub. This pub, the Eagle and Child, was a favorite hangout spot.

The group would talk about more than just literature. Lewis wrote a letter to a former student about their meetings as being theoretical to talk about literature, but usually they would talk about something better. Lewis always felt that he owed a great deal to this group in shaping his mind and his spirit.[7] Discussing thoughts and ideas would sharpen their thinking and fine-tune their writing. "Iron sharpeneth iron; so a man sharpeneth the countenance of his friend" (Proverbs 27:17). The Inklings also gave these men a sense of belonging and increased their friendship for each other. In *The Four Loves,* Lewis described his feelings about being part of this group, expressing how lucky he was to be among his betters who each brought the best, wisest, and funniest out of each other.[8]

It was a restricted group. All shared a Christian worldview and membership was by invitation only and by a general consensus of the group. They wanted people who were good and critical thinkers, but not Prima Donnas. The main people who were the backbone of the group were Lewis, Tolkien, Owen Barfield, and Charles Williams, though there were many others who would regularly join the group. These included Warren Lewis, Hugo Dyson, Nevill Coghill, and Robert Harvard. Warren began coming to the Inklings meetings in 1933 and other than his years in active military duty during World War II, he was a regular participant. Hugo Dyson was a lecturer at Reading University which was quite a distance to travel. He could not make it every week, but tried to attend as often as he could. Nevill Coghill was a long-time friend of Lewis and an original member of the group. Over time, he attended less and less. His philosophical leanings took him away from the conservative Christian view of the group. Robert Harvard was Lewis's medical doctor. He never authored a book, but he loved attending the meetings and participating in the discussions. He was nicknamed "Humphrey" after the doctor in Lewis's book, *Perelandra*. Other attendees would come sporadically or for a short time. These included Charles Wrenn, Colin Hardie, Adam Fox, Lord David Cecil, Christopher Tolkien, and others.

Charles Williams would affect the Inklings greatly though he was not originally living in Oxford. He was an author and editor for Oxford University Press, but he originally lived in London. In 1936, Lewis read

Williams's book *The Place of the Lion*. It affected him so much that he wrote him a complimentary letter inviting him to visit the Inklings. In this letter, he expressed his feeling that Williams's book was like a strange new country, speaking to him as a native tongue.

Williams had just read Lewis's book *The Allegory of Love* and wrote him an admiring note in reply. Williams mentioned he had never admired an author at the same time that the author was admiring him. He compared Lewis's work to Dante's in its understanding of the identity of love and how it fits into a religious context.[9] The two would become close friends. Lewis described their relationship as rapidly growing inward, even to the bone.

When Williams moved to Oxford in 1939, he became an active participant in the Inklings. Tolkien and Lewis had different views of Williams's work. Tolkien found his writing alien to him and sometimes distasteful. He thought some of Williams's writings were even ridiculous. But Lewis enjoyed its fanciful tone.

The Place of the Lion would have a profound and lasting effect on the writer Lewis. He would use much of the same imagery of Williams's lion for his own Aslan in Narnia. In his book, Williams described his lion character as being something not of this world, yet familiar. When some young men first meet the lion, they are visibly affected by its majesty. The lion is different from any lion they had seen at a zoo. It was bigger and seemed to grow larger by the moment. It stood in awful, lonely solitude. It was alone, yet complete by itself.[10] This description is similar to Lewis's description of Aslan.

Most of the Inklings were writers and they would bring their chapters or essays to read to each other and then critique them. They each had a profound effect upon each other emotionally, but also creatively. Tolkien would write later that Lewis enjoyed hearing things read aloud. He had a powerful memory for things he received in this way. Lewis also had a great talent for criticizing works extemporaneously. Lewis read his manuscript for *The Problem of Pain* (1940) out loud to the Inklings. It was his first book written as an apologist or a defender of Christian beliefs. He dedicated the book to the Inklings.

Throughout World War II, the Inklings continued to meet. Lewis would read his manuscripts of *The Abolition of Man* (1943), *That Hideous Strength* (1945), *The Great Divorce* (1945), and *The Lion, the Witch and the Wardrobe* (1950); Warren read chapters from a book he was writing about the age of Louis XIV; Charles Williams read parts of his novel, *All Hallow's Eve*; and Tolkien would read excerpts from *The Hobbit* and *The Lord of The Rings*. As the war continued, Jack's admirers from the United States would send him care packages of food and delicacies difficult to find in England at that time. The beginning of the Inklings meetings started off with a feast with one of these luxuries.

In 1949, the usual evening to meet for the Inklings happened in Lewis's rooms at Oxford, but no one came. The members were all moving on to other things, and their need for the Inklings was not there any more. Over the years, their discussions had sharpened their thoughts and perfected their writings, but the need for those discussions were no longer necessary.

NOTES

1. Lewis, *The Four Loves*, 46.
2. For more information, read Jacobs, *The Narnian*, 225, and Green and Hooper, *C. S. Lewis: A Biography*, 296.
3. Lewis, *Letters to Children*, Lyle W. Dorsett and Marjorie Lamp Mead (editors), 53.
4. Gormley, *C. S. Lewis*, 163.
5. Duriez, *Tolkien and Lewis*, 43–44.
6. For further information on the Inklings, read Humphrey Carpenter, *The Inklings: C. S. Lewis, J. R. R. Tolkien, Charles Williams, and their Friends.*
7. For further information, read Jacobs, *The Narnian*, 205 and Hooper, *Letters, vol. 2*, 501.
8. Lewis, *The Four Loves*, 74–75.
9. The two letters can be found in Hooper, *Letters, vol. 2*, "The Christian Scholar, Letter," Wednesday, March 11, 1936, and in Bodleian Library, MS. Eng. c6825, fol48, Letter, March 12, 1936. Green and Hooper (137) and Duriez (86) also discuss it.
10. Enjoy the entire novel, Williams, *The Place of the Lion* (London: Pellegrini & Cudahy, 1933).

CHAPTER SIX

Finding Joy

n the 1940s, another war tore apart the peaceful countryside of England. C. S. Lewis decided not to join the ranks of soldiers for this battle as he had in the First World War. Instead, he used his skills as a writer and lecturer to bring faith to the people of England and the world during that fearsome time. He realized that joy may be more difficult to find amidst tragedy, but it is still there for those who have faith in Jesus Christ and in his power to conquer the spiritual evils of the world. Lewis commented that in this world everything is upside down for "joy is the serious business of heaven."[1]

WORLD WAR II

As Great Britain prepared for another war, Lewis could have enrolled in the volunteer reserve army organized for the possible invasion of the German army. Lewis chose not to enroll. He used the excuse of age, but he wrote to a friend that his memories from World War I still haunted him, and he did not regret his decision.[2] In this world war, England itself was under attack. Lewis built a bomb shelter in his backyard and put blackout curtains on his windows, as did all of England. There were frequent air raids. Coal was rationed along with many other necessities.

When the call came for people in the country to open their homes to children from London, Mrs. Moore opened the Kilns to let children come and stay. Girls were the first to arrive. Margaret M. Leyland, one of the child refugees staying at the Kilns, remembered Jack as being very kind and considerate. He would never talk down to her. Another evacuee, Patricia Boshell, thought Lewis was the gardener. When she told him so, he burst out laughing.

The Kilns was a country home with a garden and chickens. The children should not have suffered the privations of the city where food was rationed. But Mrs. Moore tended to be stingy, and the girls often went to bed hungry. Lewis would smuggle food to them at night. He told them stories and let them look into his telescope.

It wasn't only girls who stayed at the Kilns during this time. One young man assigned to the Kilns by the government was learning disabled. Lewis, the consummate teacher, gave him reading lessons every night for about two months. He even made drawings and letter cards to help the boy learn his alphabet.

Having children stay at the Kilns awakened something in Jack. He started thinking about writing children's stories.[3] According to Roger Lancelyn Green, a fragment of the first children's story attempt by Lewis survived on a sheet of paper caught within the manuscript of "The Dark Tower." The first chapter of the book was entitled "Through the Wardrobe." The story included four children, Ann, Martin, Rose, and Peter. They were sent to a relation's home in the country to escape the war in London. The relation was an old professor. This original work was soon abandoned and would not be revisited for another ten years.

MERE CHRISTIANITY

In 1941, the British were fully engaged in the war. There was desperate concern over the outcome of the war. England needed to have faith. The director of religious broadcasting at BBC contacted Jack and asked him to give a series of talks on the radio. At first, he was taken aback by the request. He did not trust modern inventions and had never even listened to the radio. However, he soon agreed to do it.

His talks were very popular and brought a feeling of faith back to the English people. Jack used the imagery of the present conflict to discuss the ever-present war against evil here on earth and the final restoration of the rightful king. He was not "churchy," nor was he a member of the clergy, nor did he ever want to be. He wrote in *Surprised by Joy,* "Though I liked clergymen as I like bears, I had as little wish to be in the Church as in the zoo."[4] The average listener could relate to his thoughts and feelings. Lewis would receive many letters because of his talks. He tried to answer all the serious inquirers and felt it was his duty to answer them as fully as he could.

He would also speak to soldiers at military bases all over England. They were never as successful as his radio talks, probably because they seemed too much like college lectures for men going into battle.

The popularity of his radio lectures was not limited to England. The pamphlets based on these talks were gathered into a book titled *Mere Christianity*. By September 1947, Lewis was on the cover of *Time* magazine. In 1949, Chad Walsh, an American literary critic and writer, would write a book about him titled *C. S. Lewis: Apostle to the Skeptics*, which gave Lewis a great deal of fame in the United States.

The war ended on May 9, 1945. There was great rejoicing over the end of the war. For Jack and the Inklings, the joy was muted by the sudden death of their dear friend, Charles Williams, who died unexpectedly during surgery on May 15, just a week after the end of the war. Jack found Williams's death particularly hard to bear because of their close friendship. He would write Owen Barfield that he was aware of Charles's presence with him even though he was dead. He described it as a kind of brightness and tingling that he could sense close to him. To another joint friend, Anne Ridler, Lewis wrote that this experience had increased his faith in the next life greatly.[5]

HIS RELATIONSHIP WITH JOY

Jack continued to write to many people who sent him questions about his Christian faith and his writings. Joy Davidman, a friend of Chad Walsh, and a writer herself, started sending letters to Lewis in 1950. She was born into the Jewish faith, but had converted to Christianity, attributing part of her conversion to Lewis's books. She enjoyed rigorous intellectual debates with Lewis and wrote letters that were amusing and well-written.[6]

In 1952, Joy came to visit England and had tea with Jack and Warren. He enjoyed her conversation as much as he had her letters. An invitation to Oxford and then to spend Christmas at his home at the Kilns soon followed. At this time, she was still married to her husband and was the mother of two young sons, David and Douglas. Though Joy did not believe divorce was a right course of action, her husband was an alcoholic and would often become violent and abusive. She sought advice from Jack, and he told her to divorce him.

After returning to New York, Joy's relationship with her husband did not improve. In November 1953, she left her husband and decided to move to London to live. The divorce would not become final until August 1954. Her boys met C. S. Lewis for the first time that Christmas in 1953. They were disappointed with his appearance, expecting the author of the Narnia books to be something grander and more mythical, but they did enjoy exploring the countryside outside the Kilns. Jack even dedicated the

Narnia book he was currently writing, *The Horse and His Boy,* to David and Douglas Gresham.

Although Joy and Jack came from such different backgrounds, they became close companions. Their faith and interests brought them together. Both of them had powerful conversion stories to Christianity. Jack had an experience on a bus ride. Joy had an experience during a night of prayer that brought her spiritual awareness. She had felt a personage in the room with her. This person was very real to her and had made her feel alive in a way she had never felt before. This awakening enabled her to develop faith in and an understanding of a spiritual life.[7]

In early 1956, the British government refused Joy's visa. In order to stay, Joy needed to marry a British citizen. Out of the love for a friend, Lewis married Joy civilly in April 1956. At this time they did not live together, and their relationship did not change. They continued being good friends.

Tragedy struck when Joy fell to the floor in October 1956 and broke her thigh. The doctors x-rayed her bones and found she had bone cancer and did not have long to live. Joy wanted to die at the Kilns. In order to do so, they both felt a Christian marriage would be appropriate, and they were married in the hospital room by Peter Bide, an Episcopal priest.

Jack also felt the responsibility of being a part of the lives of his two stepsons. He did not know how to be a father this late in life, but he did understand what they were going through. He and his older brother had lost their mother when they were the same age as his two stepsons.

Jack stayed close to Joy's bedside. Instead of getting worse, she began to feel better. During this time, Jack realized that he truly loved Joy, not just as a friend, but as a wife. His feelings were bittersweet as he felt the happiness of true love and was forced to watch his love die before his eyes. Joy also felt romantic love for Jack as her husband. She told a friend that she now knew true love existed.

Joy continued to help Jack in his writing, including *Till We Have Faces* and *The Magician's Nephew.* When Joy felt better, they were able to travel to Ireland, and Jack took Joy to all of his favorite places. They enjoyed walks in nature and felt its healing power.

In 1960, the specter of cancer returned. Even though Joy was in pain, Joy and Jack decided to attempt one last trip to Greece. Joy's health failed rapidly when they returned home. On July 13, 1960, a mere two months after their return from Greece, Joy died in the hospital with Jack at her side.

Jack was devastated. Douglas would remember seeing Jack weep bitterly, which was the first time he had ever seen a grown man cry. They put their arms around each other and tried to comfort one another. The boys would not stay long with Jack because of his own failing health, but they did keep in contact with him through letters and visits.

Similar to their experience after the death of their mother, Warren and Jack were left alone again. They clung to each other during this empty time, which felt to them as though the holidays had ended. Warren continued to be a great comfort to his brother, as Jack had worn himself out with taking care of Joy. Though grieving and weary, he continued to write letters to his fans with Warren's help and to lecture at Cambridge.

NOTES

1. Lewis, *Letters to Malcolm: Chiefly on Prayer*, 93.
2. See Hooper, *Letters*, vol. 2, 258.
3. Green and Hooper, *C. S. Lewis: A Biography*, 303 and Duriez, *Tolkein and Lewis*, 114.
4. Lewis, *Surprised by Joy*, 272.
5. Gormley, *C. S. Lewis*, 111.
6. This is the description Warren gives to Joy's letters in his diary.
7. For more information, read Davidman, "The Longest Way Round," in *These Found the Way*, 23.

CHAPTER SEVEN

Expressing Joy

. S. Lewis was a prolific writer. His books continue to be loved today as much and sometimes even more than when they were first published. His writings span the gamut of many literary genres. He wrote fiction and nonfiction, serious adult novels and childhood fantasy, epic poetry and Christian essays, literary criticism and linguistic interpretation, and radio talks and science fiction novels.

AN OVERVIEW OF HIS WRITINGS

His first two published works were pieces of epic poetry steeped in mythology, *Spirits in Bondage: A Cycle of Lyrics* (1919) and *Dymer* (1926). These works were generally given good reviews from literary critics, but the general public did not readily respond to their negativity and anger against God.

After Lewis became a Christian, his conversion seemed to open up a great inner reserve for writing. His first book of prose was *The Pilgrim's Regress* (1933). This book is a mythological tale that uses the story as an allegory to describe Lewis's own spiritual journey and awakening to truth.

Lewis used writing to cleanse his mind or release certain mental and emotional compulsions. He wrote the poem *Dymer* to release him from what he called "Christian Dreams" or a preoccupation with daydreams about a fantasy world. He wrote a space trilogy to exorcise his fascination with space—*Out of the Silent Planet* (1938), *Perelandra* (1943), and *That Hideous Strength* (1945). These books follow the exploits of Dr. Ransom. In the first book, he is kidnapped and taken to Mars to become a human sacrifice. The other two books follow his exploits as he travels to Venus and finally fights an evil organization called N.I.C.E.

His fiction books continue with *Screwtape Letters* (1942), which follows a senior devil instructing a junior devil named Wormwood. *The Great Divorce* (1945) is a novella that discusses allegorically the ride from earth to heaven. *The Chronicles of Narnia* are the most famous of his fictional works with seven books written between 1950 and 1956. His final fictional work is an adult novel retelling the myth of Cupid and the princess Psyche titled *Till We Have Faces*. It is written through the voice of Psyche's sister, Orual, who describes the tragic story through her point of view. Lewis's lovely wife, Joy, helped write this book. He felt it was one of his best-written books.

WRITING NONFICTION

Lewis is still considered one of the great modern apologists. He wrote many nonfiction books articulating and defending the truth of Christianity. *The Problem of Pain* (1940) explores the dilemma of how a loving God can allow evil to exist. *The Abolition of Man* (1943) looks at moral relativism in schools and society. His book *Miracles* (1947) reviews the reasonableness of miracles in this world and defines them as supernatural interventions for a mortal world.

Originally, *Mere Christianity* (1952) was published in three separate books (*The Case for Christianity, Christian Behavior,* and *Beyond Personality*), but a decade later they were consolidated into one book. The title is coined from a seventeenth-century Anglican writer, Richard Baxter, who wrote during a period of time when England's Christianity was being torn apart by different factions and sects. All of England was being forced by the monarchy and Prime Minister Oliver Cromwell to choose a party, which had political and religious ramifications for them and their family. Baxter would not choose a party. Instead, he wrote if he were to pick a party, his party would be against all sects and parties that divide people. His party would be against parties. Baxter was criticized for not taking a side. In response, Baxter declared that he was taking a side. He was a "Christian, a mere Christian."[1] That was his religion and he would not be forced to change his belief.

In *Reflections on the Psalms* (1958), Lewis gives Christian insight on Judaism as found in the Old Testament. *The Four Loves* (1960) examines four types of love defined by the Greeks: storge (affection), philia (friendship), eros (erotic love) and agape (charity or unconditional love). *Letters to Malcolm: Chiefly on Prayer* (1964) portrays Lewis writing letters to a fictitious friend, Malcolm, answering his questions on prayer. *The World's Last Night and Other Essays* (1960) and *The Weight of Glory* (1949) are both collections of addresses Lewis gave as lectures or essays that he had written previously.

Surprised by Joy (1955) was written as a spiritual autobiography focusing on Lewis's search for joy and explaining how this quest brought him to Christianity. It focuses on his early childhood and leaves out a great deal of the details of his life. *A Grief Observed* (1961) is also autobiographical and centers on Lewis conquering the suffering and loss he felt after the death of his beloved wife, Joy.

Lewis also wrote academic books focusing on his knowledge of literature. *The Allegory of Love* (1936) reviews the allegorical love poetry of Western Europe from Ancient Rome to Edmund Spenser. *Rehabilitations and Other Essays* (1939) is a work composed of his scholarly essays on literary criticism. *The Personal Heresy* (1939) is coauthored by E. M. W. Tillyard and debates the question of whether poems should reflect the personality of the poet. *A Preface to Paradise Lost* (1942) is taken from lectures Lewis delivered at Oxford. Milton had a special place in Lewis's heart. He read Milton as a young boy after the death of his mother. Milton always seemed to bring Lewis solace.

English Literature in the Sixteenth Century, Excluding Drama (1954), *Studies in Words* (1960), and *An Experiment in Criticism* (1961) are textbooks that were used in universities to study literature, language, and literary criticism.

Since Lewis's death, there have been other anthologies of his works that have been published posthumously. Many of these anthologies are redundant repackaging of various older collections, but under a new title. Right after his death, there were some books published collecting his poetry (*Poems,* 1964), essays and stories (*Of Worlds: Essays and Stories,* 1966), and lectures at Oxford (*The Discarded Image: An Introduction to Medieval and Renaissance Literature,* 1964).

The letters of C. S. Lewis have been published into many anthologies, including his letters to children, to an American lady, and letters to Arthur Greeves, his lifelong friend. His diary while he was a student at Oxford has also been published relatively recently in *All My Road Before Me: The Diary of C. S. Lewis, 1922–1927.*[2]

OXFORD AND LEWIS'S CAREER

It is difficult to believe that Lewis's great success in writing did not help his career at Oxford. Yet with all of his popular success, Lewis never received a university appointment at Oxford of any greater note than his original position as a don.

Tolkien, as a friend and colleague at Oxford, explained that a don should write only two kinds of books at Oxford: books on the subject he taught in which he is considered an expert, such as literature for C. S. Lewis; or detective stories. But dons are not forgiven for writing popular works of fiction or nonfiction, especially books that are not in his sphere of expertise.

Lewis's books were internationally successful. His Christian apologetic books were hugely popular, yet Lewis had no formal theological training as a minister. Because of this, at Oxford he was not forgiven for his writing. The popularity of his books was seen as a negative mark in his academic career rather than a positive reason for advancement.[3]

It was not until much later in his life, through the help of Tolkien, that Lewis was finally offered an appointment as Professor of Medieval and Renaissance Studies at Magdalene College in Cambridge University. Lewis was originally reticent to accept the appointment because of the travel it required. He also worried about leaving his brother, Warren, alone much of the week. Warren suffered from the same problems of depression and alcoholism as their father had. Tolkien continued to persuade Lewis until he finally accepted in 1954. Cambridge was good to Lewis. Unlike Oxford, they celebrated his accomplishments and gave him the notoriety he deserved.

DEATH AND GRIEVING

Lewis always turned to writing to help him get through spiritually hard times. To help him deal with his grief after the death of his beloved wife, he wrote *A Grief Observed* under a pseudonym, N. W. Clerk. He began the book by equating feelings of grief with feelings of fear. He continued to acknowledge the deep feelings that accompany the death of a loved one, the hindrance of grief in experiencing God's love, the dilemma of prayer, and the disillusionment of faith. He ended the book with a focused decision to leave his grief and focus on the love God. Lewis realized that living righteously should be the main focus of his attention, since death is the natural end of all mortals. Since he was still alive, he shifted his attention to living the two great commandments than continuing in his grief. This book helped Lewis sort out his grief, and it has been a source of solace for many other grieving souls.

Just a year after Joy's death, Lewis's health started deteriorating. He was afflicted with an enlarged prostate, damaged kidneys, and a weak heart. Many of these health problems were directly related to a lifetime of smoking. Lewis was writing his final book during this time, *Letters to*

Malcolm: Chiefly on Prayer, which he finished in May 1963. At the end of this book, he describes to an imaginary friend, Malcolm, his understanding of the resurrection and returning to heaven: the new earth and sky will be similar to, yet not the same, as the current earth and sky; resurrected bodies will return to this new earth; the birds will sing once again, the waters will flow, and light and shadow will move across the land; and people will see their friends and they will laugh together in amazed recognition.[4]

In July of 1963, Jack wanted to visit Ireland one last time but he had a heart attack. He was revived, but he realized that he did not have long to live. He wrote in a letter to a friend that the experience of dying and then being brought back from the dead and having to die again was rather hard.[5] With his last days, he began to sort through his papers and letters with Warren. His loving brother was the last to see Jack alive. He died on Friday, November 22, 1963, in his room at the Kilns, the same day as President John F. Kennedy's assassination.

Lewis's mother had a calendar with daily quotes from Shakespeare. On the day she died, the quote had read: "Men must endure their going hence, even as their coming hither: Ripeness is all."[6] Warren had the beginning of this quote, "Men must endure their going hence," inscribed on Jack's tomb. This was a fitting memorial for both Jack and his beloved mother.

Those at his funeral were devastated at losing their dear friend. His friends would miss his friendship and letters. The world would miss his writings and his voice encouraging all mankind to live more like Christ.

Notes

1. Baxter's statement "I am a CHRISTIAN, a MERE CHRISTIAN, of no other religion" can be found in Jacobs, *The Narnian,* 213, or Christopher Hill, *The Experience of Defeat: Milton and Some Contemporaries,* (Harmondsworth, England: Penguin, 1984), chapter 7.

2. For a complete list of all C. S. Lewis books, please refer to the Appendix D.

3. A further explanation of this can be found in Green and Hooper, *C. S. Lewis: A Biography,* 340.

4. Lewis, *Letters to Malcolm,* 124.

5. For further information, see Gormley, *C. S. Lewis,* 158.

6. For a further explanation, see Jacobs, *The Narnian,* 9. This is from Shakespeare's *King Lear.*

PART TWO

DEFINING JOY

"Dearest," said Aslan very gently, "you and your brother will never come back to Narnia."

"Oh, Aslan!!" said Edmund and Lucy both together in despairing voices.

"You are too old, children," said Aslan, "and you must begin to come close to your own world . . . there I have another name. You must learn to know me by that name. This was the very reason why you were brought to Narnia, that by knowing me here for a while, you may know me better there."

Voyage of the Dawn Treader

This section uses the seven books of *The Chronicles of Narnia* series as a basis for discussing the themes of his fiction and nonfiction works in the context of modern revelation.

CHAPTER EIGHT

The Magician's Nephew: In the Beginning

debate is still ongoing as to the order in which the Narnia series should be read. A young boy and his mother were at odds on the matter, and in 1957 they wrote Lewis a letter about it. The mother believed they should be read the way they were written with *The Lion, The Witch and The Wardrobe* first and *The Magician's Nephew* just before *The Last Battle* but the boy thought they should be read chronologically with the creation of Narnia first. Lewis seemed to chuckle in his reply and confessed that he did not plan the books out ahead of time, so it probably didn't matter what order they were read in, but in the end he thought the boy was most correct.[1] As a result, this section will follow that order as well.

IN THE BEGINNING

The Magician's Nephew begins with a boy, Digory, and a girl, Polly, being thrust into the adventure of eternity. They make choices, sometimes right and sometimes wrong; they are seduced by evil; they see the beauty of goodness and pure love; and they become part of the birth of a new world, Narnia. These experiences change their childishness into eternal wisdom and knowledge. The themes and symbols of this story are more than just a fairy tale. They have embedded in them deep spiritual significance as well.

GARDEN OF EDEN PARALLELS

From the onset Polly and Digory seem to shadow much of the story of the Fall of Man. Like Adam and Eve they meet in the garden together. Soon their boredom leads them to devise an exciting diversion. They decide to explore a space in the attic that connects the row of houses where they live, even though their parents would not approve of such an activity. One of the houses seems to be vacant and they hope to find a secret place to call their own. On the appointed day both children climb into the roof space and count their way past each house, entering the attic of the home they think is empty, but they have miscounted and are in the attic of Digory's house in Uncle Andrew's study.

Uncle Andrew is a magician of sorts who lives with his two sisters. Miss Ketterley has never married and his other sister is Digory's mother. She has returned with Digory because she is deathly ill. Miss Ketterley is worried about her sister's condition, but Uncle Andrew does not think about it.

When the two innocent children first find Uncle Andrew, he leaps out of his chair in obvious joy to use these children for selfish purposes. Lewis compares him to a demon, obviously setting him up as a parallel for the serpent. He offers Polly a simple yellow ring. Polly finds the ring strangely attractive. She puts the yellow ring on her finger and immediately disappears.[2] Uncle Andrew has tricked Polly into going to another world without the means to return. Poor Digory must go after her with green rings to bring her back. He sees Uncle Andrew for who he is and warns him that all wicked, cruel magicians will be punished in the end.

The temptation for Polly is an interesting parallel to the temptation of Eve in the Garden of Eden. Like Eve, Polly knew that her parents would be upset if they were aware of what she was doing. Like Eve, her choice cast her from the world she was in, inadvertently forcing her companion to follow. Although Polly's sin was entirely innocent (she had no idea that there would be any consequence in touching the ring), she never would have experienced this danger if she had stayed in the safety of her original home. The sin she committed was not done with malice, anger, or impassioned thoughtlessness. Instead, it was something she knew she should not be doing but chose to do anyway. It is significant that the great sin which cast our first parents from Paradise and ushered in a world of sorrow was also not a cruel or violent act but an intentional choice.

SMALL SINS

In his most popular book, *Screwtape Letters,* Lewis again visits this idea of little mistakes having great consequences. Screwtape's nephew, Wormwood, is an apprentice devil trying to lead his patient from God. Screwtape commends Wormwood for getting his patient to become friends with "worldlings," people who without committing any large crimes are slowly edging further and further away from God. He warns him to not waken his patient's sense of position and to make him feel his wrong choices are trivial and easily rectified: "You will say that these are very small sins; and doubtless, like all young tempters, you are anxious to be able to report spectacular wickedness. . . . It does not matter how small the sins are provided that their cumulative effect is to edge the man away from the Light and out into the Nothing."[3]

Wormwood's encouragement to commit "small sins" is almost identical to the prophesied cunning that would run rampant in our day. Nephi prophetically describes what he sees in the latter days. In the last few pages of his writings, he says, "And there shall also be many which shall say: Eat, drink, and be merry; nevertheless, fear God—he will justify in committing a little sin; yea, lie a little, take the advantage of one because of his words, dig a pit for thy neighbor; there is no harm in this; and do all these things, for tomorrow we die; and if it so be that we are guilty, God will beat us with a few stripes, and at last we shall be saved in the kingdom of God" (2 Nephi 28:8). Nephi calls this type of rationalization false, vain, and foolish doctrines. He explains the consequence of such behavior is that our hearts will become puffed up, and we will seek to hide our choices from the Lord.

OTHER SMALL SINS

In Lewis's little-known science fiction trilogy, *Perelandra*, the second book, tells the story of the creation of a new planet. Ransom has been brought to this planet to help the first "woman," an Eve-like character with green skin, withstand temptation. Weston, an evil scientist, has been taken over by a demon and attempts to convince her to sin, by killing animals to make clothes. Ransom takes his responsibility seriously and tries to protect the queen. Every night Ransom is plagued by Weston calling his name over and over, not allowing him to sleep.

One morning, Ransom sleeps in because of his fatigue from Weston's calling. When he awakens, he finds the Lady is wearing a cape of feathers. He is concerned that Weston has taught her to kill. Instead, he has only introduced the concept of vanity. Ransom wants to show her how she looks and finds a mirror. He is hoping this will stop the continuation of sin. Initially, when she looks in the mirror, she recoils and is confused by what she sees. She feels something she has never felt before—fear and guilt.

Later, Weston tries to get her to look again in the mirror. He tempts her into trying other things that are wrong by explaining to her that she will never know if something is good unless she tries it. On the other hand, Ransom warns her that if something is not good and she tries it, she may not stop herself from doing it again, which is why it is much better not to do it in the first place. Through this interplay Lewis illustrates the danger of those first small steps that can lead us into unforeseen traps that impede us on our journey.

In *Screwtape Letters* Lewis also emphasizes that the first small steps of sin can be the most difficult to recognize but ultimately can be as devastating as larger sins. Inevitably, small sins may lead to the most serious errors if a correction in direction is not made. After Screwtape commends Wormwood for his subtle strategy, he says, "Indeed, the safest road to Hell is the gradual one—the gentle slope, soft underfoot, without sudden turnings, without milestones, without signposts."[4]

This gentle slope spoken of by Lewis echoes Nephi's prophesy when he warns those living today that Satan will lead some "by the neck with a flaxen cord, until he bindeth them with his strong cords forever" (2 Nephi 26:22).

THE GIFTS OF THE FALL

Living in a world without consequences for poor behavior, authority figures to correct us, or a code of ethics, morals, and even commandments to show us the way would be as dangerous as wandering through the desert without a map or guide. The world soon would become the slippery slope recommended by Wormwood.

After Adam and Eve's transgression in the garden, the Lord stood before them, giving them the signposts and milestones Lewis talked about.

> Unto the woman, I, the Lord God, said: I will greatly multiply thy sorrow and thy conception. In sorrow thou shalt bring forth children, and thy desire shall be to thy husband, and he shall rule over thee.
>
> And unto Adam, I, the Lord God, said: Because thou hast hearkened unto the voice of thy wife, and hast eaten of the fruit of the tree of which I commanded thee, saying—Thou shalt not eat of it, cursed shall be the ground for thy sake; in sorrow shalt thou eat of it all the days of thy life.
>
> Thorns also, and thistles shall it bring forth to thee, and thou shalt eat the herb of the field.
>
> By the sweat of thy face shalt thou eat bread, until thou shalt return unto the ground—for thou shalt surely die—for out of it wast

thou taken: for dust thou wast, and unto dust shalt thou return. (Moses 4:22–25)

Each received consequences that were custom fit to their separate divine roles. For Eve, this referred to the physical pain of mortality and childbirth, but it also included an even greater affliction. Within a few years Eve would see her own son take the life of his brother and become condemned for it. She would have to bear the emotional and spiritual pain of watching one son physically die and another son not return to the truth, becoming spiritually lost. That sorrow, greater than any other, would be hers and would encourage her to do all in her power to train, teach, and love her children in righteousness.

For Adam, he was given the challenge to provide for his family by the sweat of his brow. Through times of famine, illness, injury, and depression, he was required to work with purpose, to keep in his mind what was most important, what was worth all his efforts both physically, mentally, and spiritually. These burdens were in fact gifts that would open their eyes to the dangers around them, especially that greatest danger of all, not returning to their Father in Heaven as a family.

At the time of the Fall, our first parents were given one additional gift, the gift of enmity between good and evil. This opposition to evil was the great mediator, our Savior, Jesus Christ, who would help lead them back to their heavenly home. It is by understanding the reasons we are in this mortal existence, the purpose of our divine roles, and the power of the Savior's enmity that we are able to clearly recognize which direction we are going.

In a world filled with confusion, eternal clarity is one of the greatest blessings of the gospel light. Moroni explained the use of a black and white litmus test which will allow us to recognize even small sins when he said, "All things which are good cometh of God; and that which is evil cometh of the devil. . . . It is given unto you to judge, that ye may know good from evil; and the way to judge is as plain . . . as the daylight is from the dark night" (Moroni 7:12, 15). In an essay entitled "Is Theology Poetry?" Lewis expressed this same concept when he said, "I believe in Christianity as I believe the sun has risen, not only because I see it, but because, by it, I see everything else."[5]

A great blessing of being a member of The Church of Jesus Christ of Latter-day Saints is our knowledge of who we are, why we are here, and where we are going. This brings peace and hope in our daily existence. With that eternal perspective, no challenge seems insurmountable, as long as we look in the mirror and see ourselves honestly and stay on the right path.

THE CREATION OF NARNIA

Returning to the story of Digory and Polly, the children find themselves in a strange wood with a number of pools around them. Each pool leads to a different world and the children decide to explore. They go to a dark world. Polly wants to leave, but Digory is curious. The children come to an old castle and find a banquet hall filled with people who are frozen in time. At the end of the row of people is a woman who is both beautiful and terrible at the same time.

In the center of the room is a bell. Polly still wants to leave but Digory, in a moment of rebellion, rings the bell. The ringing begins slowly and starts to grow louder and louder with each passing minute until the sound swells to a roar. This single event, seemingly so small, would have the same growing effect as the bell. Beginning with waking up Jadis, the wicked queen of Charn, it eventually leads to the near destruction of Narnia as she becomes the White Witch years later. Jadis quickly grabs the children by the hands and ushers them out of the palace. Soon, they return to London with their evil regal visitor.

In the drab city, Jadis seems larger than life. She immediately decides she will rule this world and enlists the feeble efforts of Uncle Andrew, who waffles between abject servitude and empty pride. Jadis becomes more and more out of control. A crowd of disgruntled victims follow her. Her cab crashes and she wrenches the bar off a lamppost with superhuman strength to retaliate. The cabby shows courage and tries to stop her onslaught. He is inadvertently pulled away from earth into another world as Polly and Digory don their rings to bring an end to the brawl. They take the cabby, Uncle Andrew, Jadis, and the cabby's horse, Strawberry, along with them.

The strange ensemble enters a new pool and find themselves in pitch darkness. In the darkness, they hear one voice singing. The simple song dances all around them. Suddenly, the sky is filled with stars which seemed to sing like a great chorus with the First Voice. When the cabby sees it, he exclaims that he would have been a better man if he had known such things were possible. Strawberry, the horse, whinnies happily. As a shining light begins to fill this new planet, the children are in awe. Uncle Andrew fears the voice and looks as though he wants to creep away into the nearest rat hole. Queen Jadis, on the other hand, understands it better than them all but hates the fact that there is a magic greater than hers. She is determined to defy it.

Just a Word about the Lamppost

In the increasing light they can see that the song is coming from a Lion that is beautiful, shaggy, and bright. The witch wants to flee, Uncle Andrew wants to kill it, but the cabby tells them to hush for he is enthralled by the song. They watch as the Lion's song brings forth grass, trees, and animals. With every step, the Lion moves closer, still singing, and not really looking at them. When he is close enough, the witch takes the lamppost bar and flings it, hitting the Lion between the eyes. It does not hurt the Lion. Instead, it falls to the ground where it begins to grow, turning into a full lamp, with the light inside glowing brightly.

This is how the lamppost came to be in Narnia. It stands as an impressive symbol of Christ's ability to transform experiences or events intended to do harm into something of value. Although the rod struck him, it did not harm Aslan in the least, and through his powers of creation he changed it to a thing of benefit. The same principle is true of our lives. Whatever our challenges, with Christ, they can be for our good. Joseph Smith, who had many challenges in his life, learned this lesson while enduring a particular difficult time. He prayed to the Lord seeking relief and received this answer: "All these things shall give thee experience, and shall be for thy good" (D&C 122:7).

Lewis also recognized that through Christ, good could come out of bad. In *The Problem of Pain* he addressed the gifts of strength and character that can be had through hardship: "I have seen great beauty of spirit in some who were great sufferers. I have seen men, for the most part, grow better not worse with advancing years, and I have seen the last illness produce treasures of fortitude and meekness from most unpromising subjects."[6] These words ring especially true as we remember Lewis's own personal experiences with grief and the cruelties he endured at school. In fact, one may wonder if it is because of those experiences that Lewis became the man he was.

Facing the Consequences

After the evil queen's failed attempt to stop Aslan, she runs off. Uncle Andrew tries to run too but falls down. The newly created Narnian animals try to comfort him and meet his needs but aren't sure what he is. They mistake him for a tree and plant and water him. Digory feels he must speak to the lion and begs the horse to carry him there. He stands before Aslan, unable to look in his eyes because secretly in his heart, he is seeking something in this magical place to make his mother well.

Aslan does not answer his question but asks one instead, as Christ has done numerous times throughout the scriptures.[7] He asks Digory to tell him how the evil witch came to Narnia. In Digory's first recounting of events, he decides not to tell the complete truth. After a stern look from Aslan, he admits he woke the witch up but suggests the possibility that he was enchanted by the bell. Again, Digory backs down and confesses he was only pretending to be enchanted. How like Adam's response to being caught partaking of the fruit when he said, "The woman thou gavest me, and commandest that she should remain with me, she gave me of the fruit." And then realizing the truth of his individual responsibility, Adam adds with godly sorrow, "and I did eat" (Moses 4:18).

The idea of taking personal responsibility for our mistakes and trying to correct them is illustrated a number of times throughout the story but nowhere more pointedly than in the evil Jadis herself. When the children first discover her on Charn, Jadis admits to destroying her own world by speaking the Deplorable Word which she learned at great personal sacrifice. Although her actions caused the death of millions of people, she does not blame herself and carries no guilt because she believes her sister and her subjects forced her to do it because they would not comply with her demands. The evil witch is blinded by her selfishness, greed, and singular point of view.

In speaking of his own errors, Lewis admits that the sooner a person takes responsibility for his mistakes and turns them around, the faster he progresses: "When I have started a sum the wrong way, the sooner I admit this and go back and start again, the faster I shall get on. There is nothing progressive about being pig headed and refusing to admit a mistake. . . . Going back is the quickest way on."[8] Jadis has no hope of changing her position because she refuses to admit her mistakes. Before the eyes of Aslan, Digory, on the other hand, comes clean about his mistakes, allowing him to take the next step.

MAKING RESTITUTION AND ANOTHER GARDEN

After admitting the truth of his shortcomings, Digory is in the depths of despair. He thinks he has spoiled everything and there is no hope for his mother now. Aslan senses his concerns and instructs Digory in a way to undo the evil he has done.

Digory must travel far away to another garden and retrieve an apple that will protect Narnia for many years. Aslan turns the Cabby's horse into a flying horse and gives it a new name, Fledge. Polly and Digory set out together on their journey. When they arrive at the garden, there is a sign that tells them that they must take the fruit for another or not at all.

If they steal it, it will bring them despair. Digory was also told to enter by the gate and no other way. When he enters the garden, he meets the evil witch, who had climbed over the wall instead of entering through the gate. She had eaten of the fruit, claiming it would enable her to live forever. She tries to convince Digory to take the fruit and return to his mother to heal her. She asks, "What has that Lion ever done for you?" Digory almost gives in until she mentions leaving Polly behind. In that moment, he realizes again how evil the witch is and resists her suggestion. He takes the apple back to Aslan, and the witch runs off.

When Digory returns, Aslan says, "Well done" with a voice that shakes the earth.[9] Aslan gives Digory the honor of planting the apple so it will grow into a tree that would protect Narnia from the witch. Polly does not understand why the fruit would repel Jadis, but Aslan explained that because she had partaken of the fruit at the wrong time and in the wrong way, it would seem disgusting to her now, even though the fruit was really delicious.

Once the tree has grown, Aslan plucks an apple and gives it to Digory to feed to his mother. It will heal her. Aslan says that if Digory had stolen the apple, it may have physically healed her, but it would not have brought her joy. But this fruit Aslan offers will, just like the fruit Lehi offered his family at the tree of life, "whose fruit was desirable to make one happy" (1 Nephi 8:10). Digory's sacrifice of giving up the apple he thought would heal his mother physically ultimately is the means for fulfilling his dearest wish of all—to save his mother both physically and spiritually.

GIVING UP SOMETHING GOOD FOR SOMETHING BETTER

Lewis also illustrates this idea of sacrifice in *The Great Divorce,* a story of a busload of people going from Hell to visit Heaven. When they arrive, most do not choose to stay because they have to leave their worldly baggage behind in order to enter. In the preface to this book, Lewis explains, "I do not think that all who choose wrong roads perish; but their rescue consists in being put back on the right road. A wrong sum can be put right: but only by going back till you find the error and working it afresh from that point, never by simply going on. If we insist on keeping Hell (or even earth) we shall not see Heaven: If we accept Heaven we shall not be able to retain even the smallest and most intimate souvenirs of Hell."[10]

A transformation occurs in Digory. His impetuous errors in exploring beyond the bounds he was allowed, ringing the bell, and hiding his mistakes are each undone. He even confesses to Aslan that he almost gave into temptation and ate the fruit.

When Digory finally brings that apple to his mother's side and feeds it to her, she is healed. They eventually return to their house in the country to live happily, inviting Polly out to visit every holiday.

UNCLE ANDREW

As the story nears its end, Aslan turns to care for Uncle Andrew. Worried by his strange behavior, the kind animals have built a cage of sorts around him so that he will not hurt himself. In case he might be hungry, they throw every kind of food at him, leaving him quite a mess. For all the beauty around him in Narnia, he sees nothing but fear. The words of Aslan are growls to him because he won't open his heart to hear them. It is at this point that Aslan bemoans Uncle Andrew's fate, "Oh, Adam's sons, how cleverly you defend yourselves against all that might do you good."[11] In those words we can hear the sadness of Christ's words to his chosen people when he said, "How often would I have gathered thy children together, as a hen doth gather her brood under her wings, and ye would not!" (Luke 13:34).

Uncle Andrew leaves Narnia fearful to touch magic again but his heart is completely unchanged. His stagnant condition is described by Lewis at the end of *The Great Divorce:* "There are only two kinds of people in the end: those who say to God, 'Thy will be done,' and those to whom God says, in the end, 'Thy will be done.' All that are in Hell, choose it. Without that self-choice there could be no Hell. No soul that seriously and constantly desires joy will ever miss it. Those who seek find. To those who knock it is opened."[12]

Uncle Andrew's only desires were for selfishness and materialism. During the last years of his life, Uncle Andrew is taken in by Digory's father, where he likes to have visitors come so he can tell about his great adventure. Like the people of Charn, he is frozen in time. He never progresses or lives at all.

THE NEW KING AND QUEEN OF NARNIA

Of all the changes we see in individuals throughout the story, the most extreme is Frank the cabby and his wife, Helen. Both were originally country folk forced to make a scant living in the city. In this new land, Frank and Helen are pronounced King and Queen of Narnia. They arrive poor and rough looking. As they are dressed in finery and stand before their coronation, Helen sees in her husband all his best qualities magnified, and the harshness and quarrelsomeness he had picked up in the city washed away. Both become royalty, worthy of their callings.

In his book, *The Weight of Glory*, Lewis states, "It is a serious thing to live in a society of possible gods and goddesses, to remember that the dullest and most uninteresting person you can talk to may one day be a creature which, if you saw it now, you would be strongly tempted to worship." From their original descriptions, Helen and Frank are initially dull. They become kind and good rulers of Narnia. Lewis goes on to warn us how we should view our neighbors, "It is in the light of these overwhelming possibilities, it is with the awe and the circumspection proper to them, that we should conduct all our dealings with one another, all friendships, all loves, all play, all politics. There are no ordinary people. You have never talked to a mere mortal."[13] Understanding our divine potential and the worth of those around us encourages us to behave appropriately in every aspect of life.

NOTES

1. Dorsett and Mead, *C. S. Lewis Letters to Children*, 68.
2. The rings in this book bear a striking resemblance to a ring in J. R. R. Tolkien's *The Lord of the Rings*. Considering their friendship, it is an interesting parallel.
3. Lewis, *Screwtape Letters*, 63.
4. Ibid., 60–61.
5. Lewis, "Is Theology Poetry?" *The Weight of Glory*, 116.
6. Lewis, *The Problem of Pain*, 108–109.
7. Throughout the scriptures, Christ often uses questions to answer questions. See his dealings with the Brother of Jared in Ether 2:23; his response to the young lawyer after the telling of "the Good Samaritan" in Luke 10:36; or the last line of the story of Jonah in Jonah 4:8–11.
8. Lewis, *Mere Christianity*, 28–29.
9. Lewis, *The Magician's Nephew*, 203.
10. Lewis, *The Great Divorce*, viii-ix.
11. Lewis, *The Magician's Nephew*, 203.
12. Lewis, *The Great Divorce*, 75.
13. Lewis, *The Weight of Glory*, 45.

CHAPTER NINE

The Lion, the Witch and the Wardrobe: The Atonement

hortly after World War II, Lewis started thinking about writing a series of children's books. Lewis was writing the story for his goddaughter, Lucy, Owen Barfield's daughter. She became the character for the little girl named Lucy Pevensie who would discover Narnia. Lewis dedicated the book affectionately to the "real" Lucy who was now a young adult. The book had taken longer to mature than she had. *The Lion, the Witch and the Wardrobe* was finally published in 1950. In his dedication, Jack acknowledged the fact that Lucy was not a little girl anymore and was probably too old for fairy tales. Some day, he hoped she would start reading fairy tales once again and pick up his book to read.[1] Whether Lucy ever dusted off the book and finally read it or not is inconsequential because millions of others, young and old, have found great joy in this Christian fairy tale.

SEEKING JOY IN THE MIDST OF EVIL

In *The Magician's Nephew,* Digory and Polly bring evil into the world of Narnia through the witch, the Queen Jadis. The introduction of evil brings an opposition to all things. As the characters deal with evil, they also gain a greater understanding of their ultimate goal of joy. Opposites are necessary for them to make correct choices. This becomes a constant theme in all of the Narnia books. In *The Lion, the Witch and the Wardrobe,* this dualism is illustrated through the stark evil and selfish pleasures of the White Witch (who was originally Queen Jadis) in direct opposition to the goodness and selflessness of Aslan. The Pevensie children are each subject to her enticements, charms, and worldly delights. They must make choices in accordance with or opposition to the White Witch.

Latter-day scripture supports the enduring view of continually seeking for joy, in spite of evil forces that would try to take us away from it. We must constantly strive for this divine goal. The scriptures describe man's ultimate destiny as having joy: "Adam fell that men might be; and men are, that they might have joy" (2 Nephi 2:25). We need to choose between those actions that bring eternal joy and those actions that bring eternal heartache and pain.

From the beginning, Adam and Eve were tempted by the devil. Our earthly experiences continue the same pattern of temptation so that each of us can make a conscious choice between evil and eternal joy. "And it must needs be that the devil should tempt the children of men, or they could not be agents unto themselves; for if they never should have bitter they could not know the sweet" (D&C 29:39).

In his *Preface to Paradise Lost,* Lewis simply states what he sees as an obvious eternal principle: when we are obedient to the will of God, we are happy and we can experience glimpses of eternal joy during our earthly sojourn. When we are disobedient, we are sad and our experiences distance us from an eternal view. For all the modern scholars' wisdom, they have missed this "dazzlingly" simple fact.[2]

One of Lewis's earliest literary pieces was entitled "Joy" which he wrote under the pseudonym Clive Hamilton.[3] In this poem, he describes awakening from slumber into an understanding of joyous beauty. This realization often comes unexpectedly and ephemerally on earth. As joy leaves us, there comes an ache and longing for the feeling of joy to stay. Having joy forever with us is not meant for this existence, but for a heavenly life that is to come. Choosing to be righteous is a lifelong process of hard work with lovely moments of joy to inspire us along the way.

ASLAN, IN THE PRESENCE OF JOY

Aslan brings a feeling of joy and awe to all the Pevensie children from the first time they hear his name. When Peter, Susan, and Lucy finally see him, they are all "trembly" inside, realizing that something can be great and terrible at the same time. He looks regal, golden, and overwhelming. They speak to him, and he makes them feel comfortable in his presence.[4]

In *The Pilgrim's Regress,* the main character, John, hears sweet music and a voice that says, "Come." Then John sees a primrose garden and an island. These visions quickly pass from his mind. As the sweetness of this dream passes away, he is filled with a sad excitement. He now knows what he wants, and it fills him with a sweet desire.[5]

Susan and Lucy feel this same yearning in the presence of Aslan, the

Creator-Lion. Susan feels that a delicious smell or beautiful music has just floated by her. Lucy feels like she had just awakened to find out it is the beginning of a holiday or summer vacation. The whole sensation is lovelier than they can put into words. Aslan brings them joy. Their greatest desire is to be in Aslan's presence always.

EDMUND'S CHOICE—GOING A DIFFERENT WAY

Edmund is initially affected by the sound of Aslan's name, but the change does not last long. Edmund has already met the White Witch on his first trip to Narnia, and she has given him a taste of Turkish Delight. By partaking of this food, Edmund becomes a slave to her whims because of his lust to have more. He lies to his siblings about ever having met the witch. His nature becomes duplicitous as he finds himself wanting another taste of the delicious food to satiate his own lust. He will do anything for a bite.

All of us should beware of pleasures that become insatiable. Jesus taught us to go as far as casting away body parts that cause us to sin, especially if we cannot stop sinning: "If thy right eye offend thee, pluck it out, and cast it from thee: for it is profitable for thee that one of thy members should perish, and not that thy whole body should be cast into hell" (Matthew 5:29). Lewis alludes to these instructions of the Savior when he discusses irresistible sin: "If it becomes irresistible . . . [t]he time for plucking out the right eye has arrived."[6]

As Edmund becomes a prisoner to his lust, he also leaves the company of those who could help him stop his craving. On his way, Edmund finds a lion turned into stone and jeers at it, as if it were Aslan. He goes so far as to draw a pencil mustache and glasses on the poor beast, but it does not give Edmund any satisfaction or fun.

Edmund finally reaches the White Witch's palace. To his dismay, the pleasure he sought so desperately becomes a prison. Edmund feels the wrath of the witch because he did not bring all his siblings with him, as she had told him to do. Edmund becomes quite miserable. He drinks water, eats stale bread, and then is forced to go on a terrible journey in a sled with the witch. He is not wearing a coat or warm clothing of any kind, and the witch does nothing to protect him. He soon is covered with snow.

The White Witch initially seemed so beautiful and nice. She was charming to him at first, as long as he could provide her with what she wanted. She even went so far as tantalizing him with her kingdom, offering him the position of prince. Similarly, the devil "flattereth away . . . he whispereth in their ears, until he grasps them with his awful chains, from whence there is no deliverance" (2 Nephi 28:22).

Looking back at their initial meeting, it would have been much better if Edmund had never listened to the White Witch's lies or tasted her food. He had a feeling about the witch, but he did not heed it. Lucy had also cautioned him about her cruelty, but he still did not listen, nor believe Lucy's words of warning.

Lewis warned all Christians, "A Christian would be wise to avoid, where he decently can, any meeting with people who are bullies, lascivious, cruel, dishonest, spiteful and so forth. Not because we are 'too good' for them. In a sense because we are not good enough. We are not good enough to cope with all the temptations, not clever enough to cope with all the problems, which an evening spent in such society produces. The temptation is to condone, to connive at; by our words, looks and laughter, to 'consent.' "[7]

After having gone down the path of being with the witch, Edmund cannot, on his own willpower, break the power of her spell. It was only with Aslan's help that Edmund is ultimately saved from imminent destruction.

BELIEVING IN THE TRUTH—EVEN WHEN NO ONE BELIEVES YOU

In George Macdonald's children's story, *The Princess and the Goblin,* the virtuous Princess Irene saves a young boy, Curdie, from the goblins because of an invisible thread which only she can see. Curdie does not believe Princess Irene's story of an invisible thread.

When they return home, Irene's grandmother asks her why she is not happier about saving Curdie. The grandmother finds out it is because of Curdie's unbelief. She chides Princess Irene for being hard upon someone who does not believe. She reminds her that Irene herself probably would not have believed if she had not seen it herself.

Curdie returns home to his mother. He tells her about his disbelief of Princess Irene's story about an invisible thread that led to his rescue. His mother warns him about being a skeptic. Just because he cannot see the invisible thread, it does not prove the thread does not exist. Until he finds a better explanation, he should be more sparing in his judgment.[8]

Lewis read this book as a child and later as a converted Christian. He understood the need for believers to be understanding of unbelievers. He also acknowledged the need for unbelievers to be willing to have faith and trust those they know who are good people. Trusting in other's faith can bring them hope to believe themselves.

Lucy, the youngest Pevensie, is the first to find the wardrobe's entrance to Narnia. She is hiding during a game of hide-and-seek, and the wardrobe looked like a perfect place. This seemingly simple decision of Lucy's had far reaching consequences for herself, her family, and the country of Narnia.

Every decision we make, even when we are playing, affects our eternal life. We cannot think that because we are just having fun, that time does not count. Lewis reflected on the power of every second, "Our leisure, even our play, is a matter of serious concern. [That is because] there is no neutral ground in the universe: every square inch, every split second, is claimed by God and counterclaimed by Satan."[9]

After Lucy returns, she tells her brothers and sister about Narnia. They do not believe her at first. She refuses to recognize the experience as make-believe, and her older siblings begin to worry. Edmund even thinks Lucy is becoming "batty."

A few days later, Edmund follows Lucy trying to hide in the wardrobe in a later hide-and-seek game. He discovers Narnia for himself and meets the White Witch. Lucy sees Edmund in Narnia and is so excited to finally have a fellow believer, someone who has had the same experience as she has. However, even after being there, Edmund refuses to concede that there really is another world in the back of the wardrobe. Instead, he denies it all. Edmund allows poor Lucy to continue feeling the pressure of admitting it was all pretend.

Susan and Peter decide to go talk to Professor Digory about Lucy's story. They are worried there might be something seriously wrong with Lucy. The professor asks the children if they think Lucy is "mad" because of her stories of Narnia. They don't know what to think, but they know Lucy has always been truthful before. By talking to Lucy, the professor knows she is not mad, so he concludes that if she is not mad, and she is not lying, then, logically, she must be telling the truth.

Lewis, like the professor, knew what madness truly looked like for he had seen madness on a close and personal basis. He would never forget watching the fits of Dr. John Hawkins Askins, Mrs. Moore's brother. Dr. Askins went through a terrible time of insanity just before his death. Mrs. Moore and Lewis went to care for "Doc" during the spring of 1923 while they waited to find a hospital bed for him. He described a fit of Doc's during their final lunch together. The doctor would hoot, kick, spit, and become paralyzed, falling to the floor. At one point, Doc had looked at Lewis and said, "I'm in Hell."[10] Lewis conceded in his diary that this was the most painful experience he had witnessed in his life. Because of this experience, Lewis realized that mental anguish could be more painful than physical pain.

The other children had a hard time believing Lucy's story until they had their own experience in the wardrobe. Similarly, many people have a hard time believing another's spiritual experience with God, whom they cannot see, until they have a similar experience.

Joy Davidman, Lewis's wife, had a spiritual experience. She did not see, but felt the presence of someone in her room. She prefaced her description of the event with the statement that those who have had similar experiences or who know God will understand what she is describing; others will not listen nor understand the experience.

Jesus taught, "If thou canst believe, all things are possible to him that believeth" (Mark 9:23). Sometimes we must cry out, "Lord, I believe; help thou mine unbelief" (Mark 9:24). That simple act of faith, even in acknowledging the limitations of our belief, will enable the Lord to then take us by the hand and lift us up supporting our belief, even in things we cannot see or completely understand.

EDMUND RETURNS HOME

Edmund betrays his family, the free Narnians, and Aslan. He tells the White Witch where Aslan is meeting those who are still on his side. After his ride in the witch's sled, Edmund is miserable. He is cold, wet, hungry, and tired. They reach the ancient Stone Table, and the witch grabs Edmund and is about to slit Edmund's throat when Aslan's scouting party rescues him.

Edmund is taken back to Aslan's camp where Aslan has a private conversation with him. Then Edmund is presented to his family with the reminder that they are not to discuss what is past. Edmund shakes hands with Peter, Susan, and Lucy while he says he is sorry. In return, they express their love for him. The prodigal son returns, and he is willing to move forward.

Picking yourself up and trying again is an act of faith. Lewis wrote in a letter, "No amount of falls will really undo us if we keep picking ourselves up each time. We shall of course be very muddy and tattered children by the time we reach home. But the bathrooms are all ready, the towels put out, and the clean clothes in the airing cupboard."[11] Edmund did fall, but Aslan cleaned him up and sent him off to try again.

The Pevensie children also "frankly forgave" Edmund (1 Nephi 7:21). They did not harbor bad feelings toward him, but forgave him freely. Edmund had hurt them deeply, but they were willing to forget past hurts.

Lewis collected an anthology of George MacDonald's writings and sermons. MacDonald wrote and spoke about the importance of forgiveness, even when there is provocation for hatred and anger. He felt the greater the excuse to hate, the stronger the reason that the hater should forgive and be delivered from the "hell" of his anger. He explained, "No man who will not forgive his neighbor, can believe that God is willing, yea wanting, to forgive him. . . . If God said, 'I forgive you' to a man who hated his brother, and if (as impossible) that voice of forgiveness should reach the man, what would it mean to him? How would the man interpret it? Would it not mean to him, 'You may go on hating. I do not mind it. You have had great provocation and are justified in your hate'?"[12]

This exemplifies what the Lord taught, "I, the Lord, will forgive whom I will forgive, but of you it is required to forgive all men. And ye ought to say in your hearts—let God judge between me and thee, and reward thee according to thy deeds" (D&C 64:10–11).

THE ATONEMENT: PAYING THE PRICE FOR SIN AND DEATH

Edmund comes back, but the enormity of his sins demands greater justice. It is not enough just to say "I'm sorry." A price needs to be paid for his betrayal. The White Witch demands Edmund's life. It is her right to kill him. Aslan talks to her alone and gives her the bond of his own life. The ultimate pain and agony will be suffered by Aslan as he gives himself to be tortured and killed for the sins of another.

The White Witch thinks she has won. She shaves off Aslan's mane, muzzles him, and allows the onlooking crowd to kick, beat, and spit upon him. Just before she stabs Aslan on the ancient Stone Table, she tells him that he has lost his life and his kingdom without saving anyone, especially Edmund.

Susan and Lucy witness Aslan's degradation and murder. At sunrise, mice gnaw off the ropes that bound him, and the Stone Table breaks in two. Then Aslan's body disappears. Susan and Lucy despair that all is lost because the body is gone. Then Aslan rises in front of them, stronger and more vigorous than before. All has been restored to him, including his mane. With his newfound strength, Aslan defeats the White Witch and her evil once and for all.

The great love Aslan has for Edmund causes him to suffer this horrific death. Yet Edmund does not understand the enormity of the sacrifice that was made for him by Aslan. However, during the battle against the White Witch, Edmund fights harder than anyone and is badly hurt in the battle, risking his life to destroy the witch's wand. Lucy uses a few drops of her healing potion on Edmund but must leave him before she knows if it has worked because Aslan directs her to help the other wounded. Through this experience both children are tested.

By putting his own life on the line for others, Edmund is changed and understands more fully the magnitude of Aslan's selfless act. The Savior taught, "He that loveth his life shall lose it; and he that hateth his life in this world shall keep it unto life eternal" (John 12:25). Edmund's spiritual and physical life were restored through the healing power of Aslan and through his own willingness to do whatever it takes to undo the wrong he had done.

Another trait illustrated through this part of the story is Lucy's act of true charity. Charity is the pure love of Christ and "seeketh not her own" (1 Corinthians 13:5). Lucy makes the difficult decision to care for others before knowing if Edmund is better because Aslan asks her to do this. Her decision illustrates charity for others and the importance of obedience even in the face of hardship. When she returns to her brother, she finds him completely healed.

These beautiful images make this story a beloved allegory of Christ and his sufferings for us. It is also a theme that Lewis wrote about in other works. In the beginning of Lewis's book, *The Problem of Pain,* he quoted George MacDonald: "The Son of God suffered unto the death, not that men might not suffer, but that their sufferings might be like His."[13] Our sufferings do help us understand the suffering of our Savior.

Our Savior's sufferings did not eliminate the sins we will commit on earth or trials we will experience. He died for us even though we are still sinners, "but God commendeth his love toward us, in that, while we were yet sinners, Christ died for us" (Romans 5:8). The hope of the Atonement is that we can repent and change to become new and better people, "which hope we have as an anchor of the soul, both sure and steadfast" (Hebrews 6:19).

THE PEVENSIES ARE FOREVER CHANGED

Through these experiences in Narnia, Peter, Susan, Lucy, and Edmund are forever changed. They become kings and queens of Narnia and rule there for many years. Even Edmund is described as being "great in council and judgment." They live together in joy and become men and women of wisdom and experience.

If we allow our experiences to be shaped by the Master Builder himself, we too can find greater potential and change in what we become. Usually, Christ has a much bigger plan for us than we could ever dream. Lewis wrote,

> Imagine yourself as a living house. God comes in to rebuild that house. At first, perhaps, you can understand what He is doing. He

is getting the drains right and stopping the leaks in the roof and so on: you knew those jobs needed doing and so you are not surprised. But presently he starts knocking the house about in a way that hurts abominably and does not seem to make sense. What on earth is He up to? The explanation is that He is building quite a different house from the one you thought of—throwing out a new wing here, putting on an extra floor there, running up towers, making courtyards. You thought you were going to be made into a decent little cottage: but He is building a palace.[14]

At the end of their first adventure in Narnia, the children tell Professor Digory all about the experience. The professor understood their story because he has also been to Narnia as a child. He tells the children to look in the eyes of other people, searching for those who may know and understand their feelings. They must search for others who have also visited Narnia and had adventures there, for only they will understand their stories.

The Pevensie children continue to be a work in progress. They would come back to Narnia in other adventures. Each of their experiences changes them a little bit more, teaching them something different and making them better people.

Notes

1. Read the dedication by Lewis, *The Chronicles of Narnia, The Lion, the Witch and the Wardrobe*, 110.
2. For more insights, read Lewis, Preface, *Paradise Lost*, 71.
3. Published in *The Beacon*, 3, no. 31 (May 1924).
4. Lewis took the name Aslan from the Turkish word for lion. He found the word in a footnote of a copy of *The Thousand and One Nights or Arabian Nights* that he was reading.
5. Lewis, *The Pilgrim's Regress*, 8.
6. Lewis, *The Weight of Glory*, 43.
7. Lewis, Reflections on the Psalms, 71.
8. For the entire story, read George MacDonald, *The Princess and the Goblin*, 17.
9. Lewis, *Christian Reflections*, 33.
10. For further information on this incident, read Lewis, *All My Road Before Me*, 211–18.
11. Lewis, *Collection of Letters*, vol. II, 507.
12. Lewis, *George MacDonald: An Anthology*, 13.
13. Lewis, *The Problem of Pain*, vii.
14. Lewis, *Mere Christianity*, 205. Lewis is referencing a quote by George MacDonald.

CHAPTER TEN

The Horse and His Boy: Providence and Pride

f all the Narnia books, *The Horse and His Boy,* it could be argued, has the most exciting plotline and digresses the least into obvious religious metaphor. It begins with a poor slave boy and an escaping princess, who through a variety of little expected accidents join together to save a country, an experience that neither had ever dreamt of. Except for a few final scenes with Aslan, a reader would think it was simply a great adventure. But true to form, Lewis does explore certain gospel truths amid its pages, in particularly the concepts of providence and pride.

THE MEANING OF PROVIDENCE

Providence is a term often used by the founding fathers to mean the extent to which God interferes with natural events for our benefit. Benjamin Franklin wrote the following in a letter to Thomas Paine: "Without the belief of a Providence, that takes cognizance of, guards, and guides, and may favor particular persons, there is no motive to worship a Deity, to fear his displeasure, or to pray for his protection."[1]

Lewis also believed strongly that "whether we like it or not, God intends to give us what we need, not what we now think we want."[2] Too often in today's world, people ascribe these acts of providence to good luck or fate, rather than recognizing the hand of God in their lives. Although from the first page of *The Horse and His Boy* there are hints that a larger force is in play, certain fantastic events are clearly nothing less than the direct intervention of Aslan. Again and again, Aslan nudges circumstances into alignment: the sound of roaring lions scaring two talking horses into almost colliding, a cat comforting a boy in the middle of the night, and a huge predator chasing the horses that pushes them beyond their normal strength. All of this is done in order to save Narnia from an even more vicious predator and to soften the hearts of the proud.

This concept of direct intervention is thrilling for members of the Church because it is one of the major tenets of our belief not often shared by other denominations in the Christian community. As we study the course of events leading to the Restoration, we can see that the very trends of history were shaped to prepare the world for the gospel in its fullness again. In our individual lives we often share testimonies of minor miracles when we unexpectedly ran into someone in need of our help or avoided injury due to an impression. The heart of our faith is, as Isaiah states, "that we may see, and know, and consider, and understand together, that the hand of the Lord hath done this" (Isaiah 41:20).

ASLAN OUTSIDE HIS OWN COUNTRY

The story of *The Horse and His Boy* begins in a southern country called Calormen, where a fisherman lives with a child that he found and named Shasta. Shasta works hard but is often treated roughly by this man. One night a wealthy Tarkaan, or warlord, comes demanding food and lodging. Late that night the boy overhears his adopted father bargaining with the Tarkaan to purchase him as a slave. Unsure of what to do, Shasta approaches the warlord's great horse, who surprisingly talks to him. Bree, the talking horse, explains that he was kidnapped as a foal and has been pretending to be a dumb animal until he could escape. He tells Shasta about the freedom and beauty of a northern paradise called Narnia and the two run away together.

Everything goes well at first, and they fall into a pleasant routine as they make their way north. Then one night as they are traveling, they notice another rider who they try to avoid. Bree hears a lion and bolts forward wildly, running recklessly, as does the other horse and rider. Before long, the two horses are neck and neck with the roar of at least two lions on their tails. As they splash into an unexpected inlet by the sea, the roaring is gone but not before the other horse speaks. Bree hears the mare, Hwin, and addresses her. Hwin was also taken from Narnia as a foal and is running away with her mistress, who is a warlord's daughter raised in privilege.

The reader who knows of Aslan is certain that their meeting has been orchestrated by him, but since both Shasta and Aravis have not been raised in Narnia, they know nothing of the Lion. In their country they worship Tash, a cruel god who will be explained more in *The Last Battle,* the final book in the series. Despite their total lack of awareness of his existence, Aslan condescends to assist them. Like the words spoken to the prophet Jeremiah when Israel was being lost in wickedness, "Behold I am Lord, the God of all flesh: is there anything too hard for me?" (Jeremiah 32:27). As Aslan reaches beyond the confines of the land of Narnia, so Christ stands before all flesh, every country, whether they acknowledge him or not.

In *The Problem of Pain* Lewis speaks about people who try to erase God from their lives. He says, "They wanted some corner in the universe of which they could say to God, 'This is our business, not yours.' But there is no such corner."[3] It is a great error to think that the efforts of Deity only extend within his chosen people when every corner of the earth is his. Scripturally, we see Christ declare his divinity to the Samaritan woman at the well, and he heals the centurion's daughter, both of which remind us that he is truly God over the whole earth. In this way it seems good to read of Aslan reaching into this other land to help these two children.

PRIDE EXPOSED

That night the four fugitives sit at camp, and Bree takes command of the situation. He encourages Aravis to tell the story of her escape. She explains that her father was going to marry her to a wealthy but disgusting old man, and she attempted to kill herself rather than marry. But her mare who she did not know was a talking horse, spoke for the first time to dissuade her. When that didn't work Hwin, put her head between the dagger and the girl. At last Aravis decided to give up the idea of killing herself and to run away instead.

In order to escape from her father's house undetected, Aravis drugged a servant girl. Shasta asks if the slave would be punished, and Aravis replied that she would be whipped but that she deserved it. Bree, the proud warhorse, is angry at Shasta for interrupting the story. Both Aravis and Bree show lack of empathy for the poor servant girl, which is the first sign of their pride; this concept continues to be a powerful theme throughout the story. Lewis had strong opinions about this topic and devoted an entire section of his book *Mere Christianity* to the subject, entitled "The Great Sin." Lewis believed that "pride leads to every other vice: it is the complete anti-God state of mind."[4] As Shasta's story progresses, this anti-God state becomes more apparent.

ARRIVING AT CITY OF TASHBAAN

Back on the road to Narnia, the foursome must go through the city of

Tashbaan; there is no way around it. Hwin makes a suggestion to cut the horses' tails ragged, have them roll in the mud, and dress Aravis in rags like Shasta has been wearing all of his life. Aravis goes along with the plan until she faces the city, where she becomes upset. It isn't the rags that bothers her; it is being seen by others in them. Lewis believed this was the very definition of pride when he said, "Pride gets no pleasure out of having something, only out of having more of it than the next man. . . . It is the comparison that makes you proud: the pleasure of being above the rest. Once the element of competition has gone, pride has gone."[5]

Within the bustling city providence is again at work. As the mass of travelers move aside for guests of the king, Shasta gets jostled and ends up at the front of the press of people where he is plucked from the crowd by a visiting nobleman, Edmund, who mistakes him for a friend. Unlike the selfish, diffident boy who assisted the White Witch, Edmund is now a faithful and valiant young man who treats Shasta with patience despite the fact that he thinks he is the spoiled Corin, heir to Archenland, who has run off again.

At the palace Shasta overhears how Prince Rabadash, son of Tisroc, had come to Narnia to win Susan's hand in marriage. The prince was very polite when in Narnia, but on the trip to his land they have seen him for who he really is. Rabadash reflects each of the three traits delineated by the prophet Joseph Smith, in his revelation warning priesthood leaders against unrighteous dominion. Rabadash first tries to "cover [his] sins" by not divulging his true nature; second, he attempts "to gratify [his] pride, [his] vain ambition." His decision to court Susan is not based on feelings for her but on his concern of what the world with think of him if he fails to win the prize of Narnia. Finally, Susan realized not only does he "exercise control or dominion or compulsion upon the souls of the children of men" (D&C 121: 37) in his own kingdom, but that when she denies the prince they may quickly become prisoners instead of guests, and so the Narnians plot their escape.

Once the adults leave the room to begin executing their ruse, a boy who looks just like Shasta climbs through the window. Mirroring Mark Twain's story, the prince and the pauper trade places, and Shasta climbs out the window to head off toward the meeting place his friends had decided on before entering the city.

A NIGHT AT THE TOMBS

Shasta arrives alone at the tombs outside of Tashbaan at twilight and shivers at the shadowy stone shapes when he feels something touch his leg.

In the dark he can make out the silhouette of a large cat that stays with him all night. It is Aslan, comforting and protecting him, but in the morning he is gone. Aslan's watchful care reflects one of Lewis's six propositions about pain and suffering in this imperfect world, spoken of in his book *The Problem of Pain*. Proposition number four talks about the settled happiness and security that we all crave in this life, but that it is fleeting and short-lived, yet consistently provided. Lewis said, "Our Father refreshes us on the journey with some pleasant inns, but will not encourage us to mistake them for home."[6] Like Abraham at the altar, Elijah in the desert, and Joseph in Liberty Jail, when his children are at critical points of extreme anguish, we often see the Lord condescend, lift, and comfort. Sometimes this comfort comes as a messenger or voice, but more often it is a powerful impression that speaks to our very souls.

Within the first weeks that Oliver Cowdery began transcribing the Book of Mormon for Joseph Smith, he was given a revelation through the Urim and Thummim where we see this sort of love—this comfort at a point of fear and indecision. The Lord said, "Cast your mind upon the night that you cried unto me in your heart, that you might know concerning the truth of these things. Did I not speak peace to your mind concerning the matter? What greater witness can you have than from God?" (D&C 6:22–23).

Just as these great men were succored in their need, even so the Lord succors us in our extremities and carries us through the most difficult moments. It is also significant that after Shasta is refreshed, strengthened and protected by Aslan in the image of a cat by the next morning, the boy is back on his own. Although he is not yet out of danger, it is time for him to meet his own challenges single-handedly. Even so our Father will help us, but will also allow us to do as much as we can by our own volition. "Men should be anxiously engaged in a good cause, and do many things of their own free will, and bring to pass much righteousness" (D&C 58:27).

Aravis Finds a Friend

Right after losing Shasta, Aravis recognizes a childhood friend riding on a litter and hops into it. Lasaraleen is newly married to a wealthy man and asks Avaris to tell her story but hardly listens to a word, more concerned about her clothes, her most recent parties, and the latest gossip. In Lasaraleen we see the epitome of pride. Lewis once said, "A proud man is always looking down on things and people; and, of course, as long as you are looking down, you cannot see something that is above you."[7] Nowhere is this blindness more apparent than in this character who wants Aravis to marry her intended, who has now been promoted to the Grand Vizier, so that she can visit his opulent palaces and increase her rank in society, not caring in the least that her friend would be miserable. Rather than be discouraged, Avaris sees her old self more clearly in her friend and increases her resolve to escape from the traditions that have fed her weaknesses.

Lasaraleen takes Avaris to the back gate of the palace to escape, but they are almost found out and hide in a room where they see Tisroc, the fat ruler of Tashbaan, enter with his son Prince Rabadash and the Grand Vizier. The Narnians have just escaped. Tisroc is a ruthless ruler who cares nothing for the welfare of others. The Grand Vizier is lying prostrate on the ground and Prince Rabadash kicks him in his frustration, but Tisroc only censures the poor vizier for not continuing despite his discomfort. This total lack of concern for others is similar to the attitude of "flippancy" which means "showing a lack of seriousness that is thought inappropriate."[8]

In *Screwtape Letters* the master demon believes that the habit of flippancy is a victory of sorts: "If prolonged, the habit of Flippancy builds up around a man the finest armour-plating against God that I know. It is a thousand miles from joy. It deadens, instead of sharpening, the intellect; and it excites no affection between those who practice it."[9] As Prince Rabadash charges off to enact his plan to overthrow Archenland and kidnap Susan. Tisroc turns to the vizier and says that if his son fails, he will not come to his aid, showing the lack of affection spoken of by Lewis. This state of being "without principle and past feeling" was also referred to by Mormon, describing his people who were ripe for destruction (Moroni 9:20).

RUNNING TO SAVE NARNIA

Aravis hurries to tell Shasta of the danger. They set off in haste with the horses, traveling all day and night. Exhausted, the group slows their pace, but again providence spurs them forward. They see what looks like a cloud in the distance. It is Prince Rabadash with his two hundred armed men. This is where the price of pride begins to show itself. Although Bree has bragged of his feats in battle, it is Hwin, a smaller and weaker horse that is setting the pace. When the war horse suddenly hears the sound of a lion he passes Hwin in fear, leaving her behind to face the danger. Shasta turns to see the lion closing in on Hwin and Avaris and tries to get Bree to slow down or turn around to help them, but he just keeps going. Finally Shasta jumps from the saddle to help as the lion reaches the slower horse and slices stripes across Aravis's back. Shasta scares the lion away and it runs off.

The small band finds a hermit's gate where they are welcomed. The hermit tells the weary Shasta that he must continue and run as fast as he can to find the king. Shasta obediently races off, pushing himself to the edge of his physical abilities. Like Lewis said in *Mere Christianity*, "Christ says, Give me All. I don't want so much of your time and so much of your money and so much of your work: I want You."[10] Shasta's attitude of self-lessness and commitment qualifies him for the great inheritance that is his to come. But after giving all, still more is required.

He runs until he comes to the king of Archenland and tells him of the impending danger. The king believes the boy, recognizing immediately his resemblance to his own son. Shasta is given a horse and the group head off to the palace. Unfortunately, Shasta has never used the reins or touched the sides of a horse since Bree's pride refused to let him. Without direction his horse falls behind and he soon finds himself lost in a fog. When he can't see the way, Shasta hears a voice. It is Aslan again who guides him out of the darkness and into the light, a fitting metaphor. As Shasta breaks through the fog, he realizes that he is where he is supposed to be. In the end Narnia is saved and the king of Archenland explains that Shasta is Corin's twin, kidnapped as a baby by traitors because it was prophesied he would save their country. The family is reunited, and Shasta the slave becomes a prince, fulfilling his divine heritage.

THE HEALING OF BREE AND ARAVIS

Back at the Hermit's cottage, Bree is hesitant about moving to Narnia and suggests they stay where they are until his tail grows back. His pride will not allow him to appreciate the blessings around him. In contrast Aravis shows real humility by expressing gratitude at Shasta's selflessness and genuine concern for others. A phrase Lewis enjoyed from George MacDonald reads, "The love of neighbor is the only dungeon out of self."[11] In this story Shasta's love for his neighbor did more than that, as it seemed to be the final impetus to pull Aravis out of the dungeon of self as well.

As Avaris and the horses continue to speak, the discussion turns to Aslan. Bree, who feels he knows the most about the subject, explains to Hwin and Aravis that when people say that Aslan is a lion, it is only symbolic. They don't really mean that he has fur and whiskers. As the words are coming out of his mouth, Aslan walks up behind Bree in the flesh. The irony of the warhorse's words reflects what Lewis said about individuals who purport to admire Christ but don't believe in his divinity: "I am trying here to prevent anyone saying the really foolish thing that people often say about Him: [that is,] 'I'm ready to accept Jesus as a great moral teacher, but I don't accept His claim to be God.' That is the one thing we must not say."[12] Through their experience with Aslan, each of these characters find how real and powerful Aslan truly is.

When Aslan steps forward, Aravis and Bree fall back in terror, but Hwin steps forward despite her fear and shows total submission. This sweet mare who would be killed herself rather than see her mistress die, who gave all she had to save a country she had never visited, walks up to Aslan. He kisses the mare gently on the nose, commending her. Reminiscent of the servant with only three talents, despite her smaller size, she had done everything asked of her and received the full reward for her pure heart, "Well done, thou good and faithful servant: thou hast been faithful over a few things, I will make thee ruler over many things: enter thou into the joy of the lord" (Mathew 25:21).

A common trend in Lewis's day that still exists is the philosophy we should be excessively tolerant of any behavior. Mercy is toted and judgment of any sort condemned as unkind. Lewis refuted this stance in an essay where he said, "The Humanitarian theory wants simply to abolish Justice and substitute Mercy for it. . . . Mercy, detached from Justice, grows unmerciful. That is the important paradox. As there are plants which will flourish only in mountain soil, so it appears that Mercy will flower only when it grows in the crannies of the rock of Justice: transplanted to the marshlands of mere Humanitarianism, it becomes a man-eating weed, all the more dangerous because it is still called by the same name as the mountain variety."[13]

When Aslan explains to Aravis that he was the one who caused her injury, stripe for stripe what the servant girl received because of her escape, she realizes the extent of the pain she has caused. It is only after she could feel it herself that it was real to her. At that point her attitude changes, and for the first time she asks about the poor girl. If Aravis had understood before, she would not have needed to endure this lesson, but justice became the means through which she was able to become merciful. In a revelation devoted to explaining the concept of eternal punishment, the Lord said, "For behold, I God, have suffered these things for all that they might not suffer if they would repent; But if they would not repent they must suffer even as I" (D&C 19:16–17).

TELL NO OTHER STORY BUT YOUR OWN

When Aravis asked what became of the servant girl, Aslan answered that he would only tell each person his own story. He repeats the same words to Shasta and Bree. This is an important gospel principle—the concept that we cannot receive revelation or direction over someone else's life. We can be inspired in how to best serve them, but often when those promptings come, we have no idea why and must go forward with faith. Sometimes as soon as we make that phone call, drop by someone's home, or give someone needed items, the reason becomes clear. Other times we may never know. In the wonderful revelation known as the Olive Leaf, the Lord clearly states, "Whatsoever ye ask the Father in my name it shall be given unto you, that is expedient for you; And if ye ask anything that is not expedient for you, it shall turn unto your condemnation" (D&C 88:64, 65).

The word *expedient* means appropriate or necessary. A later revelation helps us to better define what is appropriate for us: "All truth is independent in that sphere in which God has placed it, to act for itself, as all intelligence also; otherwise there is no existence" (D&C 93:30). Our "sphere" may be within our family or calling but does not reach beyond the bounds of our God-given authority, and it is always most importantly focused on ourselves.

One wonderful thing about our stories being separate is that Christ deals with each of us individually. He sends us help, comfort, and inspiration based on our own trials, experiences, weaknesses, and strengths. Speaking through the prophet Ezekiel, the Lord said, "I know the things that come into your mind, every one of them" (Ezekiel 11:5). Ammon also bore this witness when he taught the gospel to King Lamoni's father and said of God, "He knows all the thoughts and intents of the heart" (Alma 18:32).

Lewis believed this as well. He wrote, "He has infinite attention to spare for each one of us. He does not have to deal with us in the mass. You are as much alone with Him as if you were the only being He had ever created. When Christ died, He died for you individually just as much as if you had been the only man [or woman] in the world."[14] Because Christ knows who we are, we can rejoice at the hand of providence lifting us when we fall, comforting us in the night, or even laying stripes on our backs to help us see the hurt we have caused. With each experience we can remember the Savior's words, "Lift up your hearts and be glad, for I am in your midst, and am your advocate with the Father" (D&C 29:5).

NOTES

1. *The Life of Benjamin Franklin Written by Himself,* Lippincott, 1884, 364.

2. Lewis, *The Problem of Pain,* 46.

3. Ibid., 75.

4. Lewis, *Mere Christianity,* 121.

5. Ibid., 122.

6. Lewis, *The Problem of Pain,* 116.

7. Lewis, *Mere Christianity,* 124.

8. *Encarta Dictionary*: 2007.

9. Lewis, *Screwtape Letters,* 56.

10. Lewis, *Mere Christianity,* 196.

11. Lewis, *George MacDonald,* 27.

12. Lewis, *Mere Christianity,* 52.

13. Lewis, *God in the Dock,* 294.

14. Lewis, *Mere Christianity,* 168.

CHAPTER ELEVEN

Prince Caspian: Restoring Forgotten Truth

hakespeare wrote, "Be not afraid of greatness; some are born great, some achieve greatness, and others have greatness thrust upon them." From the beginning of *Prince Caspian,* characters are thrust into situations of greatness. The Pevensie children from *The Lion, the Witch and the Wardrobe* are waiting at the train station when they feel themselves being pulled miraculously back to Narnia. Their adventures lead them to perform great acts to help save Narnia.

Prince Caspian has been born into greatness as the king's son. But he also must choose to become great as he battles his uncle, King Miraz, who has usurped the throne. There are many other Narnians who make significant choices as they try to bring Narnia back to former beliefs that have been lost. Under seemingly insurmountable odds, they want to restore Narnia's belief in Aslan through faith-filled action.

This tale is a fable of faith where many of the characters are confronted with and overcome various trials and obstacles. They must make decisions to help restore old beliefs even when they are persecuted and vilified for doing so. Some of them lose their lives in the battle for Old Narnia.

Prince Caspian is a young boy who lives during a period of apostasy, or a falling away from faith. He is taught to believe in Old Narnia by his nurse and tutor. His faith in Old Narnia leads to a battle cry of change throughout the land, thus restoring the old Narnian ways and faith in Aslan.

In Palmyra, New York, in 1820, another young boy, Joseph Smith, was also searching. He was seeking the gospel of Jesus Christ and was also confused by the new and modern beliefs of his time. Joseph was driven by a faith in Jesus Christ, which did not waver. Because of that faith, he received a vision that began the restoration of the gospel of Jesus Christ as it was in the primitive Church. Even though Joseph was tormented, ridiculed, tried, and finally murdered for his faith, he never denied his vision and mission of restoration. The work of restoration begun by the Prophet Joseph Smith continues today throughout the world as a work of faith.

There are many parallels between Prince Caspian's story of restoration of the beliefs of Old Narnia and the restoration of the gospel of Jesus Christ on April 6, 1830. Lewis would not have seen or acknowledged these parallels, since he did not know of the Restoration by the Prophet Joseph Smith. Yet they are still interesting to observe. As previously cited, "There are pearls of great price not produced in our own oyster beds."[1] Lewis may not have believed in the restoration of The Church of Jesus Christ of Latter-day Saints, but the spiritual inspirations he received while writing and speaking often underscore our own beliefs in the restored truths of the gospel of Jesus Christ.

THE APOSTASY: LOSING FAITH

Centuries after High King Peter, King Edmund, Queen Susan, and Queen Lucy reigned in Narnia, much has changed. The people of Narnia have quieted the talking animals, cast out magical creatures, enslaved the spirits of the trees, and stopped believing in Aslan. Modern Narnia is supposed to be new and revolutionary without being mired in old traditions and beliefs. The people there have rid themselves of these old ways to become a modern nation.

The Narnians are not supposed to believe in or talk about their old faith. Those who do are punished by their new king, Miraz, who is not a Narnian, but a Telmarine. The Narnian world is being turned upside down and the spirits of the people are spent because of this bitter subjugation.

During World War II, Lewis saw his world also being overturned by the ideologies of men. Differing philosophical beliefs were causing people to do terrible things to each other and lose faith in God. Lewis pointed out that this was not a new story. Satan has been putting specious thoughts in the minds of man since the beginning of time to get man to leave or change the truth. In his series of Christian lectures for the BBC, Lewis tried to help Christians return to the basic beliefs of their religion and not be confused by these other ideologies taught by modern men. He said,

What Satan put into the heads of our remote ancestors was the idea that they could . . . invent some sort of happiness for themselves outside God, apart from God. And out of that hopeless attempt has come nearly all that we call human history—money, poverty, ambition, war, prostitution, classes, empires, slavery—the long terrible story of man trying to find something other than God which will make him happy. It seems to start up all right and runs a few years, and then it breaks down. They are trying to run it on the wrong juice. That is what Satan has done to us humans.[2]

The Narnian apostasy has brought prejudice against magical creatures, including fauns, dwarfs, naiads, dryads, centaurs, and talking animals. These magical creatures have become renegades and outlaws hiding from King Miraz and his men. Finding joy in the beauty and diversity of animals and creatures in Narnia has been lost. Instead, there is a sameness that the society attempts to impose on all the people of Narnia.

Doctor Cornelius feels this prejudice as a half-human, half-dwarf; he is not accepted by either world completely. While serving as Prince Caspian's tutor, he tries to dress himself as a man. When Doctor Cornelius joins the ranks of the renegades, Nikabrik, a Black Dwarf, calls him a "half-and-halfer"[3] and offers to slit his throat. Yet Doctor Cornelius is the one who teaches Prince Caspian about the old ways of Narnia and helps educate him about the wide variety of mystical creatures.

Prince Caspian's nurse was the first to tell him stories of the Old Days. She is also part dwarf and hides this fact from the king. But when King Miraz finds out she has been telling the prince these fairy tales, he immediately dismisses her and commands the prince never to talk about such stories again. Doctor Cornelius becomes Prince Caspian's tutor and continues teaching the prince through the guise of astronomy lessons in the Great Tower, where no one can hear. These stories produce longings in Prince Caspian's heart for the days when Aslan moved among the people and the High King Peter ruled with the help of his siblings.

Others in Narnia have also been suppressing their feelings of faith. There have been nine Telmarine kings (Prince Caspian being the tenth) who have ruled over Narnia. For generations, Narnians were not able to discuss their beliefs about the Old Ways openly. The badger, Trufflehunter, who is a talking beast, declares that his faith is unchanging because he remembers the true kings of Narnia. In contrast, Nikabrik does not like men talking about these old stories. He is worried that they will get the stories mixed-up and that no good will come of such talk in their world.

Lewis realized that we may suppress spiritual thoughts or longings in order to fit into the world. Satan will try to convince us not to act on these spiritual promptings. In *Screwtape Letters,* Screwtape counsels his apprentice, Wormwood, on how to get a person to forget about feelings from the Spirit: "The more often he feels without acting, the less he will be able ever to act, and, in the long run, the less he will be able to feel."[4] Through this long time of apostasy, most of the Narnians had stopped acting upon their feelings and their knowledge of the Old Ways. The faith of the people was fading away.

THE FAITH OF FRIENDS

Lewis understood the many facets and aspects of faith. He realized that faith may have different meanings for different people. He distinguished between an intellectual faith, or acceptance that there is a God, and an active faith and trust that leads one to surrender his will to Him. He wrote, "Faith may mean (a) A settled intellectual assent. In that sense faith (or 'belief') in God hardly differs from faith in the uniformity of Nature of in the consciousness of other people. This is what, I think, has sometimes been called . . . 'rational' or 'intellectual' or 'carnal' faith. It may also mean (b) A trust, or confidence, in the God whose existence is thus assented to. This involves an attitude of the will. It is more like our confidence in a friend."[5]

In *Prince Caspian*, Lewis provides some significant examples of those who kept the faith in Narnia. Three comrades-in-arms find the unconscious Prince Caspian who had fallen off his horse during a storm. He had been fleeing from his uncle, King Miraz, who usurped his throne. Nikabrik is a Black Dwarf, Trumpkin is a Red Dwarf, and Trufflehunter is a talking badger. Each of them comes from a different background, but they are brought together in their hope to oust the king and restore Old Narnia. Each has a distinctive story of faith as he helps in the work of restoration.

Nikabrik's faith in Aslan is a result of his hate for the existing regime and his belief that Aslan may overcome the king. When he first meets Prince Caspian, he wants to kill him because he is a man. Nikabrik is partially mollified by Prince Caspian's obvious knowledge of the mystical creatures and the prince's desperate flight from his uncle. When Prince Caspian is introduced to the others, the Black Dwarfs are still suspicious of him. They only accept him as their king because he is against King Miraz.

Nikabrik wants to invite the ogres and hags to become part of their army. He does not care whom he joins forces with, as long as they are willing to fight against the existing king. He has faith in Aslan only as long as Aslan fights against the Telmarines. He does not care if it is Aslan or the White Witch who helps them, as long as their army is victorious over King Miraz.

Nikabrik's faith is based on outcomes. As their small force begins to lose the battle against the Telmarines, he seeks another source of power and strength to aid them. He suggests they seek out the power of the White Witch, since she treated the dwarfs well during her reign. He brings a hag and a werewolf to be a part of the war council to back him up with his proposal.

He questions the existence of Aslan by insisting that if Aslan really existed, he would help them in their fight. He wants the war council to call upon the power of the White Witch for aid. Nikabrik is finally killed by the evil he has brought into the war council. Prince Caspian sorrows over the body of the Black Dwarf and wisely observes that Nikabrik's hatred and lack of true faith came from a life of suffering.

Nikabrik's superficial faith was based on the results and actions he could see. As long as he could perceive Aslan's help, he would believe in him. His faith was not strong enough to generate real hope or joy, sustaining such feelings independently from life events. Those Narnians who believed only partially in the old ways did not succeed. As Lewis points out in another letter from Screwtape to Wormwood, "A moderated religion is as good . . . as no religion at all."[6]

In contrast, Trufflehunter, the talking Badger, has a constant faith in Aslan and in Old Narnia. His faith does not change even in the face of possible defeat. He never forgets the stories of the High King Peter, Aslan, and the castle Cair Paravel.

After they fight a crucial battle and lose, the council sits around a rough-hewn table discussing what to do next. Trufflehunter suggests blowing the horn to receive help from Aslan. After blowing the horn, Doctor Cornelius suggests dispatching two messengers to find those whom Aslan sends. The Doctor comments that Aslan probably would not come himself. Instead, he would send High King Peter from the past to one of the ancient places, such as to the mouth of the river or to where the lamppost still stands. Trufflehunter wants to go, but he is not fast enough to be one of the messengers.

Trumpkin's faith is not as strong and immovable as Trufflehunter's. Initially, he thinks Aslan and the High King are all just a sham.[7] But when Prince Caspian blows Susan's horn to summon help, Trumpkin offers to be one of the messengers to find the support that might come, commenting that dying here or there is all the same.

Trumpkin follows the call because of his patriotism to the cause of Old Narnia, which has become his religion. He does not believe in Aslan, but he does believe in the war they are fighting. In *Screwtape Letters,* Lewis writes about another way the devil will devalue our faith, substituting other good causes in its place:

> Let him begin by treating the Patriotism or the Pacifism as a part of his religion. Then let him, under the influence of partisan spirit, come to regard it as the most important part. Then quietly and gradually nurse him on to the stage at which the religion becomes merely part of the "cause," in which Christianity is valued chiefly because of the excellent arguments it can produce in favour of the British war effort or of Pacifism. . . . Once you have made the World an end, and faith a means, you have almost won your man, and it makes very little difference what kind of worldly end he is pursuing.[8]

Trumpkin's faith originates only in his belief that Prince Caspian is the rightful king. He does not believe that spirits live in the trees, that Aslan really exists, or that the High King Peter can improve the situation.

He does find the Pevensie children, but they are a bit of a disappointment for Trumpkin when he first meets them. He tells the children to go back home, for they would be no help at all. Each of them must prove to Trumpkin that they are worthy of the battle. Edmund fights Trumpkin with the sword and wins. Susan bests him with her bow and arrow. Lucy heals his wound with her elixir. Finally, Trumpkin concedes and lets the High King Peter lead the way.

Trumpkin's faith is based on seeing before believing. He does not understand how the same Aslan the children knew in Narnia could still be alive. When the dwarf finally sees Aslan, he is astonished. Aslan roars for him to come near and poor Trumpkin totters over. Aslan throws him up in the air and gently catches him, then asks if they can be friends. Trumpkin answers a shaky "yes." His belief in Aslan has only become a reality because he has seen him.

Trumpkin is much like the apostle Thomas. After the Savior's resurrection, all the apostles saw their resurrected Lord, except Thomas. He said that he would not believe Jesus was really resurrected until he had seen and felt the Savior's hands and side for himself. Eight days later, Jesus stood in front of Thomas and told him to touch his hands and side, so he would stop being faithless and become believing. Jesus said, "Thomas, because thou hast seen me, thou hast believed: blessed are they that have not seen, and yet have believed" (John 20:29).

In contrast, Doctor Cornelius continues believing in secret, even when there is no physical evidences on which to base his faith. He tells the prince the stories of the fauns, talking beasts, and dwarfs, even though he has never seen them and is not even sure if they exist. He is a learned man of the Narnian world, yet he does not let his learning overpower his faith. He tells Prince Caspian that these mythical creatures probably do not exist anymore. Sometimes, he thinks he hears a Dwarf-drum or sees a glimpse of a Satyr dance. These small moments will revive his hopes and dreams.

When the Doctor finds himself a part of the renegades, he is able to see for himself that his hope was not in vain. His knowledge of the Old Ways brings the Prince and his forces to the ancient Cair Paravel and Aslan's How using it as their headquarters. His wisdom would assist Prince Caspian throughout his days as a ruler of Narnia.

THE TRIAL OF LUCY'S FAITH

The Pevensie children had seen Aslan, walked with him, talked with him, and knew of his goodness, mercy, and wisdom from their previous visit to Narnia. When they are called back to Narnia, they do not know where to go or what to do. The children spend many days trying to deal with this situation. While they are hiking, Lucy thinks she sees Aslan and has the strong spiritual impression that they are to go up the face of a rock, rather than the much simpler and more logical way of down by the river gorge. She tells her siblings her feelings. They cannot see Aslan nor do they feel the same spiritual promptings as Lucy. As a group, they decide to go the easy way. Lucy faces a decision over whether to follow the group on the path she knows is wrong or go up the rock face alone. Lucy follows her siblings weeping as she walks, going against her spiritual desires and impressions.

During that night, Aslan comes to her. He tells her to wake up her siblings and the dwarf from a much-needed sleep and follow him. The others do not see or hear him. She needs to lead the way. She complains to Aslan that no one will believe her. Aslan explains she must follow him, even if no one else does.

No one wants to go with Lucy. Their delicious sleep has too great a hold on them, besides they cannot see Aslan. Lucy tells them if they do not follow her, she will go forward on her own. Finally, they decide to go along with Lucy because of the difficult trials they had the day before after not following her promptings. They travel far during the night, never seeing Aslan and only proceeding according to Lucy's directions.

Susan is the worst about not wanting to go with Lucy. She threatens to stay by herself, rather than leave in the middle of the night. Finally, after their long climb, Susan admits that she did know, deep inside, that Lucy had seen Aslan. But she was too tired to attempt the difficult rock climb, and her physical need for sleep stops her from acknowledging those feelings. Lucy's brothers and sister had become too caught up with what was happening around them to take the needed time to meditate and seek answers from Aslan.

Listening for spiritual promptings that have been sent our way should almost always be our first priority in life. Satan wants us to stop listening. He will turn up the volume of the busyness and noise in our lives, which can eventually lead to our destruction if we let it. In *Screwtape Letters*, Screwtape teaches Wormwood, "The game is to have them all running about with fire extinguishers whenever there is a flood, and all crowding to that side of the boat which is already nearly gunwale under."[9] Unlike their sister Lucy, Peter, Edmund, and Susan were too involved in their problems to take time to observe and listen for spiritual answers.

HAVING FAITH IN ASLAN

Moroni taught, "Wherefore, dispute not because ye see not, for ye receive no witness until after the trial of your faith" (Ether 12:6). A witness of our faith in Jesus Christ usually comes with a price. The price is often in overcoming a difficult trial or a temptation.

As sin is resisted, one gains a greater understanding of the strength of the temptation. Lewis realized this concept when he wrote, "A silly idea is current that good people do not know what temptation means. This is an obvious lie. Only those who try to resist temptation know how strong it is. . . . You find out the strength of a wind by trying to walk against it, not by lying down."[10] It is usually not until after we have resisted temptation that we receive a blessing or a witness from the Lord.

Initially, Lucy follows her siblings against the wishes of Aslan. After her mistake, Lucy vows to be obedient to Aslan and resist the temptation to follow her own wisdom, no matter what. Lucy trusts Aslan enough to do what he asks, even when it goes against common sense and what the others think. Aslan gives Lucy additional courage and strength when she buries her head in his mane and then talks to him face to face.

Joseph Smith, like Lucy, had to stand firm in his testimony, even though many others ridiculed him. He was often tempted to reject his testimony of the Restoration, but he did not vacillate from what the Lord had told him to do, "for I had seen a vision: I knew it, and I knew that God knew and I could not deny it, neither dared I do it; at least I knew that by so doing I would offend God, and come under condemnation" (JS—H 1:25).

This unwavering faith did not take away his trials. Instead, it strengthened him in the face of his trials. While in Liberty Jail, Joseph Smith called out for God, pleading for His help and presence. The Lord responded to his pleadings with words of consolation and peace: "My son, peace be unto thy soul; thine adversity and thine afflictions shall be but a small moment; And then, if thou endure it well, God shall exalt thee on high; thou shalt triumph over all thy foes" (D&C 121:7–8).

THE BATTLE BETWEEN OLD AND NEW NARNIA

When the young Prince Caspian first tells his uncle about Aslan and the stories of Peter, Edmund, Susan, and Lucy, the king thinks it is nonsense. King Miraz cannot imagine two kings, like Peter and Edmund, ruling at the same time. As king of New Narnia, Miraz is selfish and unable to see beyond himself and his own desires for power and money.

After Prince Caspian leaves his uncle's court, he encounters a different group of subjects. They see him as their rightful king and arm him with swords, helmets, and mail shirts. The centaur Glenstorm asks him when they will start the battle. At first Caspian is surprised. The centaur explains that he has looked to the heavens trying to identify the time for the battle to restore Old Narnia and has determined that the time is now.

The battle is hard and many are killed. In the end, it is King Miraz's own pride that results in his downfall. A final challenge is issued to King Miraz by the High King Peter. At first, King Miraz declines the challenge, realizing that Peter has the force and strength to win the battle. But his own soldiers plot against him and play to his vanity. He accepts the challenge to fight Peter. King Miraz's soldiers suppose that win or lose, they will have a victory.

What the Telmarines do not realize is that Aslan and the High King are powerfully connected. Peter is acting as the servant of Aslan. As such, he will have his help. The battle between the two men is ferocious and there are times when it is uncertain who will win. Peter is finally victorious, leaving King Miraz lying on his face but still alive. The merciless Telmarine soldiers yell "Treachery!" and run after the small Narnian army, stabbing to death their own king as they run past him.

Lewis felt the power of nature was a great force for good in his life. Given these feelings, it is appropriate that the spirits of the trees and woods, the Dryads, Hamadryads, and Silvans, bring about the final victory over the Telmarines. Just before the Narnian army is overtaken and destroyed, the Telmarine soldiers see the walking trees and think it is the end of the world. These spirits are terrible yet beautiful. The Telmarine warriors turn and run with fright until they are stopped at the river's edge, where they throw down their weapons of war in complete defeat.

Originally, Prince Caspian's small army had tried to fight the army of King Miraz by themselves. It was not until Peter came and defeated the wicked king that the tide turned. Aslan and his spirits of nature then conquered the Telmarine army, and the victory was won—the restoration of Old Narnia was complete!

Before the Prophet Joseph Smith could restore The Church of Jesus Christ of Latter-day Saints, he needed to receive the priesthood keys and the authority to do so. First, the Aaronic Priesthood was restored along with the keys of the gospel of repentance. On May 15, 1829, John the Baptist, who was acting under the direction of Peter, James, and John, conferred upon Joseph Smith and Oliver Cowdery the Aaronic Priesthood, and they were baptized in the Susquehana River. Oliver Cowdery described this event using the imagery of nature: "What joy! what wonder! what amazement! While the world was racked and distracted—while millions were groping as the blind for the wall, and while all men were resting upon uncertainty, as a general mass, our eyes beheld, our ears heard, as in the 'blaze of day'; yes, more—above the glitter of the May sunbeam, which then shed its brilliancy over the face of nature!" (JS—H 1:71, footnote).

The Apostle Peter, who became the prophet of the primitive Church after the death of Jesus Christ, together with his counselors, James and John, returned to the earth to give Joseph Smith the keys of the Melchizedek Priesthood. Peter was acting under Christ's direction to restore the authority of the priesthood to the earth once more. The conferring of these priesthood keys made possible the restoration of the fulness of the gospel of Jesus Christ on the earth today.

MISSIONARY WORK—RESTORING NARNIANS TO THE TRUTH

While the Telemarines are being defeated, Aslan travels around his kingdom, liberating the hearts and minds of his people. Some of them want to be liberated while others do not. Aslan passes a school for girls and most of the girls run away when they see the lion. Only one girl,

Gwendolen, stays and follows him. At another school, a mistress teaching a class of boys feels a longing in her heart when she sees Aslan. Initially, she shakes her head "no" at Aslan's invitation to come to him. She cannot leave her duties as a teacher. Her pupils look out the window to see what is happening. They are frightened and run when they see the lion, but their teacher decides to leave and follow Aslan.

Finally, Aslan meets a little child who is crying because her aunt is on her deathbed. Aslan visits the aunt, who is the nurse who originally taught Prince Caspian the stories of Narnia. She immediately recognizes Aslan and thinks he has come to take her back to his home. Instead, he heals her and she is able to ride on his back to see her precious Prince Caspian once more.

Bringing the message of the Restoration to the world is the work of all members of The Church of Jesus Christ of Latter-day Saints. It is a message of healing. Many who hear it will accept it willingly and immediately, while others will reject it. Missionaries have been sent throughout the world to preach the gospel to all nations. "Wherefore the voice of the Lord is unto the ends of the earth, that all that will hear may hear" (D&C 1:11).

After his death, the Savior visited the spirit world and organized the work of carrying the light of the gospel to those who were in spirit prison. These had been in spiritual darkness, but now, could be taught the gospel and thus be liberated. "And the chosen messengers went forth to declare the acceptable day of the Lord and proclaim liberty to the captives who were bound, even unto all who would repent of their sins and receive the gospel" (D&C 138:31).

THE TAIL OF REEPICHEEP

Great faith is not just found in those with great appearances. Sometimes, people can be misjudged because of the color of their skin, the size of their physical stature, or the way they dress. These outward signs often do not reflect the person within. The Lord reminded the prophet, Samuel, "Look not on his countenance, or on the height of his stature . . . for man looketh on the outward appearance, but the Lord looketh on the heart" (1 Samuel 16:7).

An example of misjudging someone because of size is Reepicheep, the head soldier mouse of Narnia. Prince Caspian has to suppress a laugh when he first meets Reepicheep. After laughing himself, Doctor Cornelius refers to the warrior mouse as a valiant beast.

During the final battle with the Telmarines, the mice join the fray by stabbing the feet of the Telmarine soldiers. When the war is over, Reepicheep is brought to Aslan on a litter with many wounds. Lucy uses her diamond bottle to save the brave warrior. When Reepicheep jumps up to thank Aslan and Lucy for his good health, he notices his tail has been cut off. Reepicheep is embarrassed and ashamed. He asks for his tail to be replaced for the sake of his dignity and honor. Aslan points out that he might be placing too much importance on his tail.

Then, all of Reepicheep's mouse friends draw their swords. If Reepicheep must go without a tail, all of them will cut off their tails too. Aslan exclaims that he is overcome by the kindness and love of the other mice, and he restores Reepicheep's tail.

The Savior taught about the perfect law of love. He taught his disciples to love one another as he loved them (John 15:12). As we live the gospel of Jesus Christ, we become filled with charity, which is the "pure love of Christ, and it endureth forever; and whoso is found possessed of it at the last day, it shall be well with him" (Moroni 7:47). We become the people of the Lord as we are baptized and are "willing to bear one another's burdens, that they may be light; Yea, and are willing to mourn with those that mourn; yea, and comfort those that stand in need of comfort" (Mosiah 18:8–9). Society would be dramatically different if all people lived the perfect law of love.

There were many who could have been blamed for the evil done in Narnia. Yet, Aslan offers his healing and peace to all who will accept it, even to the Telmarine soldiers. George MacDonald felt that forgiveness was the most important requirement for true deliverance and healing to occur: "No doubt God takes what wrong there is, and what provocation there is, into the account: but the more provocation, the more excuse that can be urged for the hate, the more reason . . . that the hater should [forgive, and] be delivered from the hell of his [anger]."[11]

The Telmarines are offered the opportunity to join Narnia or to go back to their world. The strife of Narnia is transformed into reconciliation. There is a restoration of peace as belief in Aslan is restored and the people are free to live the Old Narnian ways once more.

NOTES

1. Kimball, "The Christian Commitment: C. S. Lewis and the Defense of Doctrine," 197.
2. Lewis, *Mere Christianity,* 49–50.
3. Lewis, *Narnia,* 355.
4. Lewis, *Screwtape Letters,* 67.

5. Lewis, *Awake,* 137.

6. Lewis, *Screwtape Letters,* 46.

7. Lewis, *Narnia,* 387.

8. Lewis, *Screwtape Letters,* 34.

9. Lewis, *Screwtape Letters,* 138.

10. Lewis, *Mere Christianity,* 143.

11. Lewis, *George MacDonald,* 13.

CHAPTER TWELVE

The Voyage of the Dawn Treader: Journey of Faith

he Voyage of the Dawn Treader is the only book in the chronicles that has no single villain. Although in their quest to find the seven lost lords the small crew does face many dangers, their greatest challenge is dealing with their own weaknesses. This journey admittedly brings about vast changes in the character of Eustace, Lucy and Edmund's spoiled cousin, but it also changes the Pevensie children and King Caspian.

Lewis's great love of classic literature shows through as the *Dawn Treader* heads into unchartered seas to face strange islands, reminiscent of the great epic sagas. But like Lewis's other books, there is still purpose in this tale and lessons he expects the reader to pick up, especially the danger of vices. In *Screwtape Letters*, the evil Screwtape observes, "Hence nearly all vices are rooted in the Future. Gratitude looks to the past and love to the present; [but] fear, avarice, lust and ambition look ahead."[1]

As King Caspian, Lucy, Edmund, and Eustace search for the lost lords, they find that each nobleman has fallen prey to one of these vices, and sometimes they fall prey to them as well. Making such errors is the nature of moving forward. Perhaps this book is a warning for us, as we each progress on our life's journey, to watch out for the most common pitfalls along the way.

A SUMMER WITH EUSTACE

The story begins with Lucy and Edmund stuck at their aunt and uncle's house for the summer, trapped with their annoying cousin, Eustace. Peter is spending the summer being tutored by Professor Kirke, very similar to Lewis's own pleasant experience with Professor Kirkpatrick. Susan is with her parents in America, so the two other children are left behind. Eustace comes from a school that does not believe in punishment, and his parents enjoy his outlandish behavior, but his cousins can't endure it. Lucy and Edmund try to hide in their bedroom, but Eustace barges in. On the wall is a picture of a wonderful ship in the shape of a dragon that Lucy thinks looks like a Narnian ship. Eustace thinks that Narnia is just a stupid imaginary country his cousins have made up, but as he stares at the picture it comes alive. Before long they are pulled into the waves and rescued by King Caspian's crew.

After a warm reunion with the Pevensie children and a couple of choice words from Eustace, King Caspian explains his quest. Since he has established peace in Narnia, he has decided it is his responsibility to sail out and find the seven exiled lords who had been loyal to his father. Beyond the lost islands, which they are soon approaching, is a part of the sea entirely unknown to his people.

Reepicheep, the Chief Mouse of Narnia, is accompanying them as is Lord Drinian, the captain, and about thirty other men, who have each volunteered for the honor of voyaging to the end of their world. Some even hope that when they get to the edge, Aslan's country will be waiting for them.

USING A JOURNAL TO COPE WITH STRESS

Eustace feels like a prisoner and constantly complains about his situation. King Caspian has given his large upper cabin to Lucy and is sleeping in a small lower room with Eustace and Edmund. Although all of them are in the same situation, Eustace has an incredible knack for feeling he is the most ill-treated of anyone on the ship. The only thing Eustace has to help him cope is a small notebook and a pencil which he uses as a journal.

After the death of his wife, C. S. Lewis also kept a journal that had an incredible impact on him as he faced the grieving process. Lewis wondered if writing his feelings out was really helping. He said, "I must have some drug, and reading isn't a strong enough drug now. By writing it all down (all?—no: one thought in a hundred) I believe I get a little outside it. . . . In so far as this record was a defence against total collapse, a safety-valve, it has done some good."[2]

It is significant that there has also been direction by LDS Church leaders that each of us should keep a journal. Recently, President Henry Eyring spoke of a journal he has kept of how the hand of the Lord has touched his family. For years he kept the record faithfully, never missing a day. That book has proved to be a great strength to his entire family.[3]

The Lost Islands

Soon the *Dawn Treader* arrives at the last known part of Narnia, the Lost Islands, which has not been visited by anyone from their country in many years. The first of the three islands, Felimath, seems to be uninhabited and its large grassy mounds look inviting. King Caspian, Lucy, Edmund, Eustace, and Reepicheep decide to walk across it to stretch their legs while the boat sails around. As they come to a valley in the center, they are ambushed and tied up. The leader of the unkempt gang, Pug, is a slave trader and brings them to their ship to sell them at the slave market.

As they pass an inn, a fine gentleman insists on purchasing one of them. He takes King Caspian and tells him that he reminds him of his master who had died. Caspian guesses that this must be one of the lords he was seeking, and Lord Bern bows before his new king. Lord Bern explains that he left his fellow travelers because he was afraid to continue on the voyage. He is now married and has a family and lands. Although Lord Bern despises the slave trade, he has felt there was nothing he could do about it. King Caspian, on the other hand, is determined to act, and so a plan is conceived.

To his credit, Caspian continually acts on his impressions whereas Bern withdraws from trying to help change his society. In *Screwtape Letters* Lewis warns, "The more often [one] feels without acting, the less he will be able ever to act, and, in the long run, the less he will be able to feel."[4] Luckily for Bern, as soon as the King pushes him into taking the first steps, he begins to act independently for the good of all and changes that trend in his life.

Forgiveness as a Weapon

With only thirty armed men, Lord Bern realizes the young king is in a precarious situation. He sends word to his close friends who trumpet the arrival of the king of Narnia to the largest city of the Lost Islands. As he walks up to the governor's castle, King Caspian sees the guards lounging around the courtyard and in various doorways. He immediately calls them forward and censures them for their disgraceful dress and conduct, but because he wants his return to be a joyful occasion, he gives them the day off and several caskets of wine to celebrate. They leave happily and he replaces the guard with his own men.

Walking into the castle proper, the king uses the same tactics. The governor tries to put off the king, telling him that nothing can be done until it is brought before a committee with the proper paperwork. Lords

Bern and Drinian turn over the table, and drag the pathetic man over to the king who explains that the past duty that should have been paid to the throne must come from his own pockets. The governor suddenly becomes very upset. The king forgives him of his debt, relieves him of his duties, and sets Lord Bern as the new Duke of the Lost Islands.

The act of forgiveness may be a greater gift for the forgiver than for the person that caused the offense. In Lewis's portrayal of Prince Caspian's forgiveness, the guard's and governor's gratitude left them compliant enough for him to reassert his authority. With that edge, the King, Lord Bern, and his guards close down the slave market. King Caspian also reunites with his friends, and they continue on their journey.

EUSTACE GETS WHAT HE DESERVES

The crew heads out to the uncharted waters, past the Lost Islands, and sails for about two weeks. They then go through a terrible storm and lose two of their water barrels. Unsure of how long it will be before they see land, they decide to ration food and water. Everyone is struggling, but we see through Eustace's journal that he feels especially abused. One night, feeling feverish, he sneaks up to the water barrel and is caught by Reepicheep. Everyone is awakened and Eustace is forced to apologize but feels no remorse, more upset about being caught than about his own behavior. In the end, he blames the mouse.

Lucy pities her cousin and begins to share her ration of water with him, but he cannot even feel gratitude, convincing himself that girls really need less water than boys, and it should have been divvied up like that in the first place. In Eustace we see the heart of someone entirely "past feeling," much like Laman and Lemuel (1 Nephi 17:45). Through his selfishness, Eustace loses the ability to feel anything but contempt and anger, and mopes in his room until they reach land again.

Finally, land is in sight and the storm-damaged ship pulls safely into the harbor of a small island that looks uninhabited. The men find wild goats to eat and fresh water, but Eustace balks the next morning as they begin listing all the work that needs to be done before they can cast out to sea again. With no one watching him, Eustace leaves, planning on returning when the work is complete. As the fog thickens, however, Eustace realizes he is lost and finds himself in a strange valley near a pool. In the dim light, he sees a great dragon lumber from its lair and drink, then fall over dead. Suddenly the rain pours down in torrents, and the only place to run for shelter is the dragon's cave. There Eustace finds treasure and falls asleep on the mounds of gold and jewels where he thinks selfish, "dragony" thoughts.[5] In the morning he wakes up and has changed to a dragon.

Eustace flies to the bay in his dragon form and everyone soon guesses what has happened. Ironically, it is Reepicheep with whom he had the most contention who gives him the most comfort, telling him that many great people have had the same or worse trials and still recovered. With his new abilities, Eustace finds many ways to help. As he begins to feel the rewards of his efforts and the gratitude of those around him, Eustace starts to see himself differently, and for the first time he wonders if he might have been wrong in the way he behaved.

TAKING OFF THE DRAGON SKIN

That night Eustace sees a lion. Although as a dragon Eustace could physically take the animal, he still fears him. He follows the lion to a clear fountain and is told to undress and bathe. Eustace scratches at his skin and many scales fall off. He pulls and pulls out of his skin but as he is about to bathe he realizes there is another layer underneath. He scratches at that layer and works until it is off, but there is still another scaly skin below. The third time he turns to the lion in frustration who says he will undress him. The lion takes his claw and slices deeply, right to his heart, and peels the thick skin away. Eustace says it hurts but feels so good to be free of it. After he bathes, he comes out of the water a boy. Aslan dresses him and Eustace returns to the ship a new person.

Eustace's transformation occurs because he allows Aslan to remove his dragony exterior. No matter how hard he tried, he could not do it on his own. Only Aslan had the power to take away the barriers that were not allowing Eustace to progress. In a letter to an Anglican nun, Sister Penelope, who was a theologian, writer, and fan to whom he later dedicated the second book of his space trilogy, Lewis included this poem:

THE APOLOGIST'S EVENING PRAYER

From all my lame defeats and oh! much more
From all the victories that I seemed to score;
From cleverness shot forth on Thy behalf
At which, while angels weep, the audience laugh;
From all my proofs of Thy divinity,
Thou, who wouldst give no sign, deliver me.
Thoughts are but coins. Let me not trust, instead
Of Thee, their thin-worn image of Thy head.
From all my thoughts, even from my thoughts of Thee,

O thou fair Silence, fall, and set me free.
Lord of the narrow gate and needle's eye,
Take from me all my trumpery lest I die.[6]

Lewis's wish in this poem is for Christ to "take from [him] all [his] trumpery." Although we cannot diminish our own efforts in the repentance process, the fact is only through Christ can we be completely changed. We need the power of the Atonement to change our hearts. Like King Lamoni's father who said, "I will give away all my sins to know thee" (Alma 22:18), that willingness to abandon sin is a key element. Yet even more important is the willingness to turn to Christ and recognize that true repentance comes only through him. Elder Richard G. Scott put it this way: "Of all the necessary steps to repentance, the most critically important is for you to have a conviction that forgiveness comes in and through Jesus Christ. It is essential to know that only on His terms can you be forgiven. You will be helped as you exercise faith in Christ."[7]

Often Christ's terms are not what we expect. Like Namaan with leprosy who went to the prophet Elisha to be healed, too often the road to repentance may seem too humiliating or we may feel misunderstood and lose the blessing that could be ours.[8] Our preconceptions of the process of our transformation must not be a stumbling block in our progression. One of Lewis's most well-known quotes from his book *Mere Christianity* addresses this idea but originally came from the words of George Mac-Donald. He tells us to imagine that we are a living house and that God has come in to make some repairs. At first he fixes the things we knew are broken but then he starts doing more, knocking out walls and putting up new wings—and it hurts. The problem is that we thought we "were going to be made into a decent little cottage but He is building a palace."[9]

Those painful renovations, like the thick dragon's skins being ripped off Eustace, are pain with purpose, even if we can't see the purpose just yet. As Paul said, "For now we see through a glass darkly; but then face to face: now I know in part; but then shall I know even as also I am known." (1 Corinthians 13:12). Perhaps this is why the first principle in the gospel is faith in the Lord Jesus Christ. The faith to expose our weaknesses to him, to show him our soft underside, to be willing to do what it takes to remove even the most callous dragon skin and become what only He knows we have the potential to be, no matter the cost—that is the faith that will save us.

TEMPTATION TOO STRONG TO RESIST

As the *Dawn Treader* moves on, they come to an island with two streams. Starting at the west they hike around to the other side where they find an old, rusty sword and suit of armor. After looking around they come to a lake so clear that they can see the bottom where a golden statue of a man lies. Edmund dips his spear in the water and discovers that anything touching the water turns to gold. The statue on the bottom is one of the lost lords. King Caspian immediately realizes the power that such wealth could bring and swears all his comrades to secrecy upon death. His reaction has the rest of the crew worried and they frankly rebuke him. They call the island "Deathwater" and quickly leave.

The possibility of unlimited wealth is a temptation that is more than King Caspian can deal with, and he is fortunate to have friends that lift him away from that place. A scripture that is often misquoted speaks of not being tempted beyond what we can bear. "There hath no temptation taken you but such as is common to man: but God is faithful, who will not suffer you to be tempted above that ye are able; but will with the temptation also make a way to escape, that ye may be able to bear it" (1 Corinthians 10:13). This escape provided by God for our temptations is explained in more detail by Alma as he spoke to Zeezrom: "But that ye would humble yourselves before the Lord, and call on his holy name, and watch and pray continually, that ye may not be tempted above that which ye can bear, and thus be led by the Holy Spirit, becoming humble, meek, submissive, patient, full of love and all long-suffering" (Alma 13:28). Here the prophet Alma clarifies that often the escape comes prior to the temptation. Our preparations as we read the scriptures daily, pray on a regular basis, and work on improving our choices then become the armor of God that protects us from any temptation. What Paul was saying is that we all have the ability to overcome anything thrown at us if we rely on Christ.

In the previous example, Caspian's escape from temptation was his friends. If he had been surrounded with less than desirable associates, like Edmund was in *The Lion, The Witch and The Wardrobe,* he may not have been able to break free of this weakness. Lewis also taught this concept: "A Christian would be wise to avoid, where he decently can, any meeting with people who are bullies, lascivious, cruel, dishonest, spiteful and so forth. Not because we are 'too good' for them. In a sense because we are not good enough."[10]

It is only when we are planted firmly on the rock of our Redeemer that we truly can withstand any temptation, "that when the devil shall send forth his mighty winds, yea, his shafts in the whirlwind, yea, when all his hail and his mighty storm shall beat upon you, it shall have no power over you to drag you down to the gulf of misery and endless wo, because of the rock upon which ye are built, which is a sure foundation, a foundation whereon if men build they cannot fall" (Helaman 5:12). That is our great escape that comes with every temptation.

ONE SIDE OF THE STORY AND THE INVISIBLE MONOPODS

The next island the *Dawn Treader* encounters has a large green lawn with an English-style house in the distance. As the landing party makes their way to the structure, Lucy falls behind, trying to get a rock out of her shoe. Alone sitting by a tree she hears a *thump, thump* all around her and voices conspiring to stop them from returning to their ship. Lucy runs to warn the others, but by the time they make it to the shore, they are surrounded by an invisible enemy.

The Duffers believe they were once a beautiful people but were "uglified" by the evil magician who rules them. They were so tired of seeing each other that one night they snuck up the stairs and found a spell in the book of spells that would turn them invisible. It worked so well that it turned the magician invisible as well, and he walks so softly they aren't sure if he is still alive. The spell can only be broken by a girl, and Lucy volunteers rather than have her friends fight a battle against rivals they cannot see.

When Lucy climbs the stairs she is afraid, believing the stories told by the Duffers. Everything she sees seems ominous and scary. She finds the book and on reading the spell that turns all things unseen visible, she is surprised to see Aslan. He responds by saying that she should know he is always there and would follow the rules. She finds out that the magician was established by Aslan to help the Duffers, but that they refuse to learn.

Even their uglification was really one of the magician's attempts to improve their lives. The Duffers were once common little dwarfs whose job was to mind the garden so that they would have food for themselves. Every day they would walk half a mile up a hill to get water from a spring rather than using the stream that passed right by the garden. No matter what the magician said, they continued in their error, so he turned them into bouncing monopods. Their new form was a blessing but they could not see it.

The Duffers' problem is a common one. Too often we don't recognize challenges as the blessings they are. In a letter to his friend Lewis confessed, "The great thing, if one can, is to stop regarding all the unpleasant things as interruptions of one's 'own,' or 'real' life. The truth is of course that what one calls the interruptions are precisely one's real life—the life God is sending one day by day."[11] The magician's efforts toward the Duffers were constantly for their benefit, as are God's dealings with his children. If we can recognize the true intent of unexpected changes in our lives, we can be free of the short-sightedness that plagued the Duffers and kept them from both happiness and progression.

THE THREE SLEEPING LORDS

On the final island, they see the last three lords sitting at Aslan's table with a great feast spread before them, which they are unable to partake of because they are asleep. As Caspian, Lucy, Edmund, Eustace, and Reepicheep walk up to the table, they do not eat for fear it was the food that caused the unnatural sleep that has obviously lasted for years. They stay and guard the sleeping noblemen. In the night a beautiful woman emerges from the mountain. Her father, Ramadu, also comes forward and tells of how the lords fought at the table about going to the end of the world. One wished to continue while the others were ready to turn back. In the heat of argument, one of the lords grabbed the stone knife used by the White Witch to kill Aslan. Because it was forbidden, a deep sleep came upon them. The only way to remove the sleep is for someone to go to the ends of the earth and stay there.

After feasting at the table, the group leaves and comes to a place where the water is sweet. Drinking it, they realize it is all they need to live. The water even gives them the ability to withstand greater light because it comes directly from Aslan's country. In *Mere Christianity* Lewis looks at the history of civilizations and bemoans their attempts to create a society apart from God. He believes the reason great civilizations crumble is because they try to run on the "wrong juice."[12] In contrast, as the *Dawn Treader* grows closer to Aslan's country, they see the benefits of the "right" juice, even the living water of Christ.

A GLIMPSE OF ASLAN'S COUNTRY

As the group journeys to the end of their world, the ship comes to a large wave of water standing still. Through the wave, they see a beautiful land. Reepicheep pulls his small raft aboard the dingy and makes his goodbyes. This trip to Aslan's country is something he had planned for his whole life. The children—Eustace, Lucy, and Edmund—also know it is time for them to go, but the impetuous young King suddenly does not want to be left behind. He stomps off to his cabin where Aslan visits him, telling the King his time is not yet. We see in Caspian the same sentiment spoken by Joseph Smith that even the glory of the telestial or lowest kingdom "surpasseth all understanding" and his desire to go there was great.

In Lewis's book the *Great Divorce,* a busload of passengers go from hell to heaven, but when they see heaven, they choose not to go in. Caspian seems a perfect foil, wanting to enter but being told it was not yet his time. Like Lewis says at the end the *Great Divorce,* "All that are in Hell, choose it."[13] Perhaps the same is true for heaven, but they do not get to choose when they are permitted to enter. The farewell is difficult but soon the *Dawn Treader* heads back to Ramadu's island. Caspian will marry Ramadu's daughter and rule in peace for many years.

THE END OF THEIR WORLD AND THE BEGINNING OF OURS

After some time Reepicheep puts out his little coracle, or raft, and leaves on his own. As he heads toward the wave, he is lifted up and that is the last the children see of him. Finally, Lucy, Edmund, and Eustace see land, where the sea touches sand and then grass. They get out and walk to a fire where a lamb stands that asks them to eat until they are filled, just like the disciples were asked after Christ's resurrection.[14] It is at this point that the lamb turns into the Lion.

> "Dearest," said Aslan very gently, "you and your brother will never come back to Narnia."
>
> "Oh, Aslan!!" said Edmund and Lucy both together in despairing voices.
>
> "You are too old, children," said Aslan, "and you must begin to come close to your own world now . . . But there I have another name. You must learn to know me by that name. This was the very reason why you were brought to Narnia, that by knowing me here for a little, you may know me better there."[15]

Of any passage in the chronicles of Narnia, this is the clearest declaration of Lewis's purpose in his wonderful children's books. As we keep his intent in mind, we can see new perspectives that encourage us to work harder toward feeling the love and devotion in our own hearts that these children feel toward Aslan. In an essay that Lewis wrote called "A Mind Awake" he spoke of the two levels of faith. The first level involves simply an intellectual assent that God exists. But the second level is trusting in Him as a friend.[16] It is this confidence, trust and even love that is the foundation of our faith in the living Christ, "which is the gift of God unto all those who diligently seek him" (1 Nephi 10:17).

NOTES

1. Lewis, *Screwtape Letters,* 76.

2. Lewis, *The Problem of Pain,* 9–10.

3. Henry B. Eyring, "O Remember, Remember," *Ensign,* Nov. 2007, 66–69.

4. Lewis, *Screwtape Letters,* 67.

5. Lewis, *Voyage of the Dawn Treader,* 97.

6. Lewis, *Letters,* vol. II, 527, or *Poems,* 143.

7. Richard G. Scott, "Peace of Conscience and Peace of Mind," *Ensign,* Nov. 2004, 15.

8. See 2 Kings 5:1–27.

9. Lewis, *Mere Christianity,* 205.

10. Lewis, *Reflections on the Psalms,* 71.

11. Lewis, *They Stand Together,* 499.

12. Lewis, *Mere Christianity,* 50.

13. Lewis, *The Great Divorce,* 75.

14. See Luke 24:42–43.

15. Lewis, *Voyage of the Dawn Treader,* 269–70.

16. Lewis, *A Mind Awake,* 137.

CHAPTER THIRTEEN

The Silver Chair: Continual Battle against Evil

L ewis took the title for his book on his own conversion, *Surprised by Joy,* from a sonnet by Wordsworth, which is thought to be about Wordsworth's beloved daughter who died at the age of four. The poem tells of someone in the droves of grief who suddenly remembers a wonderful experience about the deceased and is "surprised by joy," but then remembering his loss "that thought's return was the worst pang that sorrow ever bore."[1] The sonnet is without hope, but Lewis's use of it divulges his faith in Christ's ability to reunite us with our loved ones and fills us with ultimate joy. It seems to be an answer to Wordsworth's sorrow.

In *The Silver Chair,* pain and grief are the great motivators that cause Prince Rilian to seek revenge for his mother's death, King Caspian to leave for Aslan's country, and Jill and Eustace to come to Narnia in the first place. But in the end through Aslan, as in Christ, all pain is turned to joy.

THE EXPERIMENTAL HOUSE

After the Lewises' mother died, Warnie was sent to boarding school. A few years later Jack joined him, and this began some of the worst years in Jack's life. One of the biggest difficulties was the allowance and even encouragement of bullying. Although the headmaster was committed to an insane asylum and the school closed shortly after the Lewis boys left, the scars lasted a lifetime. In the first scenes of *The Silver Chair,* Jill Pole is crying behind the gymnasium at her school, the Experiment House, hiding from a gang of bullies much like Lewis must have faced himself at that age.

The Experimental House is considered a progressive school where the headmistress enjoys psychological discussions with children instead of punishing them. The result is that often instead of being corrected, these children became her favorites. The irony of this schoolmaster's misconception of showing pity to some at the expense of hurting many more is similar to a malady common in our society, that of misplaced benevolence.

Today it may be easier for some to be kind to people far from them than to those within their realm of influence, like people who willingly support humanitarian groups in other countries, but can't be bothered to watch a neighbor's child for a few minutes. Or the person who loves doing "Meals on Wheels" but when asked to bring dinner to a new mother, becomes frustrated. If we aren't careful, we can find ourselves slipping into selfishness without ever realizing it.

Screwtape described it this way: "Do what you will, there is going to be some benevolence, as well as some malice, in your patient's soul. The great thing is to direct the malice to his immediate neighbours whom he meets every day and to thrust his benevolence out to the remote circumference, to people he does not know. The malice thus become wholly real and the benevolence largely imaginary."[2]

What a far cry this attitude is from where Lewis thought we should be. In *Mere Christianity* he tells us that our service shouldn't only be directed to people around us but that the amount we give should stretch our hearts. "I am afraid the only safe rule is to give more than we can spare . . . if our charities do not at all pinch or hamper us, . . . they are too small. There ought to be things we should like to do and cannot do because our charitable expenditure excludes them."[3]

FINDING THE STREAM

Eustace from the *Voyage of the Dawn Treader* discovers Jill crying behind the school building and the two begin to talk. Jill remarks how much he has changed from the year before, and Eustace mentions his experience in Narnia. He decides to visit there again. He tells Jill to point to the east and call Aslan's name three times. Nothing happens except that they are suddenly found by the out-of-control children, who start to chase them. Soon Eustace and Jill come to a gate in the wall that surrounds the school. It is never unlocked but hoping to escape a beating, Eustace turns the handle, and they run forward. The gate closes behind them, and Eustace yells at Jill to stop. She doesn't right away but turns around to find a huge cliff. Trying to help her back to safety, Eustace falls off himself, head over heels. Suddenly Aslan appears, blowing Eustace to safety. Aslan walks quietly away.

Alone, Jill lies down on the ground and starts crying. After a while she realizes she is incredibly thirsty. Looking around, she finds a stream, but sees Aslan beside it. Her fear will not allow her to approach what she knows will satisfy her. She asks if there is another stream, and Aslan tells her no. Then she asks if he will eat her, and Aslan says he has eaten many people, even whole kingdoms. Finally, she approaches and drinks, quenching her thirst.

Jill did not understand the principle being taught. King Benjamin addressed this principle in his powerful address when he said, "There shall be no other name given nor any other way nor means whereby salvation can come unto the children of men, only in and through the name of Christ, the Lord Omnipotent" (Mosiah 3:17). As Christ said himself, "I am the way, the truth, and the life: no man cometh unto the Father, but by me" (John 14:6). Lewis put it this way in *Mere Christianity,* "God cannot give us a happiness and peace apart from Himself, because it is not there. There is no such thing."[4] There is no other stream that will quench our thirst.

FOUR COMMANDMENTS TO OBEY

After Jill drinks her fill, the lion asks about Eustace. She admits that he fell because of her, and Aslan tells her why she was brought to Narnia. He gives her four signs that she must not forget and that will make her way easier. The signs are similar to commandments and they are meant to help her in her task to find the missing prince, son of King Caspian.

Unlike Eustace who entered Narnia as a spoiled child, Jill is merely unfamiliar with how to obey and less capable of it, not rebellious. Through this adventure she will grow from a forgetful child to an obedient and faithful follower of Aslan. This transformation comes as a result of Jill's efforts even when they don't follow the plan exactly. Her growth is a clear illustration of the principle Lewis taught at the end of *Mere Christianity* where he said,

> The command Be ye perfect is not idealistic gas. Nor is it a command to do the impossible. He [Christ] is going to make us creatures that can obey that command. He said (in the Bible) that we were 'Gods' and He is going to make good His words. If we let Him—for we can prevent Him, if we choose—He will make the feeblest and filthiest of us into a god or goddess, a dazzling, radiant, immortal creature, pulsating all through with such energy and joy and wisdom and love as we cannot now imagine. . . . The process will be long and in parts very painful; but that is what we are in for. Nothing less. He meant what He said.[5]

Because Jill is willing to follow Aslan's directions, he will "make good his word" and helps the children achieve their goal, even when they do not follow exactly. This combination of individual efforts, coupled with the power of Christ, is the way in which we are most able to progress. It is a true reflection of the importance of works, coupled with grace, allowing us to become our full potential. When asked concerning his belief about the part that works plays in the gospel compared to grace, Lewis replied, "I have no right really to speak on such a difficult question, but it does seem to me like asking which blade of a pair of scissors is the most necessary."[6]

Lewis illustrates through this book the importance of following the commands of the Lord in our personal progression. The four commands given to Jill are:

1. When she sees Eustace again, Jill is supposed to tell him to greet an old friend at once.

2. They should journey to the north to find a ruined giant city.

3. They must do what the writing says that she finds in the city.

4. She will recognize the lost prince because he will be the one who will asks her to do something in the name of Aslan.

Jill promises that she will repeat the signs often and not forget them. Then she steps off the cliff in the ultimate leap of faith, and Aslan blows her gently to Narnia.

FAILING ON THE FIRST SIGN

Jill arrives in Narnia as the entire town is gathered to bid farewell to an old king leaving on his ship. She finds Eustace but is distracted by the talking animals and bright clothing. Eustace does not really want to listen to Jill and does not recognize anyone. By the time the ship sails, it is too late. The opportunity to obey the first command is past. The old king was Caspian. Time in Narnia is different than time on earth, and he is near the end of his life, whereas Eustace has only aged a few months.

King Caspian is sailing to Aslan's Country and may never return. Fortunately, a large owl notices them and introduces them to the court, but tells the children to tell no one of their quest to find the lost prince. They are invited to the palace. That night, the owl flies the two children to an old belfry where they are told that many brave knights have gone in search of the prince, but have never returned. No one is permitted to look again. Had they asked the king directly he would have agreed, but in his absence they will be forbidden to attempt it. If Jill and Eustace are to continue their quest, they will have to do the best they can on their own. The owls fly the children to a small village in a swamp where a Marshwiggle called Puddleglum becomes their guide.

A Word on Puddleglum

With a small body, long limbs, and webbed feet and hands, Puddleglum seems like a frog-like humanoid, but his character is worth examining. When the children first arrive, they are exhausted. He warns them about how poorly they will sleep but prepares a soft bed for them. When he makes them dinner, Puddleglum worries they will hate his cooking, but it is delicious. As the three begin their journey across giant country in compliance with the second sign, his cautious words seem to change. When food is scarce and the chill sets in, he marches onward, now sounding optimistic, but in actuality not changing at all.

In times of ease we may seem to be obedient, but in times of trial realize that our discipleship is only skin deep. Puddleglum's character, commitment, and behavior are completely consistent, no matter the circumstance. Lewis explored this idea in his writings and worried that sometimes we may only be pretending to be followers of Christ: "If I am a field that contains nothing but grass-seed, I cannot produce wheat. Cutting the grass may keep it short: but I shall still produce grass and no wheat. If I want to produce wheat, the change must go deeper than the surface. I must be ploughed up and re-sown."[7] A mowed grass field and wheat field may look similar but it is when they grow out that the differences are clear. Puddleglum's character shines as the trio meets many challenges because his heart is sown with the right stuff.

Recognizing Evil

If sin was not immediately self-satisfying, why would anyone do it? Temptation is by definition tempting, appealing, and simply enjoyable. The only problem is that joy through sin is always temporary and often not nearly as fun as it seemed. Lewis put it this way, "We are half-hearted creatures, fooling about with drink and sex and ambition when infinite joy is offered us, like an ignorant child who wants to go on making mud pies in a slum because he cannot imagine what is meant by the offer of a holiday at the sea. . . . We are far too easily pleased."[8]

Jill and Eustace encounter many people who distract them from completing their goal. As they make their way across the cold wasteland of the northern country, they come to a bridge. On the other side a beautiful lady dressed in green is riding with a knight in shining armor. She tells the travelers of Harfang, a great house of giants who will welcome them, warm them, and feed them. The children can think of nothing else and brave their way across a valley of rocks, which is the ruined giant city they are searching for. However, they do not recognize it because their focus is finding a warm bed. This temptation sidetracks them from their true purpose.

When they arrive, they are welcomed by the giants. At first they think it is a wonderful place, although they are soon dressed in doll clothes and kept prisoner. Looking from the window to the land they just passed, they realize that they had traveled right through the ruins. From their view they can also read the huge writing which says, "Under me." The three decide to escape through the kitchen where they find out the giants were going to eat them in a "man pie." The giants see them escaping and chase them to the path of the ruins. The little group find a crack that they can squeeze into, inadvertently following the third command, or sign. Their attempt to return to their quest has given this sign through grace itself.

THE UNDERWORLD AND MEETING THE PRINCE RILIAN

Soon Jill, Eustace, and Puddleglum are met by a great number of "Earthmen," little gnome-like creatures, who lead them through twisting tunnels to an underground sea and finally to the castle. As they are about to go to the dungeon, a young man calls them to his room. He is a loyal follower of the queen and sings her praises. The children do not like him. He explains that he has a terrible enchantment. Every night he turns into a serpent, so he must be bound to the silver chair or no one will be safe. He asks the three if they will stay with him since the witch will not be there that night to help him, and they agree, mostly out of curiosity.

After being bound to the chair, he begins to change but in attitude only. He begs them in the name of Aslan to cut his bonds. Puddleglum immediately recognizes the sign, but in their fear the children are still unsure. Jill wishes she knew what to do, when Puddleglum responds that she already knows. Due to their friend's insistence, they cut the prince's bonds. He immediately snatches up his sword and attacks the silver chair until it is just a pile of small silver slivers.

Prince Rilian explains that ten years earlier he went on a picnic with his mother, Ramadu's daughter. A green snake bit her while she lay resting and despite their greatest efforts, she died a few days later. Determined to avenge her death, the young prince returned to that place and found a beautiful lady dressed in green who enchanted him. Through magic he thought she was good and kind during the day, but each night the enchantment wore off, and he would realize the truth. So the lady tied him in the silver chair every night so he wouldn't escape. Meanwhile, the witch has been digging a hole with her army of "Earthmen" through the ground to Narnia. Once through, her army plans to enslave the kingdom, and she will wed Prince Rilian, becoming the ruler of Narnia.

THE END OF THE GREEN WITCH

As they are speaking, the Witch enters the room. She does not seem to react but sweetly walks to the fire, throwing in some powder that fills the room with a musty smell. Then she takes a mandolin and plays softly as she speaks to the group. Like many philosophers of our day, the witch denies the existence of anything other than that which is right before her eyes. Her enchantment seems to blind the others, weakening their faith. Soon she has almost convinced them that there is no Narnia, no sun, and no Aslan. Puddleglum gathers all his strength and stomps on the fire, stating bravely that he will go on believing Alsan and hoping for better until the day he dies.

Both Puddleglum's actions and words have an astonishing effect on the group, and the spell is lifted. Despite his foot being badly burned, Puddleglum's actions turned the entire group around. Although he was the only person injured on their journey, Puddleglum is also the only one to resist the greatest temptation of all. Lewis spoke of this when he said, "A silly idea is current that good people do not know what temptation means. This is an obvious lie. Only those who try to resist temptation know how strong it is. . . . You find out the strength of a wind by trying to walk against it, not by lying down."[9]

Once the witch realizes her deception is ineffective, she turns into a green serpent. Puddleglum, Eustace, and Prince Rilian immediately leap upon the monster and whack off its head with repeated blows. The death of the witch also brings the end of her influence. As the witch's enchantments die, the lights go out, and everyone runs to a bit of light shining through a hole. Jill stands on Puddleglum's back and is soon lifted through the gap, where a group of Narnians have gathered to celebrate the start of winter. Before long everyone is rescued, and Rilian tells all Narnia his story. They conclude that the Green Witch must have been the same sort as the White Witch. In the final analysis, they conclude that these witches always mean the same thing in every age, but go about a different way of getting it.[10]

THE END BUT NOT

As they return back to the palace, the King returns. Aslan had appeared to Caspian while he was at sea and told him to return where his son would be waiting. Rilian stands as the king is brought out of the ship on his bed and their hands clasp in love, but soon that love turns to grief as the old king dies. The children are sad when suddenly Aslan steps forward and says, "I have come."

Although they did not follow all the signs, they have accomplished what they were brought to Narnia to do. Now it is time for them to leave. Aslan breathes, and the children stand still while all of Narnia blows away. They are by the stream again and in the water they can see the dead king. Aslan asks Eustace to stick a thorn into his paw. Eustace obeys and a thick drop of blood falls in the water. As it covers the dead body, they can see his grey hair regaining its color, his wrinkles going away, and his cheeks growing round and fresh. Then Caspian leaps from the water, a young man. He laughs with "astonished joy."

The children ask Caspian if he is a ghost, but he tells them as long as he is in Aslan's country he is real, although in Narnia he might be a ghost. This theory of Lewis's is similar to his portrayal of the spirits in *The Great Divorce*, where the spirits in hell are vague and ethereal. But when an ethereal man with the lizard on his back decides that he will kill the lizard to go to heaven, he turns solid and the lizard transforms into a shining stallion that runs up to the stars with the man now on his back.[11]

It is quite clear that Lewis does not have a complete understanding of the physical resurrection or the fullness of eternity, but he does have an incredibly strong witness that it will be glorious, which is a truth we share. As James says, "Blessed is the man that endureth temptation: for when he is tried, he shall receive the crown of life, which the Lord hath promised to them that love him" (James 1:12).

Modern revelations add and clarify this promise: "And thus, if ye are faithful ye shall be laden with many sheaves, and crowned with honor, and glory, and immortality, and eternal life" (D&C 75:5), and "raised to endless happiness to inherit the kingdom of God" (Alma 41:4), and "which was prepared for them from the foundation of the world, and their joy shall be full forever" (2 Nephi 9:18).

NOTES

1. Here is the complete sonnet from http://www.bartleby.com/145/ww427.html
   Surprised By Joy—Impatient as the Wind
   Surprised by joy—impatient as the Wind
   I turned to share the transport—Oh! with whom
   But Thee, deep buried in the silent tomb,
   That spot which no vicissitude can find?

Love, faithful love, recalled thee to my mind—
But how could I forget thee? Through what power,
Even for the least division of an hour,
Have I been so beguiled as to be blind
To my most grievous loss?—That thought's return
Was the worst pang that sorrow ever bore,
Save one, one only, when I stood forlorn,
Knowing my heart's best treasure was no more;
That neither present time, nor years unborn
Could to my sight that heavenly face restore.

2. Lewis, *Screwtape Letters,* 28.

3. Lewis, *Mere Christianity,* 86.

4. Ibid., 50.

5. Ibid., 205–6.

6. Ibid., 148.

7. Ibid., 198.

8. Lewis, *Weight of Glory,* 29.

9. Lewis, *Mere Christianity,* 143.

10. Some commentaries claim that the Green Witch was Jadis from *The Magician's Nephew,* but Lewis makes it very clear on page 240 that although she is the same "kind of witch," the Green Witch was a different individual.

11. Lewis, *The Great Divorce,* 111–14.

CHAPTER FOURTEEN

The Last Battle:
An Anti-Christ, the End of the
World, and Final Judgment

he Last Battle is Lewis's apocalyptic tale of the end of Old Narnia and the joyous beginning of New Narnia. An unwilling deceiver tricks the Narnians into believing he is Aslan, succeeding in his deception, except for an elect few who realize he is an imposter. There is a final battle that seems hopeless, but miraculously changes into an adventure of hope and faith. There is a final judgment for all Narnians present and past. Finally, the Old Narnia becomes a New Narnia that is more real and vibrant. The original world seems to be a mere cardboard copy of the deep and rich new one. Of course, Aslan creates and rules over the New Narnia, bringing everlasting joy to all who live there.

In this story, there are many symbolic similarities with New Testament imagery, especially those in the book of Revelation. Lewis is not trying to be prophetic, merely uplifting. The parallels are there to help us examine our own understanding of the end of our lives, whether it is by death at old age or a worldwide apocalyptic destruction, in a way that brings hope rather than despair.

AN UNWILLING DECEIVER

It starts with Shift the ape, who sees a lion pelt in the water. He gets his "friend," Puzzle the donkey, to retrieve it for him from the cold stream. Their relationship is not much of a friendship as Shift constantly uses and manipulates Puzzle for his own purposes rather than thinking about what Puzzle wants. Puzzle does not believe he is very smart, so he lets Shift tell him what to do. Shift sees the possibilities of the lion skin and immediately starts to work. He sews it into a coat for Puzzle. Puzzle does not want anything to do with it, but Shift keeps assuring him that Aslan would be pleased with their plan to imitate him. They can get some things they want, like a few extra bananas and lumps of sugar. In this way, Shift convinces Puzzle to become a false Aslan.

In the Book of Mormon, a few people also convinced others to believe in false prophets. Shem, the first anti-Christ of the Book of Mormon, taught people the things they wanted to hear mingled with lies. He convinced them that there would be no Christ. He is confronted by Jacob and asks for a sign. Shem is struck by the power of Lord. Just before he dies, he tells the people "that he had been deceived by the power of the devil" (Jacob 7:18). Later, Korihor persuades many people to not believe in Christ and also to pay him for his preaching. He also asks for a sign and is struck dumb. Korihor wrote on a tablet that the devil deceived him by appearing unto him "in the form of an angel . . . And [Korihor] taught [his words] because they are pleasing unto the carnal mind" (Alma 30:53). For both of these men, the devil left them once they had done his bidding. They were not supported by the devil for their work. They were told what to say by the devil.

The ape, Shift, also becomes Puzzle's mouthpiece whenever he appears to the Narnians. The ape is masterminding a deep deception trying to undermine the faith of all Narnians. He is having them believe in this fake Aslan, so they will forget the real one.

Puzzle becomes an unwilling victim. He is put into a shack on the top of Stable Hill where he is forced to stay all day. At night, the ape brings him out to show all the Narnians that Aslan has truly come back. There is a large bonfire so the Narnians can see Puzzle, but the shadows in the dark make his lion costume harder to see. Shift is the only one who talks. Puzzle becomes a prisoner in the stable going without food or water because no one remembers to feed him. All the sugar promised him never appears.

Christ warned believers to beware of those who would try to deceive men and women of this world. He said, "Take heed that no man deceive you. For many shall come in my name saying, I am Christ; and shall deceive many" (Matthew 24:4–5).

Most of the Narnians are taken in by the fake Aslan. They are initially excited by the thought that Aslan has returned. When Aslan has been with them previously, he has always been a righteous ruler. His ways have always been good to follow. But soon, he begins telling them to ruin their land and give up their freedom. Even King Tirian is initially excited about the prospect of Aslan returning. However, when he hears the commands to the Narnians, he questions how Aslan could allow such dreadful deeds to happen.

Moroni gave a standard by which we can know what is good: "That which is of God inviteth and enticeth to do good continually; wherefore, every thing which inviteth and enticeth to do good, and to love God, and to serve him is inspired of God" (Moroni 7:13). Moroni goes on to tell us that we are required to judge, but we must be careful not to judge that which is evil to be good or good to be evil, for "the way to judge is as plain . . . as the daylight is from the dark night" (Moroni 7:15).

Not all the Narnians are deceived. King Tirian, Jewel the unicorn, and Roonwit the Centaur all judge righteously. They figure out that this cannot be Aslan because of the works he is requiring of his subjects. These few stand for the truth, even unto death, willing to stand up for the true Aslan.

FREEDOM VERSUS SLAVERY

From the beginning, Shift's plan is much deeper than he ever tells Puzzle. He contacts the rulers of Calormen to come, originally as merchants. They start to use the animals as beasts of burden, rather than allowing them to live freely. The Narnians are put into slavery to work in Calormen mines underground, the Narnian trees are cut down and sent to Calormen, and all of the Narnian resources are taken away.

Their freedom was originally taken away because they allowed it to be taken from them. They did not judge wisely. Shift told them that Aslan was different. Because he was different, he was asking them to do different things than they had done before. He was not really enslaving them, but allowing them to work for wages. Later, the Calormenes took away their disguise of being merchants and brought soldiers with spears and other weapons of war. The slavery was now real. It would have been difficult for them to get out of their slavery even if they had wanted to at this point.

Many of us who think we are "free" are actually slaves to social pressure, other people's opinions, or the overpowering desire to belong to a particular circle of friends. Our masters may take different forms, but in the end, we have still allowed ourselves to become slaves. If we continue in our slavery for too long, it will be almost impossible to get rid of our taskmasters. Lewis reminds us:

> People who believe themselves to be free, and indeed are free, from snobbery, and who read satires on snobbery with tranquil superiority, may be devoured by the desire in another form. It may be

the very intensity of their desire to enter some quite different Ring which renders them immune from the allurements of high life. An invitation from a duchess would be very cold comfort to a man smarting under the sense of exclusion from some artistic or communist coterie. Poor man—it is not large, lighted rooms, or champagne, or even scandals about peers and Cabinet Ministers that he wants: it is the sacred little attic or studio, the heads bent together, the fog of tobacco smoke, and the delicious knowledge that we—we four or five all huddled beside this stove—are the people who know.[1]

THE HOPE OF KING TIRIAN

King Tirian and Jewel come upon some Calormenes whipping a free Narnian horse. The king deals rashly with these men and kills two of them. However, Tirian and Jewel are ashamed of their dreadful deed and allow themselves to be taken prisoner. Tirian is brought before the ape and the Calormene leader, Rishda Tarkaan. When he tries to tell the confused Narnians about the deception being played upon them, the king is knocked down, tied to a tree, and left there in complete despair.

While King Tirian is tied to the tree, he calls out to Aslan for help. He even offers his own life if Aslan will come and help save Narnia. He calls for the children from another world, the friends of Narnia, to come and help. When he gets no reply, he becomes hopeless.

After the death of his wife, Lewis also felt hopeless. Even though he had a testimony of Christ, the reality of his situation became too much for him to bear. In his book *A Grief Observed,* Lewis discusses the process he went through in order to get his faith back. Initially, his grief almost felt like fear. He physically experienced sensations similar to being afraid, such as thirst, a fluttering in his stomach, disorientation, and uncontrollable tears. Slowly, the beginnings of hope came back into his life. He felt his wife's presence with him as he started to think more about her feelings than his own. He speculated that the dead, when they see us, see us more clearly than they did while with us on the earth. Their understanding has grown and their vision has cleared. While she was alive, Joy saw Lewis's faults and his realities, without becoming disenchanted with him.[2] The hope of her love which continues beyond the grave moved him forward.

Lewis came to realize the answer to the questions he had been asking God had been all practically answered in the scriptures. All he needed to live by was the two great commandments of loving God and loving his neighbor. Lewis understood that he need to get on with his life and start doing the things God required of him.

King Tirian is helped in his time of need by the small and meek creatures. The mice, rabbits, and moles bring Tirian food and drink, just like Narnian mice who gnawed Aslan's cords and ropes to free him the night he gave his life for Edmund.

At the final battle, King Tirian calls all Narnians to fight against the Calormenes. The little animals—the mice, moles, rabbits, and squirrels—hop to his side to help with the battle. Very few of the other animals side with their King. Most of them cannot make up their minds.

Jesus taught, "And blessed are the meek, for they shall inherit the earth" (3 Nephi 12:5). The weak things of this world will conquer the strong. The Lord does this so people will realize they cannot rely upon their own strength or others' strength, for only the Lord's strength will enable them to conquer the world. "The weak things of the world shall come forth and break down the mighty and strong ones, that man should not counsel his fellow man, neither trust in the arm of flesh—But that every man might speak in the name of God the Lord, even the Savior of the world" (D&C 1:19–20).

After being free, King Tirian feels the grief of losing his kingdom, his friends, and possibly, his faith. Then, he has a vision or a dream where he sees seven people around a table. They seem to be able to see him, too. He is unable to speak to them, but they can obviously see him. At first, he is frustrated by this momentary glimpse. Waking from the dream is the worst moment of his life.

Ten minutes later, Jill and Eustace magically appear by his side. His prayers are heard. Nothing has changed about his dire circumstances, but everything has changed because he has a glimmer of hope. His faith is renewed. He knows he must now get to work, doing what needs to be done in order to save Narnia and himself.

DWARFS ARE FOR DWARFS

King Tirian, Jill, and Eustace find Puzzle and realize the ape's lie. When they see the donkey in the ill-fitting lion skin, they wonder how anyone could have been deceived by such a costume. They decide to wait until the bonfire, when all the Narnians are gathered, to uncover Puzzle and prove to all the truth.

While they are walking, the group comes across dwarfs being taken by Calormenes to work in mines. They battle their captors and set the dwarfs free. In order to help the dwarfs understand the truth, they show them Puzzle, the would-be Aslan. The dwarfs do not know how to take the truth. They decide never to be taken in by anyone again. Instead of thanking King

Tirian, they accuse the king of saving them just to use them and reign over them once again. They do not want to have a king anymore, nor will they ever bow to Aslan. Their motto becomes "Dwarfs are for dwarfs!"

After they leave, a single dwarf comes back, Poggin, who thanks them and wants to help. He still believes in Aslan and does not let the deception and lies of others take away his faith.

After the Savior healed ten lepers, only one leper, a Samaritan, returns to thank him. Jesus asks the man, "Were there not ten cleansed? But where are the nine?" (Luke 17:17). The Savior then says to him, "Arise, go they way: thy faith hath made thee whole" (Luke 17:19). Poggin is similar to this single leper. It is his faith that keeps him whole and gives him the right perspective on things.

Later, in the final battle, the dwarfs fight only for themselves. They kill the horses that come to help King Tirian and they kill the Calormenes. The few dwarfs that are left alive after the battle have been thrown into the stable door which leads to an unexpected world of unparalleled beauty. Peter, Jill, Eustace and Tirian have eaten the marvelous fruit found there and are enjoying the bright summer afternoon. But the dwarfs sit in a tight circle, thinking they are trapped in a dark, smelly stable and will not be "deceived." Aslan even tries giving them delicious food and drink, but all they see is stable food, not the feast Aslan has prepared for them. Their selfishness and lack of faith blinds their spiritual eyes forever.

TASH VERSUS ASLAN

Throughout the Narnian books, the message that there is an absolute right and wrong is continually emphasized. The standard does not change over time or with different rulers. The definition of correct choices and evil choices is established through the ultimate ruler, Aslan. Yet, it is not from him, but his father, the Emperor, that this standard is established. Those who choose evil and those who choose good will receive their reward, and Aslan will be their final judge.

Lewis lived during a time of progressive thinking. These modern philosophers proposed different moral standards. They advised modern society to allow changes in their moral standards in order to be current with the modern world. Lewis cautioned against these changes in morality. Standards regarding sexual purity and virtue are eternal and do not change with time.

When I was a youngster, all the progressive people were saying, "Why all this prudery? Let us treat sex just as we treat all other impulses." I was simple-minded enough to believe they meant what they said. I have since discovered that they meant exactly the opposite. They meant that sex was to be treated as no other impulse in our nature has ever been treated by civilized people. All others, we admit, have to be bridled . . . it is like having a morality in which stealing fruit is considered wrong—unless you steal nectarines.[3]

These lies about freeing our sexual urges and passions are still a real part of modern philosophical thinking today. They spout a double standard that will only bring confusion and worse. Moroni spoke to those who would deny the gospel of Christ. He reminds all of us, "For do we not read that God is the same yesterday, today, and forever, and in him there is no variableness neither shadow of changing? . . . Come unto the Lord with all your heart, and work out your own salvation with fear and trembling before him" (Mormon 9:9, 27).

The deception engineered by Shift, the ape, leads to the destruction of many Narnians' faith. He deceives the Narnians with a false Aslan. They in turn must decide who to believe. They cannot follow this new Aslan without rejecting the old.

The Calormene people have also created a god called Tash. Shift claims that Aslan and Tash are the same being. They even change the name of Aslan to "Tashlan" reflecting the blending of the two. The Narnians and even many of the Calormenes become confused. They do not know who to believe. Many of the Narnians are in physical and spiritual pain and do not know where to turn.

In *The Problem of Pain,* Lewis explains how important it is that we remain open to the lessons the one true God wants to teach us, even in painful situations, "As St. Augustine says somewhere, 'God wants to give us something, but cannot, because our hands are full—there's nowhere for Him to put it.' Or as a friend of mine said, 'We regard God as an airman regards his parachute; it's there for emergencies but he hopes he'll never have to use it.' "[4]

Tash, the god of the Calormenes, looks nothing like the lion, Aslan. He has a birdlike head, four arms, and wings, yet walks like a man. Aslan eventually explains that he and Tash are opposites. No evil service can be done for Aslan. He would not accept it. No pure and good service can be done for Tash for he would not accept good works. The deception of the ape and the slavery of the Calormenes have corrupted the minds of the Narnians. They do not know how to make right decisions or who to turn to for spiritual guidance.

In the last days, the Lord also looks at the corruption that has entered into the hearts of his people. He sees that their minds have been altered and their spirits deceived and mourns, "And my vineyard has become corrupted every whit; and there is none which doeth good save it be a few; and they err in many instances because of priestcrafts, all having corrupt minds" (D&C 33:4).

THE FINAL BATTLE

Before the final battle, all the Narnians are told the truth. They understand that Puzzle and Tash were never Aslan. Yet, for many, their faith has been forever damaged. King Tirian calls for them to fight with him. Very few have the courage or the faith to join him. The last few Narnians stand against a huge Calormene army with reinforcements from twenty ships.

The Old Testament prophet Joel describes the final battle on earth, "A day of darkness and of gloominess, a day of clouds and of thick darkness . . . A great people and a strong; there hath not been ever the like. . . . A fire devoureth before them and behind them a flame burneth . . . yea, and nothing shall escape them" (Joel 2:2–3).

In the battle, the chief Calormene, Captain Tarkaan, has ordered all who can be saved to be thrown into the stable as an offering to Tash. King Tirian fights hard for his country and his people. While he fights, Tirian notices that he is being steered toward the stable door. In his final moment in battle, he grabs Captain Tarkaan and takes him into the stable along with himself.

Captain Tarkaan immediately sees Tash, whom he has worshipped but not really believed. Tash looks at him and takes him under his wing, not a gesture of protection, but of destruction. Tash is then ordered to leave with his prey, and Captain Tarkaan has become a human sacrifice to Tash.

King Tirian now looks around him and sees a beautiful green garden rather than a lowly stable. The world seems endless. Waiting for him are the other faithful helpers of Narnia. These brave fighters have been miraculously washed clean and dressed in new clothes. The hopeless battle has now turned into something glorious.

In like manner, after the final battle on Earth, the Lord will restore all that has been ruined. Those who have been faithful will be dealt with in a wondrous fashion, "And ye shall eat in plenty, and be satisfied, and praise the name of the Lord your God, that hath dealt wondrously with you . . . And your sons and your daughter shall prophesy, your old men shall dream dreams, your young men shall see visions" (Joel 2:26, 28).

THE FINAL JUDGMENT

Aslan now returns in all his power and might. He roars for "Time," the great giant who has been slumbering until he was called. The seven faithful kings and queens of Narnia stand on Aslan's right side. They are Peter, Edmund, and Lucy Pevensie, Eustace Scrubb, Jill Pole, Polly Plummer, and Digory Kirke. The giant sounds his trumpet and the stars fall down from the sky like humans filled with light. This is the end of Narnia. All things are being wiped clean and made new.

Lewis predicts that when the Lord comes in his majesty and power, it will also be the end of our world as we know it: "But I wonder whether people who ask God to interfere openly and directly in our world quite realize what it will be like when He does. When that happens, it is the end of the world. When the author comes on to the stage the play is over."[5]

In Narnia, all creatures, both great and small, now assemble outside of the door of the stable. They must walk past Aslan and look into his face. If they look at him with fear and hatred, they go to Aslan's left side. The talking Narnians turn into ordinary beasts and they disappear into a huge black shadow. If they look at his face with love, even though they may still feel fear, they enter the door on Aslan's right. All Narnians who have died are brought back to life for this final judgment.

Owen Barfield described how our life experiences will later come back to us as a shout, "Each great experience is 'a whisper Which Memory will warehouse as a shout.' "[6] In our final judgment, we will remember all that we have done for good and ill to others. These memories will come back to us as a shout and cause the same division to happen at the end of our world. Jesus describes it as the separation of the sheep from the goats: "And before him shall be gathered all nations: and he shall separate them one from another, as a shepherd divideth his sheep from the goats: And he shall set the sheep on his right hand, but the goats on the left. Then shall the King say unto them on his right hand, Come, ye blessed of my Father, inherit the kingdom prepared for you from the foundation of the world" (Matthew 25:32–34).

Those who have been faithful move farther in and higher up into the kingdom prepared for them. Those who have not been faithful enter outer darkness.

After the judgment, the faithful Narnians watch the final destruction of their beloved Narnia. Dragons and giant lizards roam their world, tearing up all vegetation and leaving it a barren rock. The dying sun turns blood red and the moon is about to join with the sun when, finally, the giant grabs the sun and squeezes it into oblivion. There is total darkness and extreme cold. The door is shut, and everyone mourns the death of Old Narnia.

BELOVED EMETH AND PUZZLE

The group of seven finds themselves in a beautiful wood. They are walking together peacefully. They are surprised to meet a young Calormene soldier named Emeth. He had offered himself as a willing sacrifice in order to see the face of Tashlan, a mix of his god Tash and the Narnian god, Aslan. Emeth is doing this out of a simple faith in his god. As he walked into the shack on Stable Hill, King Tirian comments on how this brave young Calormene is worthy of a better god than Tash.[7]

Emeth tells his story. He realized his people were using lying and trickery to destroy Narnia. He was sickened by it. He had always been a true believer of Tash. He was upset by their use of the only god he knew. After entering the stable garden, he reflected upon all the things he had seen. Aslan finally found him. He was overcome by the lion's presence and bowed to him. Aslan touched his forehead and talked to him.

Emeth confessed that he was a servant of Tash. Aslan commented that all the service Emeth had done for Tash was counted as service done to Aslan because it was righteous service. Emeth had spent all his days seeking God, and Tash was the only god he knew. He had tried to be faithful. Aslan told him that we all eventually find what we truly seek and he had now found it. Aslan called him, "Beloved," and Emeth marveled that he would be allowed to live in Aslan's country.

The Lord will find those who are truly seeking him. There are many who are pure in heart who do not know where to find their Lord. The Church of Jesus Christ of Latter-day Saints has the special commission to preach the gospel to all the world for the gathering of these elect ones. The Lord has said, "And even so will I gather mine elect from the four quarters of the earth, even as many as will believe in me, and hearken unto my voice" (D&C 33:6).

The group also finds Puzzle in this beautiful new world. His coat is a lovely silver color and his face is an honest one. Jill runs up to him and gives him a hug. Puzzle still feels uneasy. He is worried about what will happen when he sees or talks to Aslan in person. Aslan soon seeks out Puzzle and tells him to come to him. Puzzle is nervous. Aslan talks to him in the same calm manner as he talked to Edmund after his betrayal. Puzzle leaves the interview with a smile on his donkey face.

Even though we are commanded to judge between evil and good, we cannot judge another person's heart. The Lord warns us, "I, the Lord, will forgive whom I will forgive, but of you it is required to forgive all men" (D&C 64:10).

OLD NARNIA AND NEW NARNIA

As they live in this new world, the Narnians begin to realize that this new world is more like Narnia than the world they saw destroyed. Narnia is not dead, but this world is the real Narnia. Everything means more in New Narnia. They can run and not be weary. They do not feel afraid. They can do impossible things, like swim up waterfalls, run so fast they seem to be flying, and see things far away as if they were up close.

Reading the scriptures often causes us to wonder about our earthly experience, the world we live in, and the ugliness of the world around us. We wish we could live in a heavenly realm. In a letter, Lewis pointed out to a friend that such reveries might be a testimony to the fact that we are not, in essence, temporal beings, but spiritual beings: "You say the materialist universe is "ugly." I wonder how you discerned that? If you are really a product of a materialistic universe, how is it you don't feel at home there? Do fish complain of the sea for being wet? . . . Notice how we are perpetually surprised by time. ('How time flies! Fancy John being grown up and married? I can hardly believe it!') In heaven's name why? Unless, indeed, there is something in us which is not temporal."[8]

As they go farther up and farther in, they began to change more. Their eyes could even see their world differently. Lucy can focus her eyes on something very far away and see it in her mind's eye as if it were right in front of her. She could now interact with all the splendors around her. Lewis comments, "We cannot mingle with the splendours we see. But all the leaves of the New Testament are rustling with the rumour that it will not always be so."[9]

Believing in truth and living the truth changes you. There is a rebirth that happens as we give all to the Lord. We are able to squelch the natural man tendencies. We stop wanting the pleasures of the world and seek eternal joy. Lewis wrote,

> Christ says, "Give me All. I don't want so much of your time and so much of your money and so much of your work: I want You. I have not come to torment your natural self, but to kill it. No half-measures are any good. I don't want to cut off a branch here and a branch there, I want to have the whole tree down. . . . Hand over

the whole natural self, all the desires which you think innocent as well as the ones you think wicked—the whole outfit. I will give you a new self instead. In fact, I will give you Myself: my own will shall become yours."[10]

This change can happen to you and to others around you. You can see the change in others because of the way they look and act.

This is the end of the Narnia books. Not because the story ends, but because the things after that were too great and beautiful to write.[11] For Lewis, this would be the end of his story. But, the stories do still continue in the hearts and minds of children throughout the world.

NOTES

1. Lewis, *The Weight of Glory*, 141.
2. For further information, read Lewis, *A Grief Observed*, 686.
3. Lewis, *God in the Dock*, 319–20.
4. Lewis, *The Problem of Pain*, 95.
5. Lewis, *Mere Christianity*, 65.
6. *The Quotable Lewis*, Martindale and Roots, 425.
7. Lewis, *The Chronicles of Narnia*, 728.
8. Lewis, *Collection of Letters, vol. III*, 76.
9. Lewis, *The Weight of Glory*, 33.
10. Lewis, *Mere Christianity*, 196–97.
11. Lewis, *The Chronicles of Narnia*, 767.

PART THREE

LIVING JOYFULLY

Joy is the serious business of Heaven.

C. S. LEWIS

This section examines some of the most notable references to C. S. Lewis by modern apostles and prophets.

CHAPTER FIFTEEN

A New Voice among the Saints

n January of 1971, three magazines, the *Ensign,* the *New Era*, and the *Friend*, arrived for the first time on the doorsteps of about 350,000 homes. As readers opened their copies of the *Ensign,* they found a message from President Joseph Fielding Smith. In its first few pages he introduced the magazine's purpose as another effort to help all Church members stay closer to the Lord. The prophet promised that these new magazines could be a great influence for good if they would be read consistently.[1]

In the first issue of the *New Era*, Neal A. Maxwell, who had recently been appointed commissioner of education,[2] wrote a response in a new column entitled "Questions and Answers" that fielded gospel questions from teenagers and young adult members. The first inquiry was written by a college student who had become confused by the comments of his roommates. His question stated simply, "Do we still believe in the Second Coming?" Commissioner Maxwell stated that the Church is clearly committed to this belief and went on to tell of the attitude we need to have in facing it. He warned us to react without overreacting. He asked how many of us today might have made fun of Noah building his ark or laughed about it cynically in private.

Pleading with the youth and all members of the Church alike, Elder Maxwell ends his article by reaffirming the importance of gaining a testimony of the reality of Christ's return before it occurs. He closes with the words of C. S. Lewis, "When the author walks on to the stage, the play is over."[3]

With this intriguing answer, two things occurred for the first time in the Church. The unique literary voice of Neal A. Maxwell was heard throughout its general membership, and the words of C. S. Lewis were carried into the forum of Latter-day Saint thought through an official Church publication.[4] It would seem that a door had opened, allowing the truths that C. S. Lewis so clearly illustrated through his simple but direct language to be shared with the Saints at large.

During that same year, C. S. Lewis would be quoted four more times. Two additional references were in the *New Era* by commissioner Maxwell and one reference in the *Ensign,* encouraging parents to read *The Chronicles of Narnia,* among other good books, with their children.[5]

C. S. LEWIS IN GENERAL CONFERENCE

Interestingly, it was over six years after Lewis was quoted in the new Church magazines before his words were finally mentioned in a general conference address. In October of 1977, Elder Paul H. Dunn stood at the pulpit in the Tabernacle on Temple Square and spoke of a widow who used to get angry with her husband for leaving his hat on the sewing machine when he got home from work. She would often scold him about it. Then one day, he suddenly caught pneumonia and died. Afterwards, she wished she could have seen the old hat hanging on her sewing machine. Elder Dunn asked why we so often treat those we love with less care than we should. Then he repeated Lewis's advice, "Take care. It is so easy to break eggs without making omelets."[6]

This simple line is so indicative of Lewis's insightful style for many reasons. It reminds us of how we should treat others based on the teachings of Christ, using a straightforward analogy or parable. The words are easy to understand, almost simplistic. Yet there is a deeper meaning that causes one to pause and think more profoundly.

Elder Dunn cited as his reference Elder Richard L. Evans,[7] who wrote a book of quotes that was published in 1963, the year of Lewis's death. After this first reference, C. S. Lewis quotes continued to pop up with stunning regularity in general conference. His words continued to influence LDS writers and General Authorities because of their Christian emphasis and their testimony of the Savior.

LEWIS AND THE APOSTLES

C. S. Lewis has been quoted approximately one hundred times in Church magazines, almost one-third of those citations being from general conference.[8] The majority of those references came from Neal A. Maxwell, a clear admirer of the Christian apologist. Elder Maxwell quoted

Lewis frequently in his private writings and was the first to quote him in Church publications. He was the apostle who most often used Lewis's references, providing nineteen total citations, four of those in his general conference addresses.

Elder James E. Faust was next, referencing C. S. Lewis seven times in the last twenty years. Elders Jeffrey R. Holland and Marvin J. Ashton each had four references with Elder Dallin H. Oaks at three. Most others that quoted him did so only once, but on the average C. S. Lewis's ideas have been used to assist in illustrating gospel truths between two and three times a year. As a matter of fact, there have only been two years where Lewis was not mentioned in Church magazines since 1971. First, in 1973 there was no reference of his works, but the following year there were five citations and the year after that four. Again in 2002 he was not quoted, but the year before he had been quoted five times.

Perhaps the reason Lewis is quoted so often is because he discusses mankind's frailties through the "small sins" of everyday life. His voice is not one of a university professor, but has an "every man" quality, as though he is struggling beside us, which enables people of all kinds to relate to his message. But along with his personal weaknesses and trials, C. S. Lewis openly witnesses time and again of his personal faith in Christ as both a partner in helping us overcome our challenges in this life and as our Savior in giving us the opportunity to share in His glory in the next. It is this powerful testimony of the Savior that rings true to members of the Church.

C. S. LEWIS AND THE WOMEN OF THE CHURCH

Another significant group that has quoted C. S. Lewis frequently is the women of the Church. Fifteen references come from women, which is proportionately higher than their male counterparts.[9] One of the most touching references by C. S. Lewis was not made by a woman at all but by Elder James E. Faust in an address given at a BYU devotional and later expanded as a conference address. Here, Elder Faust mentioned his great love and gratitude for his eight beautiful granddaughters,[10] and refers to a portion of a letter Lewis wrote about the importance of homemaking.

This quote was used earlier by General Relief Society President Barbara B. Smith in addressing the women of the Church at the height of the battle over women's rights.[11] In clarity Lewis explains that the purpose of every career is to support the most important career of all, that of homemaker.[12] Here, again Lewis has an incredible knack for taking an eternal principle that has become tarnished and misunderstood by worldly standards, and shining it up, holding it forward, and removing any doubt of its truth.

MORE TO COME

The next chapters will focus as much on the words of the General Authorities of the Church as they do on quotes by C. S. Lewis. Having given you an overview of the context of Lewis's quotes, we will now explore the concepts surrounding how they were utilized in the forum of the Church. As you read, you will see again the great testimony C. S. Lewis had of Christ as our Redeemer and the pure intent of a man trying to live as a true disciple, but you will also see the added light and knowledge of the fulness of the gospel brought to us by inspired men called through the power and authority of Jesus Christ to lead his church in our day.

First, we will explore Elder Maxwell's words on discipleship and how C. S. Lewis shared this worthy goal to "give [Christ] all." Next, we'll look at the "weight of glory," a complex essay by Lewis and a phrase used only once in the Bible but twice in modern revelation. In this essay Lewis speaks of the "five heads" or certainties of our reward in the eternities. In modern revelation, a wider view of that ultimate reward has been given to us, which expands on the morsels of truth expressed by Lewis.

The next chapter speaks of the role of women. For a man who spent the majority of his life as a bachelor, Lewis had a great respect for the role of homemaker. Recently, our leaders have had much to say on this topic as the family continues to fall prey to the cultural pressures of the world. There have been a number of wonderful stories about women who have made the "first feeble attempts" to stretch in those areas and have been greatly blessed for their efforts.

President Ezra Taft Benson's talk on pride has echoed through the years in our hearts, in our lesson manuals, and through the words of Church leaders today. President Benson referred to Lewis's words as the kernel of his remarks, growing to express scriptural examples and individual instances that we should be aware of.

Lewis's first book to become an international success was *Screwtape Letters* and from its pages much has been quoted about temptation and the wiles of Satan. Modern day apostles and prophets have consistently warned us to be aware of temptations and specified how we can avoid them.

Finally, we focus on joy. This was the constant theme of Lewis's life and the hope of his existence. It seems beyond coincidental that he would call the book on his conversion *Surprised by Joy* and then marry his wife Joy near the end of his life, surprisingly finding love as well. Lewis constantly spoke of it, yearned for it, and we pray it is as glorious as he dreamed. Like the wonderful homecoming of a missionary to his family, related by Elder Holland, we can imagine Jack racing home, into the arms of his Savior—the ultimate joy.

NOTES

1. Joseph Fielding Smith, "Message from the First Presidency," *Ensign*, Jan. 1971, 3.
2. Bruce C. Hafen, *A Disciple's Life*, 343.
3. Lewis, *Mere Christianity*, 65, and Neal Maxwell, "Q&A: Questions and Answers," New Era, Jan. 1971, 9.
4. Although C. S. Lewis is used as a source in *Richard Evans' Quote Book* (see endnote 7) and is discussed in a wonderful article in BYU Studies in 1971, a thorough search of past general conference talks and *Improvement Era*s from 1940 to 1970 yielded no C. S. Lewis references per Gospelink.
5. Elliott D. Landau, "Of Books, Children, and Parents," *Ensign*, May 1971, 31.
6. Paul H. Dunn, "We Have Been There All the Time," *Ensign*, Nov. 1977, 24, and Richard L. Evans, *Richard Evans' Quote Book* (Salt Lake City: Publisher's Press, 1971), 169.
7. Richard L. Evans was an apostle who was a writer, producer, and announcer of "Music and the Spoken Word" for forty-one years from 1930 to 1971.
8. See Appendix A for a complete list of C. S. Lewis quotes used in Church magazines from 1971 to 2008. Thirty references out of ninety-six are from conference issues.
9. Statistics based on 4 out of 28 conference citations by women and 13 out of 141 female speakers, based on general conference issue contents for *Ensign*, Nov. 1977, Nov. 1987, Nov. 1997, and May 2007 (including Relief Society and Young Women's sessions).
10. James E. Faust, "A Message to My Granddaughters: Becoming 'Great Women,' " *Ensign*, September 1986, 16.
11. Barbara B. Smith, "Women for the Latter Day," *Ensign*, Nov. 1979, 107.
12. Warren Lewis, ed., *Letters of C. S. Lewis* (London: Geoffrey Bles Ltd., 1952), 62 (per *Ensign*, Nov. 1979 reference).

CHAPTER SIXTEEN

Discipleship: Imagine Yourself a Living House

n the late autumn of 1998, universities across the world celebrated the hundredth anniversary of C. S. Lewis's birth by holding centenary conferences focused on his writings and insights. Brigham Young University was one of those schools and asked Neal A. Maxwell to be the keynote speaker.[1] Elder Maxwell had been struggling in his battle with leukemia at the time. After fifteen months of remission, the cancer was back. He had undergone radiation that June and was currently enduring regular injections to keep the disease at bay.[2] Standing before an audience of over two thousand,[3] he expressed his gratitude for being able to attend.[4]

Elder Maxwell touched briefly on many different dimensions of C. S. Lewis's works that he would have loved to address, including his wit and points of theology common to both Lewis and LDS beliefs. Instead of speaking on those topics, he chose to limit his remarks to C. S. Lewis's insights into how challenging being a disciple of Christ truly is.[5]

Discipleship was a common theme for Elder Maxwell, encompassing many areas of the gospel. During this presentation, he touched on faith and repentance, understanding the nature of God, temptations and distractions, misery versus joy, our natural selves, taking up the cross daily, and the first and great commandment, using C. S. Lewis excerpts in every instance. A few months later, Elder Maxwell crystallized all of these aspects of discipleship into a single common component, or the "grand key," in a talk given to BYU students and later published as an *Ensign* article. He said that when we submit our wills to the Lord, we know we are on the path of discipleship.

PUTTING ON CHRIST

Elder Maxwell went on to explain that the way we become disciples is through the first and great commandment, "Thou shalt love the Lord thy God with all thy heart, and with all thy soul, and with all thy mind" (Matthew 22:37; see also Deuteronomy 6:5). Chiding us slightly, Elder Maxwell warned that too often our actions are in more compliance than our minds and hearts.[6] It is this struggle against our human stubbornness that C. S. Lewis understood so well and illustrated so clearly through his writings, as shown in this excerpt Maxwell used to clarify this point, "We are bidden to 'put on Christ,' to become like God. That is, whether we like it or not, God intends to give us what we need, not what we now think we want."[7]

Maxwell explained that it is not enough to simply live the commandments as is evident by the story of the rich and righteous young man who came to Christ asking, "Good Master, what good thing shall I do, that I may have eternal life?"[8] Living the commandments is only the beginning. God intends to give us "customized commandments,"[9] unique to each of us, delivered through personal revelation.

The principle of responding to inspiration with submissiveness was one of the original barriers to Lewis's acceptance of Christ. In the end, it also became the basis of his conversion to Christianity. He says of his experience, "I was holding something at bay, or shutting something out . . . I felt myself being, there and then, given a free choice. I could open the door or keep it shut . . . I chose to open, to unbuckle, to loosen the rein."[10] Lewis understood from the inside out the struggle of following personal directives from the Lord, which was reflected in his poignant words.

IMAGINE YOURSELF A LIVING HOUSE

In the years before his conversion to Christianity, Lewis came across the writings of the Scottish minister George MacDonald, which impacted him greatly. He later joked that a young atheist who didn't want to be a Christian needed to be more careful in his reading.[11] He went on to say that George MacDonald had influenced him more than any writer despite the fact he was very religious.[12] Lewis's first interest in MacDonald's writings was his fairy tales and fantasy novels, but soon his attention expanded to MacDonald's sermons. Lewis was the first to admit that the quality of MacDonald's writings was lacking, but he saw in them a genius.

Lewis tried to explain his feelings in the introduction to George MacDonald's anthology which he edited, saying that MacDonald's writings shock us to the core, leaving us more fully awake than we could have thought possible.[13] Lewis also admitted that he never tried to hide the fact that he considered MacDonald his master and used his insights often in his writings.

One such quote comes at the end of Lewis's *Mere Christianity*. Lewis discusses "putting on Christ" and then explains that this is not just a special exercise for the top of the class, but a responsibility for the whole of Christianity.[14] At the conclusion of his address, Lewis finds he must borrow a parable from George MacDonald:

> Imagine yourself as a living house. God comes in to rebuild that house. At first, perhaps, you can understand what He is doing. He is getting the drains right and stopping the leaks in the roof and so on: you knew that those jobs needed doing and so you are not surprised. But presently he starts knocking the house about in a way that hurts abominably and does not seem to make sense. What on earth is He up to? The explanation is that He is building quite a different house from the one you thought of—throwing up a new wing here, putting an extra floor there, running up towers, making courtyards. You thought you were going to be made into a decent little cottage: but He is building a palace. He intends to come and live in it Himself.[15]

This is perhaps the most popular of Lewis's quotes in the Church, used in two general conferences, an *Ensign* article by Elder Maxwell, and three of Maxwell's other publications.[16] In October of 1972 while still Commissioner of Education, Neal A. Maxwell wrote an article for the February *Ensign* entitled "The Value of Home." After warning us that "there is no way to have an arms' length relationship with God," Elder Maxwell describes this relationship more clearly, explaining that submitting ourselves to his will is the only way to grow spiritually. The parable of the living house then illustrates the importance of not getting comfortable in our role as people with special responsibilities, while accepting our weaknesses. Elder Maxwell goes on to remind us that the paths of Christ and the world have always headed in different directions and are constantly becoming more disparate.[17]

Marvin J. Ashton also used this parable as an example of the fact that change hurts. In his conference address entitled, "Progress through Change" given in October of 1979, Elder Ashton explained that there is always pain in change. He told us that life is a series of ups and downs but the best growth happens when we are at our lowest.[18]

In 1984, Elder John K. Carmack was called to the Seventy and was asked to speak in the upcoming general conference. During his brief address, he told the congregation of the surprise phone call he had received from Elder Hinckley just a few days before. Elder Hinckley informed Elder Carmack that the prophet wanted to speak with him and Sister Carmack and asked if they could catch the next flight to Salt Lake and be in his office by the next morning. Then Elder Hinckley added that Elder Carmack should not worry.

Laughingly, he confessed that these words did not help. He and his wife spent most of the night without sleep until in the early morning hours the Spirit brought them peace and they were able to sleep a little. Elder Carmack encouraged members not to forget their early morning prayers and then paraphrased the story of the living house, giving credit to George MacDonald. He began with the same entry line to imagine we are a house and emphasized the phrase, "When Christ comes in, it hurts abominably."[19]

This mirror to Elder Ashton's sentiments of the pain in change may be disconcerting, unless our eyes are focused on the end result. Elder Carmack reminds us that Christ's love is tough. He refers to a quote by Dr. M. Scott Peck, author of the best-seller *The Road Less Traveled;* Peck says that everyone who asks, "What is God's love leading to?" comes to the same terrifying conclusion that he wants us to become like him. Preparing for Godhood hurts abominably, but the gift of this path is peace.[20]

C. S. Lewis expounds on this same concept right after telling the living house parable. He explains that as a young child he often had toothaches. He knew his mother would give him something to make the pain go away, but he also knew that she would take him to the dentist who would cause him more pain in other places, sometimes places that hadn't begun to ache yet. The dentist never just stopped with the immediate problem but wanted everything to be clean. This is the same way that Christ works when we invite him into our lives. He will clean up immediate issues and fix ones that haven't begun to hurt yet.

GIVE ME ALL

Within the two chapters of *Mere Christianity* that discuss putting on Christ and the living house parable, there are a number of other references that have been used by general authorities to illustrate the surrender of will that is necessary for discipleship and the ultimate purpose of our existence, which is to become perfect. In the chapter entitled, "Is Christianity Hard or Easy?" Lewis begins by presenting the scenario of a man who has desires that may not be necessarily "good." He attempts to do what's right, while secretly hoping in the end there will be enough time to do what he really wants. The problem with this sort of thinking is that "the more you obey your conscience, the more your conscience will demand of you."[21]

If you constantly hold on to part of your natural self, Lewis concludes there are only two alternatives. Either you will stop trying to be good at all, or you will be the sort of person who is constantly whining because no one notices all the good you do for others. In the latter case, you might as well have "remained frankly selfish." It is in this context Lewis makes the following statement, "Christ says, 'Give me All. I don't want so much of your time and so much of your money and so much of your work: I want You. I have not come to torment your natural self, but to kill it . . . Hand me over the whole natural self . . . [and] I will give you a new self instead. In fact, I will give you Myself: my own will shall become yours.' "[22]

In October of 1991, Elder Robert L. Backman bore witness of the importance of this surrender, quoting the above excerpt and adding his personal witness of his willingness to submit his will to the Savior because of his faith, trust, and love in him.[23] These powerful words echo the foundation of the sacrifice required of true followers of Christ, "even that of a broken heart and a contrite spirit" (D&C 59:8).

THE FIRST FEEBLE EFFORT

Lewis continues on this same theme in his next chapter in *Mere Christianity* entitled "Counting the Cost." He explains that when Christ said, "Be ye therefore perfect," he didn't mean if you weren't perfect he would not help you. Instead, he meant if you would surrender yourself to him, then he would not stop helping you until you were perfect—no matter the pain or difficulty it may cost you in this life. Lewis wanted his readers to understand that perfection did not have to be accomplished in a moment. He said, "This Helper who will, in the long run, be satisfied with nothing less than absolute perfection, will also be delighted with the first feeble, stumbling effort you make tomorrow to do the simplest duty."[24]

Heidi Holfeltz Parker, a counselor in the Macon Georgia Ward Primary, had a touching article published in the *Ensign* in 1991 which reiterated this point. She began by telling about an acquaintance who was an active member of the Church and started a business with a friend. When the economy began to turn, he sheltered company money in his children's bank accounts. When bankruptcy ensued, the partner lost everything, including his home, while the Church member was able to continue living at the same lifestyle.

Sister Parker would sometimes think how grateful she was that she was not a hypocrite like the member had been, until she remembered an experience which happened a few years earlier. She had just given birth to her daughter and it was time to go home from the hospital. She asked a nurse if the receiving blanket, which was cute, came with all the other things the hospital gave her. From the nurse's reply, she knew it was probably not to be taken, but she took the blanket anyway. She struggled over the issue for months until she finally surrendered. She informed the hospital, made payment for the blanket and her conscience was able to rest.[25]

It is imperative for all disciples of Christ to recognize and resolve the incongruities of their lives. Sister Parker cites another example from the life of Stephen R. Covey and his wife. They were parenting a young son who was lagging behind socially, athletically, and academically. When nothing they tried seemed to work, they realized perhaps it was they who needed to adjust. By showing their son unconditional love rather than pushing him to improve, he was able to blossom and realize his full potential.[26]

Sister Parker encouraged each of us to make a list of our incongruities. If we begin to feel defeated, we should look at the list. We need to remind ourselves that the Lord is "delighted by the first feeble, stumbling effort." She concluded with a warning that choices not in alignment with our divine goals both sap our energy and block the Spirit.[27] The incongruities mentioned by Sister Parker are those bits and pieces of the natural man we refuse to give up. They develop into stumbling blocks in our becoming who the Lord wants us to be.

NOT IDEALISTIC GAS

The last paragraph of Lewis' discussion on perfection ends with an oddly worded phrase,

> The command 'Be ye perfect' is not idealistic gas. Nor is it a command to do the impossible. He is going to make us into creatures that can obey that command. He said (in the Bible) that we were 'gods' and He is going to make good His words. If we let Him—for we can prevent Him, if we choose—He will make the feeblest and filthiest of us into a god or goddess, dazzling, radiant, immortal creature, pulsating all through with such energy and joy and wisdom and love as we cannot now imagine . . . The process will be long and in parts very painful; but that is what we are in for. Nothing less. He meant what He said.[28]

Although C. S. Lewis's definition of Godhood is different from what Latter-day Saints believe, the hope of an infinite wonderful reward because we willingly turned our hearts to Christ is a shared belief, as is our firm testimony that it will not be easy to do so.

In his 1995 *Ensign* article, Elder Alexander B. Morrison told the story of an ancient King named Gilgamesh, who went in search of such a reward. This story, preserved on clay tablets, dates back to at least 700 B.C., although it is generally thought to be much older. The epic speaks of Gilgamesh's search for immortality after the death of his friend. His journey takes him through many adventures, such as returning back to nature and experimenting with the pleasures of life. Gilgamesh finally decides immortality is not for man. "Life, he concluded, is bounded by the cradle and the grave."[29]

Elder Morrison explains that our understanding of our eternal natures not only extends beyond the grave but to our premortal existence as well. We did not begin at birth and we do not end at death. This knowledge gives us the hope that we can once again return to our heavenly home. But the condition for that entry is the submission of our wills to his, a necessary part of the path to perfection.

Affirming the veracity of Christ's statement in Matthew, Elder Morrison quotes Lewis per above, adding "The command 'Be ye . . . perfect' is not one that can be executed overnight, or even by the end of mortality. It takes much, much longer to overcome all our mortal weaknesses. Christ's resurrection, which assures our own immortality, provides us time to at least seriously attempt to pursue the goal of perfection. Had he not been resurrected . . . there would be no hope for us mere mortals."[30]

Ending with his gratitude for our Savior, Morrison returns to poor King Gilgamesh, who like so many around us, never understood that if it were not for the Savior, man could never enjoy the blessing of immortality.[31] We can have eternal glory and be changed, if we choose to walk that path that leads to Christ our Savior.

LAST WORDS

Just two months before his death, Elder Maxwell spoke again at general conference in May of 2004. In this sweet address he reminisced "informally and gratefully" on twelve remembrances from his past. Touching on how drastically life can change, Elder Maxwell spoke of going from administering the sacrament in his home ward one year and in a foxhole the next. He gave examples of parenting and spoke of his sister who, though blind from birth, still taught school for thirty-three years. He spoke of people who look to the world for solutions to their problems and compared them to C.S. Lewis's scene of people rushing around with fire extinguishers trying to stop a flood.[32] Then he told of traveling with Sister and Elder Russell M. Nelson when their flight was cancelled, and they wondered if they should return to the hotel. The man at the airport replied with dignity, "Sir, you never go back to the hotel." He warned of "give-up-itis" and encouraged us to persevere through all seasons of life.

Finally, he ended his remarks by repeating his earlier statement about remembering the Lord's mercy. He also added a gentle plea, saying, "As you submit your wills to God, you are giving Him the only thing you can actually give Him that is really yours to give. Don't wait too long to find the altar or to begin to place the gift of your wills upon it!"[33] This is the path to discipleship, the path to perfection, the path to Christ.

NOTES

1. A book was compiled of the most significant addresses given at the symposium entitled, *C. S. Lewis, the Man and His Message: An LDS Perspective* by Robert L. Millet and Andrew C. Skinner, Bookcraft, 1999.

2. Hafen, *A Disciple's Life*, 553–5.

3. This number was originally found on http://www.sltrib.com/1998/Dec/12061998/utah/65273.htm. Unable to find it with the original address. This is a copy of the one taken off that URL in 1998.

4. For the full text of Elder Maxwell's address, see Millet, *C. S. Lewis, the Man and His Message: An LDS Perspective*, 8.

5. Ibid., 8.

6. Maxwell, "Insights from My Life," *Ensign*, Aug. 2000, 9–10.

7. Lewis, *The Problem of Pain*, 46–47.

8. As quoted by Maxwell, "The Pathway of Discipleship," *Ensign*, Sept. 1998, 8.

9. Ibid, 9.

10. Lewis, *Surprised by Joy*, 224.

11. Ibid., 191.

12. Ibid., 213.

13. Lewis, *George MacDonald*. xvii.

14. Lewis, *Mere Christianity*, 166.

15. Ibid., 174.

16. Marvin J. Ashton, "Progress Through Change," *Ensign*, Nov. 1979, 61; John K. Carmack, "Upheld by the Prayers of the Church," *Ensign*, May 1984, 76; Neal A. Maxwell, "The Value of Home Life," *Ensign*, Feb. 1972, 4; and (per endnote 54 of Mary Jane Woodger article) Neal A Maxwell, *All These Things Shall Give Thee Experience*, 29; and Maxwell, *That Ye May Believe*, 111.

17. Maxwell, "The Value of Home Life," *Ensign*, Feb. 1972, 4.

18. Ashton, "Progress Through Change," *Ensign*, Nov. 1979, 61.

19. Carmack, "Upheld by the Prayers of the Church," *Ensign*, May 1984, 76.

20. Dr. Scott M. Peck, *The Road Less Traveled,* 1978.

21. Lewis, *Mere Christianity,* 171.

22. Ibid., 167.

23. Robert L. Backman, "Jesus the Christ," *Ensign,* Nov. 1991, 8.

24. Lewis, *Mere Christianity,* 172.

25. Heidi Holfeltz Parker, "Am I What I Appear to Be?" *Ensign,* Oct. 1991, 28.

26. Stephen R. Covey, *Seven Habits of Highly Effective People,* 20 (per *Ensign* footnote.)

27. Heidi Holfeltz Parker, "Am I What I Appear to Be?" *Ensign,* Oct. 1991, 30–31.

28. Lewis, *Mere Christianity,* 174.

29. N. K. Sanders, ed., *The Epic of Gilgamesh: An English Version with an Introduction* (New York, New York: Penguin Books, 1972), 61–118.

30. Alexander B. Morrison, " 'I Am the Resurrection and the Life,' " *Ensign,* Apr. 1995, 36.

31. Ibid.

32. Lewis, *Screwtape Letters,* 117–18 (per *Ensign* article).

33. Neal A. Maxwell, "Remember How Merciful the Lord Hath Been," *Ensign,* May 2004, 44.

CHAPTER SEVENTEEN

"The Weight of Glory": Yearning for Home and Possible Gods and Goddesses

erhaps one of the most controversial statements that C. S. Lewis ever penned was in his short essay entitled, "The Weight of Glory." Near the conclusion of this essay, later preached as a sermon in a church in Oxford in 1942, Lewis stated, "It is a serious thing to live in a society of possible Gods and Goddesses, to remember that the dullest and most uninteresting person you talk to may one day be a creature which, if you saw it now, you would be strongly tempted to worship."[1] Out of context this quote sounds incredibly reminiscent of Lorenzo Snow's couplet, "As man is, God once was, and as God is, man may become." Much to the chagrin of evangelical Christians, some Church members have presented it as such in their individual writings. In reading Lewis's essay in its entirety, however, it is clear this was not his intention.[2] Still, great truths can be found throughout this beautiful sermon which has been quoted in part nine times in Church magazines, five of which were in general conference.[3]

THE WEIGHT OF GLORY

Upon first perusal of this essay, it may seem Lewis's thoughts meander through a maze of unrelated topics, making one wonder if Lewis was really certain where he would end up at the onset. Part of what makes C. S. Lewis such a profound writer is that this meandering is always purposeful, and in the end, you are standing beside him wondering how you got there. His final powerful words usually bring a new perspective to tired topics.

Even the title "The Weight of Glory" is cryptic; it refers to a line written by Paul in one of his epistles to the Saints in Corinth and is only used once in ancient scripture. Paul, who had been suffering great persecutions in his missionary service, declared, "We are troubled on every side, yet not distressed; we are perplexed, but not in despair; Persecuted, but not forsaken; cast down but, not destroyed." Then after expressing gratitude to Christ and his great sacrifice for us Paul continues, "For our light affliction, which is but for a moment, worketh for us a far more exceeding and eternal weight of glory" (2 Corinthians 4:8–9, 17). It is curious how C. S. Lewis pulled this unique three-word phrase out of the Bible for the basis of this critical sermon.

Even more interesting is the fact that this same phrase is used twice in latter-day revelation. The first instance was shortly after the restoration when the infant Church was warned to repent and seek the Spirit through prayer as they proceed: "These things remain to overcome through patience, that such may receive a more exceeding and eternal weight of glory, otherwise, a greater condemnation" (D&C 63:66). Both the latter-day scripture and ancient scripture are directed to disciples of Christ serving amid great persecution. In this instance, the concept of our eternal weight of glory is in absolute contrast to condemnation. This context suggests that "weight of glory" has something to do with our eternal reward.

The second latter-day scriptural reference to "weight of glory" is found in section 132 of the Doctrine and Covenants and sheds the most light on this phrase. Speaking of those who have not made eternal covenants in the temple, the scripture reads, "Therefore, when they are out of the world they neither marry nor are given in marriage; but are appointed angels in heaven, which angels are ministering servants, to minister for those who are worthy of a far more, and an exceeding, and an eternal weight of glory" (D&C 132:160). This "weight of glory" could then be understood to be our responsibility in the kingdom of God. Whether on earth now or in the heavenly realm, it is our eternal responsibility as disciples of Christ to stand against temptation and persecution and fulfill our God-given obligations whatever our circumstances. As we do, we become more capable of serving him, increasing our abilities, and handling a heavier load; thus, we obtain a greater eternal "weight of glory." Through Lewis's essay, we can see that he understands, in part, this concept. Yet modern revelation both clarifies and deepens our understanding of this eternal truth.

WHAT IS OUR REWARD

C. S. Lewis begins his sermon with the observation that if you were to ask twenty men in the world what they thought the highest virtue was, their answer would probably be unselfishness. If you were to pose the same question to Christians, their answer would be love, taking a much more positive approach to life. Similarly, the world looks at church services as a place of self-denial. Although there are some temporal things that followers of Christ must deny themselves momentarily, the aim of the gospel is not denial but "the unblushing promise of reward." Lewis wonders if we too often forget the reward part saying, "We are half-hearted creatures, fooling about with drink and sex, and ambition, when infinite joy is offered us, like an ignorant child who wants to go on making mud pies in a slum because he cannot imagine what is meant by the offer of a holiday at the sea. We are far too easily pleased."[4]

Marvin J. Ashton used this quote in his 1992 Conference address about homesickness. Elder Ashton had been asked to visit a young missionary whose intense yearnings for home were causing poor performance and getting in the way of his reaching his potential as a missionary. Instead of being a hindrance, Ashton stated that a healthy emotional connection to home and the love and security felt there can be a great blessing in our lives. This principle also applies to those same longings for our heavenly home. Reminding the congregation of their premortal life with God as their Father and Christ as their brother, Elder Ashton said we knew this life would be a time of testing and probation—and most would agree it has been just that.[5]

Then Elder Ashton spoke of hurricane victims who felt the tragedy of never being able to return home again. He encouraged us to remember Satan's goal—that he would have us never return home. Satan tries to distract us from who we are by keeping us so busy, we don't think about eternal things. Elder Ashton warned Church members about becoming like the type of athlete who is more worried about the jogging suit he is wearing than actually training for the race.[6]

To illustrate this concept he quoted C. S. Lewis as quoted above. Then he added these words of Mormon, "Why are ye ashamed to take upon you the name of Christ? Why do ye not think that greater is the value of an endless happiness than that misery which never dies—because of the praise of the world?" (Mormon 8:38). Elder Ashton ends by encouraging us to find in our hearts the proper yearning for our heavenly home, which will act as a motivator, lifting us through each day and encouraging us to do the right.[7]

BECOMING SIDETRACKED FROM OUR GOAL

In "The Weight of Glory," Lewis allays claims that obedience for the purpose of receiving a reward is somehow mercenary. He believed that the hope of our reward for obedience to God should be a driving force in our lives. He explains it is only mercenary to work for a reward that is not the natural consequence of our efforts. The example he uses is that of love and marriage. If we marry because we are in love, that is not mercenary because marriage is the natural reward of love. If, however, we marry for money, then we are acting inappropriately.

He goes on to explain how a student, for example, may not enjoy his immediate studies to learn the Greek language, but works hard because of his long-term goal of being able to someday understand beautiful classic Greek poetry in its original language. Finally, with the student's hard-won understanding, he can then enjoy what was previously out of his reach. The problem lies in the student who, bored on his road to improvement, takes a break from studying Greek to enjoy some English poetry. It is not a bad thing, but it is not the same as learning Greek. Some may even try to rationalize the student's behavior by claiming his study of poetry in general will prepare him to enjoy Greek poetry more. Unless he actually learns the Greek language, his detour will only hinder him.

Speaking of the Christian's tendency to get sidetracked from his true purpose, Lewis states that if eternal good is our true destiny, then any other good is but a detour.[8] This concept of other good pursuits pushing us away from our ultimate goal is a common theme in many of Lewis's writings. Wormwood, the apprentice devil in *Screwtape Letters,* is taught by his uncle that such a diversion can be a valuable tool in leading astray the well-intentioned. Describing in detail the path of this demise, the veteran devil writes,

> Let him begin by treating Patriotism or Pacifism as a part of his religion. Then let him, under the influence of partisan spirit, come to regard it as the most important part. Then quietly and gradually nurse him on to the stage at which religion becomes merely part of the "cause," in which Christianity is valued chiefly because of the excellent arguments it can produce in favour of the British war effort or of Pacifism. Once you have made the World an end, and faith a means, you have almost won your man, and it makes very little difference what kind of worldly end he is pursuing.[9]

Dallin H. Oaks spoke of "powerful ideas" in his 1995 general conference address. He used the above quote to illustrate how surprisingly easy it is to get our priorities mixed up.[10] Elder Oaks described with clarity the basic concepts that should be at the very foundation of our thinking. These include our relationship to God and our relationship to one another. As we understand what it really means to be God's children, we become more aware of the familial connections we have to every person on the earth—that we are all brothers and sisters. These two powerful ideas increase our love and service.[11]

Elder Oaks goes on to explain that love can be a great impetus in our efforts to do good. He illustrates this point with a quote from Arthur Henry King who said, "Love is not just an ecstasy, not just an intense feeling. It is a driving force. It is something that carries us through our life of joyful duty."[12] When that love is focused on Jesus Christ and we keep him as our first priority, then we can stand as Paul who said in contrast to the foolish Athenians searching for some new thing: "For I determined not to know any thing among you save Jesus Christ, and him crucified" (1 Corinthians 2:2).[13]

RUNNING FASTER THAN WE HAVE STRENGTH

In an *Ensign* article, Valerie Holladay makes the point that there are other members who may not have a problem with being sidetracked, but they are running too fast down the right path. Too often these good people either become "burnt out" or sidetracked in their own busyness. Sister Holladay used a reference of C. S. Lewis repeating the words of St. Augustine to warn the "over-active" that "God wants to give us something, but cannot, because our hands are full—there's nowhere for Him to put it."[14]

Sister Holladay suggested that in order to listen to the still small voice, which will not compete with other voices of the world, we should schedule time to ponder. To create this quiet time even in the fullest life, she gave the following suggestions:

1. Decide your time alone is worth it. Schedule an appointment with yourself in your planning book.

2. Get up earlier. Christ arose "a great while before day."[15] Sometimes an extra hour or so in the morning can make a huge difference in your day.

3. Write in a journal focusing on your feelings instead of your activities.

4. If you still can't find a time to ponder and worship, pray for the knowledge or ability to create one.

Elder Rex D. Pinegar spoke in his 1982 general conference address about searching for the strength to meet life's challenges as he watched his daughter face the demands of leaving home to go to college. Elder Pinegar reminded members that even if we are making good decisions, life is hard. No matter what age we are, we each have specific challenges to overcome.[16] But he warned against looking at these obstacles as blocking our way along the path of discipleship. Instead, he encourages us to look at our struggles as C. S. Lewis advised, "The great thing, if one can, is to stop regarding all the unpleasant things as interruptions of one's 'own,' or 'real' life. The truth is, of course, that what one calls the interruptions are precisely one's real life—the life God is sending one day by day."[17]

Later, Elder Pinegar referred to Tolstoy's statement, "Faith is the force of life."[18] Faith is a way to face our trials more like the stripling warriors who "fought with such miraculous strength; and with such mighty power."[19] He ends with a charge for the faithful not to fear the challenges before them, but to face them patiently with faith and reminds us that if we do, God will reward us with the power to overcome whatever hardships, disappointments, or trials stand before us.[20] Through faith, we can continue to move forward with our eye on the ultimate reward no matter how difficult the way.

THE FIVE HEADS

Lewis's "The Weight of Glory" sermon continues as he returns to the Bible in search of a clearer definition of the ultimate reward of the righteous. Through study Lewis reduced the promises of the scriptures to "five heads" or in other words, five specific aspects of our ultimate prize. These promises include:

1. We shall be with Christ.

2. We shall be like Him in some way.

3. We shall have "glory."

4. We shall, in some sense, be fed, feasted, or entertained.

5. We shall have some sort of official position in the universe— ruling cities, judging angels, being pillars of God's temple.

It is interesting that after Lewis lays out these five blessings of righteousness, he then balks at his own conclusion. The biggest problem he has is why there is any need for other "heads" than the first. Being with Christ, in his mind, should be sufficient on its own. Despite this feeling, he can understand most of these gifts, except one—the concept of glory. At first he said it seemed to him that the concept of glory was either fame or luminosity. One seemed "wicked and the other ridiculous."[21]

Lewis then begins to dissect this idea of glory to clarify it. He decides that fame could be better described as good report or appreciation by God for our appropriate choices. This "divine accolade" is given in the parable of the talents, "Well, done, thou good and faithful servant" (Matthew 25:21–23). Although great care must be given not to have this turn to the deadly poison of self-admiration, Lewis can see, in the end God will turn his face to each individual with either an expression of joy and glory or an expression of sorrow and anger. He agrees that glory would be a far superior outcome.

As for the luminous aspect of glory, Lewis points to the scriptures describing us as shining as the Morning Star. At this point, Lewis's love for the classics is exposed, for he sees in these words a hint of the same spirit as the ancient Hellenistic artists. Both in mythology and poetry the powers, beauties, and glories of nature are combined with man or given to men who become fictionally more than mortals. Lewis maintains these fantasies may be an echo of reality, for when we see the wonders of divine nature within our souls it awakens a desire to become part of it. Unfortunately, as mortals "we cannot mingle with the splendours we see. But all the leaves of the New Testament are rustling with the rumour that it will not always be so. Someday, God willing, we shall get in."[22]

Neal A. Maxwell spoke of these same feelings, inklings whenever we see great beauty, which make us aware of something greater within ourselves. He told of how Joseph F. Smith observed that now and again we may feel a spark of forgotten memories that reminds us of our heavenly home.[23] Elder Maxwell then whole-heartedly agrees with Lewis that "the pages of the New Testament are rustling with the rumour," but Maxwell adds that this is not all. The Bible's pages are not the only ones witnessing of this truth; thanks to the Prophet Joseph Smith, many more pages of scripture are rustling with truth and light for those willing to read them.[24]

THE WEIGHT OF OUR NEIGHBOR'S GLORY

Lewis ends his section on the luminosity of glory by quoting St. Augustine who said that "the rapture of the saved soul will 'flow over' into the glorified body." Unsure of the meaning of this physical change, Lewis neither wants us to suppose we will be simple ghosts or that our bodies will be resurrected with "numb insensibility," only that our glory will be great. Lewis addresses those who would attempt to imagine it, warning them not to try.

Pulling his audience from these lofty but vague sentiments back to the mortality of our existence, Lewis states, "The cross comes before the crown and tomorrow is a Monday morning."[25] Through this phrase Lewis implies that our daily task is to bear the cross of this mortal existence, the burden of feeling Christ's love but being apart from him, the weight or price of glory.

Then he adds that there is another important burden we cannot forget which is the weight or load of our neighbor's glory. But it is a load that can only be carried with humility, Lewis states, for it will break the backs of the proud.

The Lord teaches us this principle in latter-day scripture. While instructing the early Saints about what they must do to earn the crown of eternal life, Christ proclaimed through revelation: "Wherefore, be faithful . . . succor the weak, lift up the hands which hang down, and strengthen the feeble knees. And if thou art faithful unto the end thou shalt have a crown of immortality, and eternal life in the mansions which I have prepared in the house of my Father" (D&C 81:5–6). This is the opposite of self-promotion, instead it is "promot[ing] the glory of him who is your Lord" (D&C 81:4) by caring for the needs of others. This is the greatest weight of glory; it is the weight that Christ carried for each of us in his great Atonement.

NOTES

1. Lewis, *Weight of Glory*, 45.
2. When Lewis penned the words, "it is a serious thing to live in a world of possible Gods and Goddesses," it is quite clear that he was looking at the Greek definition of *god* and *goddess*. In case there is any question, Lewis delves deeply into his beliefs of the relationship between God and Man in a chapter of his book *Mere Christianity* entitled "Making and Begetting." In answer to the question about whether we are actually the sons and daughters of God, Lewis clearly states, "What God begets is God; just as what man begets is man. What God creates is not God; just as what man makes is not man. They may be like God in certain ways, but they are not things of the same kind. They are more like statues or pictures of God." Earlier in the same volume, he also says, "God made us: invented us as a man invents an engine." The LDS references to this quote used in general conferences focus not on our potential for Godhood but on our perspective of our fellow man as we serve him and the ultimate reward of our behavior.
3. See Appendix A.
4. Lewis, *Weight of Glory*, 45.
5. Marvin J. Ashton, "A Yearning for Home," *Ensign*, Nov. 1992, 21; a similar concept of our heavenly home was discussed in Elder Maxwell's 1971 *New Era* article where

he quoted Lewis saying, "No amount of falls will really undo us if we keep picking ourselves up each time. We shall of course be very muddy and tattered children by the time we reach home. But the bathrooms are all ready, the towels put out, and the clean clothes in the airing cupboard." See Appendix A for details.

6. Ibid.

7. Ibid., 21.

8. Lewis, *Weight of Glory,* 47.

9. Lewis, *Screwtape Letters,* 34.

10. Dallin H. Oaks, "Powerful Ideas," *Ensign,* Nov. 1995, 25.

11. Ibid.

12. Arthur Henry King, *Abundance of the Heart,* 84.

13. The previous verse also shows the conviction of Paul. 1 Corinthians 2:1: "And I, brethren, when I came to you, came not with excellency of speech or of wisdom, [but] declaring unto you the testimony of God."

14. Valerie Holladay, "Walk in the Wilderness," *Ensign,* July 1998, 46, quoting C.S. Lewis, *The Problem of Pain,* 95.

15. See Mark 1:35.

16. Rex D. Pinegar, "Faith—The Force of Life," *Ensign,* Nov. 1982, 24.

17. Lewis, *They Stand Together: The Letters of C. S. Lewis to Arthur Greeves,* 499.

18. Tolstoy, *How I Came to Believe,* 40.

19. See Alma 53:20 and Alma 56:47, 56.

20. Rex D. Pinegar, "Faith—The Force of Life," *Ensign,* Nov. 1982, 26.

21. Lewis, *Weight of Glory,* 33.

22. Ibid.

23. Neal A. Maxwell, "Premortality, a Glorious Reality," *Ensign,* Nov. 1985, 15, quoting *Gospel Doctrine,* 5th edition, Salt Lake City: Deseret Book, 1939, 14.

24. Ibid., 15.

25. Lewis, *Weight of Glory,* 33, also quoted by Maxwell in " 'Shine As Lights in the World,' " *Ensign,* May 1983, 9.

CHAPTER EIGHTEEN

C. S. Lewis and Women

or almost twenty years, large stacks of cards and letters arrived daily at the Kilns, C. S. Lewis's country home in Headington Quarry, near Oxford. He felt an obligation to answer each one personally. Every morning when the mail arrived, with the help of his brother Warnie, Lewis sat with his nib pen and inkwell, reading and composing individual responses for several hours. At his death many of these letters were collected and later published. In response to one such letter he wrote, "The housewife's work . . . is surely in reality the most important work in the world. What do ships, railways, mines, cars, and governments, etc. exist for except that people may be fed, warmed, and safe in their own homes? . . . We wage war in order to have peace, we work in order to have leisure, we produce food in order to eat it. So your job is the one for which all others exist."[1]

THE JOB FOR WHICH ALL OTHERS EXIST

At a time of intense conflict over women's issues, Barbara B. Smith, General Relief Society President, repeated this quote in a General Relief Society meeting in 1979. She began her remarks by telling the story of Esther and emphasizing her uncle's response to the queen's dilemma, "Who knoweth whether thou art come to the kingdom for such a time as this?" Sister Smith stated that each woman today has a similar challenge to face—to be a holy woman.[2] Then she referred to the words of Eliza R. Snow, another General Relief Society President who presided during the women's suffrage era, which was another time of social advancement and confusion over women's roles.

Sister Snow clarified the responsibility of women in the Church: "It is

the duty of each one of us to be a holy woman . . . There is no sister so iso-
lated, and her sphere so narrow but what she can do a great deal towards
establishing the Kingdom of God upon the earth."[3]

Detailing the method for attaining those aims, Sister Smith suggested
that setting and achieving realistic goals was the key, so that we could feel
the joy of victory over self.[4] She illustrated that victory by sharing the
example of a dear friend with twelve children who was meeting her personal goals of daily exercise and scripture reading amid the tremendous
challenges of raising a large family. Sister Smith stated that although her
friend might not know it, C. S. Lewis wisely said that homemaking "is
surely in reality the most important work in the world."[5]

Sister Smith then spoke of brave women willing to leave their homes
in a time of war to do their visiting teaching and attend their Church
meetings. She touched on valiant women who sacrifice to stay home with
their families, while clearly stating that women who must work outside the
home for the right reasons should feel happy and confident with that decision. Finally, Sister Smith concluded her remarks reminding the women
of the Church to be like Esther who fortified herself in preparation and
then moved forward with strength, wisdom, and vision.[6]

A MESSAGE TO MY GRANDDAUGHTERS

About seven years later Elder James E. Faust also used C. S. Lewis's
quote about homemaking in a touching article called "A Message to My
Granddaughters: Becoming 'Great Women.' " He encouraged his granddaughters to choose their own paths and challenged them each to reach
her own potential—to become a great woman.[7]

Then Elder Faust clarified that the word *great* doesn't necessarily
mean that you will have an incredible career as a doctor, lawyer, or business executive, although those are possible directions for your life to take.
Instead, he clearly believes that a great woman is much more.[8] He goes on
to say that as women his granddaughters are born with gifts unique and
are apart from men. To further explain this point, he uses the words of
Spencer W. Kimball, who taught that faithful women agreed to certain
assignments in the premortal life, just as some men were foreordained to
priesthood responsibilities there. He said that although the veil is drawn
and we can't remember the details now, we will still be held accountable
for those things we have previously agreed to do.[9]

In this context, Elder Faust urged women to get an education and gain
marketable skills, but he also warned that too often women are encouraged to have it all. With sweet sincerity he entreated his granddaughters

and the female membership of the Church as a whole not to abandon the full-time career of mother and marriage. He reminded them that a person's salary does not determine their importance.[10] Then he added, "There is, however, no more important job than homemaking. As C. S. Lewis said, it is the one for which all others exist."[11]

Turning to the mother of an old missionary companion, Elder Faust speaks of Sister Isabelle Bangerter, a mother of eleven outstanding children, who he holds to be an example of a truly great woman. Then returning to President Kimball's remarks he quotes, "Among the real heroines in the world who will come into the Church are women who are more concerned with being righteous than with being selfish. These real heroines have true humility, which places a higher value on integrity than on visibility."[12]

In May of 1998, President Faust again addressed the Young Women of the Church in a General Young Women's meeting. At this time he repeated a few of the same things he had mentioned earlier to his granddaughters, but added some significant points. He warned them not to be fooled by the world's definition of happiness. Today some people may claim it is foolish to be a full-time mother. They might charge that it is not challenging and is filled with drudgery, but President Faust made the point that whatever career you choose will have some things you enjoy and others that are obligations.[13] Looking at the big picture, he again turned C. S. Lewis's words that homemaking is the most important career in the world. He encouraged education but focused on the great blessings of serving others in the home. He reminded the young women that the Prophet Joseph taught that angels could not be restrained if they lived up to their privileges.[14]

In his concluding remarks, Elder Faust encouraged each woman, young and old to hold still and listen to the whisperings of the Holy Ghost and then follow the impressions they know are right. This is the way we can reap the blessings prepared for us.[15]

THE DUTY OF MEN TO HONOR WOMEN

One year later in a spring general priesthood session, Russell M. Nelson spoke to the men of the Church on this very subject. In his address entitled, "Our Sacred Duty to Honor Women," Elder Nelson recalled that a number of years ago the First Presidency issued this statement: "Motherhood is near to divinity. It is the highest, holiest service to be assumed by mankind. It places her who honors its holy calling and service next to the angels." At another time, the First Presidency said, "The true spirit of the

Church [is to] give to woman the highest place of honor in human life."[16] Elder Nelson explained that the scriptures teach, "In the celestial glory there are three heavens or degrees; And in order to obtain the highest, a man must enter into this order of the priesthood [meaning the new and everlasting covenant of marriage]; And if he does not, he cannot obtain it" (D&C 131:1–3).

In this context Elder Nelson explained that the most important day of his life was taking his wife to be married for all eternity in God's holy temple because without that, he would not have the highest blessings of the priesthood available to him.[17] Then this insightful apostle, using the words of Paul, implored husbands to love their wives. He even suggested some ways that husbands could show their love including doing dishes, changing diapers, or caring for a crying baby.[18] When we remember the significance of this eternal relationship, our willingness to love and serve each other will naturally increase. Elder Nelson went on to warn against the ongoing trends to devalue the appropriate role of women.[19]

SATAN'S ATTACK AGAINST THE FAMILY

It is precisely because mothers are so crucial to our Father's plan that Satan works to demean them and destroy the family. In a 2001 general conference address, Sheri Dew focused on the fact that Satan concentrates his efforts on destroying righteous motherhood. He knows the crucial effects of worthy mothers on the rising generation, for without them the kingdom of God will not move forward.[20]

Satan's campaign against women and the home has had devastating effects on the world at large, reflected in a variety of social ills, such as increased divorce rates, drug abuse, sexual promiscuity, violent crime, and suicide. As Richard G. Scott noted in a 1996 Conference address, a large amount of the crime, violence, and sorrow we see in the world today is due to the breakdown of the nuclear family. All the government programs and social plans cannot replace having a mother in the home.[21] Although Church members have not been exempt from the effects of the weakening family unit, a number of recent studies have revealed some interesting facts.

In 1994, Elizabeth VanDenBerghe wrote a fascinating *Ensign* article, based on research into faith-based families, with some studies focusing specifically on Church members. The results consistently showed that the benefits of organized religion are most clearly observed in devout homes. Sister VanDenBerghe referred to C.S. Lewis's maxim that "a moderated religion is as good for us as no religion at all."[22] Her article presented numerous reports showing time and again the safety found in living devotedly to gospel principles rather than just obeying when it is convenient.

In a 1985 study of various religious groups, including Catholics, Protestants, and Latter-day Saints, researchers found Latter-day Saints had the highest marriage rate and lowest divorce rate, and couples married in the temple were significantly less likely to divorce.[23] Dr. David Larson, President of the National Institute for Healthcare Research, concluded that the results were surprising and clearly showed that religious people as a whole have happier marriages, lower divorce rates, and less problems with their children.[24]

Another study focused on LDS families with large numbers of children. Unlike previous studies which showed children from large families to be emotionally disadvantaged, receiving less attention and affection, commitment to the gospel made a significant difference. The study concluded that mothers of large, devoted LDS families tended to be more affectionate, understanding, and accepting because these women made decisions based on a philosophy of eternal importance rather than temporary pursuits.[25]

Perhaps most significantly, a 1992 Gallup survey concluded that religious faith and practice is a primary source of happiness, with 93 percent of committed religious people consistently categorizing their lives as "very happy."[26] In his *Ensign* article, "Eternalism vs. Secularism," Elder Maxwell used another C. S. Lewis quote to reiterate this point, explaining that throughout history when people attempt to "invent some sort of happiness for themselves outside God, apart from God" the results are disastrous.[27] Later in that same chapter of *Mere Christianity* Lewis goes on to say, "God cannot give us a happiness and peace apart from Himself, because it is not there. There is no such thing."[28]

THE FIRST FEEBLE ATTEMPTS

A mother looking for that happiness decided to try harder to turn to the Lord and make changes in her life. She found strength in the power of this statement from Lewis, "This Helper who will, in the long run, be satisfied with nothing less than absolute perfection, will also be delighted by the first feeble, stumbling effort you make tomorrow to do the simplest duty."[29] Vicki Mason Randalls described her first feeble, stumbling effort in trying to be a better mother in her 2003 *Ensign* article, "Mom, Are You There?" Sister Randalls had a successful career but felt prompted to leave her job to stay home with her teenage children who were getting into more and more mischief. Although her children weren't thrilled at the prospect and it was a financial strain on her family, she felt strongly that she had to do it.[30]

She explained that at first nothing magical happened. Her son continued to get in trouble but she was right there with him. Her mother battled for five weeks with cancer and lost, but Sister Randalls was right there beside her. She told of her daughter crying over a young man she had given her heart to who didn't understand the gospel. She cried right there with her. Sister Randalls then told of her successes. Her daughter was later married in the Denver Colorado Temple. Her son became an Eagle Scout and graduated. She asked herself if staying home had contributed to these changes and she had to admit it had.

Quality time is sometimes toted by experts but what Sister Randalls learned was that nothing can replace quantity. It is imperative that a mother is there at the crossroads when her children make pivotal decisions. But what encouraged Sister Randalls most was her confidence that our Father in Heaven will give us the gifts and strength we need to accomplish what he has asked of us.[31] She concluded with her conviction that it is never too late to be a better mother and the changes we make will be felt for generations.[32]

Through this experience Sister Randalls had come to understand what Elder Maxwell meant when he said, "When the real history of mankind is fully disclosed, will it feature the echoes of gunfire or the shaping sound of lullabies? Will what happened in cradles and kitchens prove more controlling than what happened in congresses?"[33] As stated by Lewis, homemaking, and creating a stable home "is surely in reality the most important work in the world."[34]

NOTES

1. *The Collected Letters of C. S. Lewis,* vol. III, Hooper, ed., 62.

2. Barbara B. Smith, "Women for the Latter Day," *Ensign,* Nov. 1979, 107.

3. Snow, *Woman's Exponent,* 15 Sept. 1873, 62.

4. Barbara B. Smith, "Women for the Latter Day," 107.

5. *The Collected Letters of C. S. Lewis,* vol. III, Hooper, ed., 62.

6. Barbara B. Smith, "Women for the Latter Day," 107.

7. James E. Faust, "A Message to My Granddaughters: Becoming 'Great Women,'" *Ensign,* Sept. 1986, 16.

8. Ibid.

9. Ibid.

10. Ibid.

11. Ibid., quoting Lewis in Hooper, *The Collected Letters of C. S. Lewis,* vol. III., 62.

12. Ibid.

13. James E. Faust, "How Near to the Angels," *Ensign,* May 1998, 95.

14. *Teachings of the Prophet Joseph Smith,* comp. Joseph Fielding Smith (1977), 226.

15. James E. Faust, "How Near to the Angels," 95.

16. In James R. Clark, comp., *Messages of the First Presidency of The Church of Jesus Christ of Latter-day Saints,* 6 vols. (1965–75), 6:178. In 1935 the First Presidency stated, "The true spirit of the Church of Jesus Christ of Latter-day Saints gives to woman the highest place of honor in human life" (in Messages of the First Presidency, 6:5), per Russell M. Nelson, "Our Sacred Duty to Honor Women," *Ensign,* May 1999, 38.

17. Russell M. Nelson, "Our Sacred Duty to Honor Women," 38.

18. Ibid.

19. Ibid.

20. Sheri L. Dew, "Are We Not All Mothers?" *Ensign,* Nov. 2001, 86.

21. Richard G. Scott, "The Joy of Living the Great Plan of Happiness," *Ensign,* Nov. 1996, 74.

22. Lewis, *Screwtape Letters,* 43, mentioned by Elizabeth VanDenBerghe, "Religion and the Abundant Life," *Ensign,* Oct. 1994, 32.

23. Howard M. Bahr, "Religious Intermarriage and Divorce in Utah and the Mountain State," *Journal for the Scientific Study of Religion* 20, no. 3 (Sept. 1981): 251–61, as cited in Elizabeth VanDenBerghe, "Religion and the Abundant Life," 36.

24. Elizabeth VanDenBerghe, "Religion and the Abundant Life," 40.

25. Melvin L. Wilkinson and William C. Tanner III, "The Influence of Family Size, Interaction and Religiosity on Family Affection in a Mormon Sample," *Journal of Marriage and the Family* 42, no. 2 (May 1980): 297–304.

26. George H. Gallup Jr. and Timothy Jones, *The Saints among Us* (Ridgefield, Conn.: Morehouse Publishing, 1992), 43, as quoted by VanDenBerghe.

27. Neal A. Maxwell, "Eternalism vs. Secularism," *Ensign,* Oct. 1974, 69.

28. Lewis, *Mere Christianity,* 50.

29. Vickie Mason Randalls, "Mom, Are You There?" *Ensign,* Oct. 2003, 68.

30. Ibid.

31. Ibid.

32. Ibid.

33. Margaret D. Nadauld, "The Joy of Womanhood," *Ensign,* Nov. 2000, 14–16 from Maxwell, "The Women of God," *Ensign,* May 1978, 10–11.

34. *The Collected Letters of C. S. Lewis, vol. III.,* Hooper, ed., 62.

CHAPTER NINETEEN

Pride: "The Great Sin"

ne of C. S. Lewis's great talents was his empathy toward human weakness and relating it in so personal a way as to open the reader's eyes to a new perspective. In a letter to his editor and close friend Arthur Greeves, Lewis exposed one such temptation, which was bothering him. He wrote about finding himself posturing in front of a mirror one morning, practicing the clever things he was going to say and imagining how clever his student would think he was. Then when he forced himself to stop it, he felt clever for doing that. Lewis bemoaned that fighting pride was like battling the hydra, as soon as you cut off one head, another rises in its stead.[1]

Expanding on this theme, Lewis dedicated an entire essay in *Mere Christianity* to the concept of pride entitled "The Great Sin." He began with a riddle of sorts, asking what vice is no man in the world free of, most don't even know they are guilty of, and does not bother you to possess it yourself but only to see it in other people. The answer was, of course, pride. Here again Lewis was concerned because he believed that most of us do not understand this principle. He went on to explain that pride is "the essential vice, the utmost evil," "the complete anti-God state of mind," and its antithesis stands at the center of Christianity.[2]

BEWARE OF PRIDE

Some forty years later a modern-day prophet, Ezra Taft Benson, encouraged the entire Church membership to focus on reading the Book of Mormon. He stood at the Tabernacle pulpit during the 1989 April general conference and commended those faithful Church members who were striving to flood the earth and their lives with the Book of Mormon.

President Benson reminded the congregation that this sacred volume was written for our day. Then he asked an intriguing question about the fallen Nephite nation, "Why did they fall?"[3] Using Mormon's words, he answered, "Behold, the pride of this nation, or the people of the Nephites, hath proven their destruction."[4] The prophet added this scriptural warning to the modern-day Church, "Beware of pride, lest ye become as the Nephites of old."[5]

Pleading for our faith and prayers, President Benson soberly acknowledged that this issue had been weighing on his mind for quite some time.[6] What followed was one of the most powerful and remembered addresses that Ezra Taft Benson ever delivered. This hallmark address has been referred to in over forty *Ensign* articles, at least fifteen general conference addresses, and an edited version was reprinted in the October 2003 issue of the *New Era*.[7] Large excerpts are also included in over twelve gospel doctrine lessons and referred to in Primary, Aaronic Priesthood, Relief Society, and other Church manuals.[8]

During this address, President Benson quotes Lewis's definition of pride and reiterates some of the same basic truths. But, it is the prophet, President Benson, who puts these truths into a scriptural framework and comments on them as a living oracle of God. He enumerates the effects of pride and ends with specific suggestions to rid our hearts of this spiritual cancer.[9] This is a feat which Lewis found still somewhat of a mystery, saying he wished he had been able to do more himself.[10]

THE CENTRAL FEATURE OF PRIDE IS ENMITY

After reminding the Saints of the Nephite destruction and our similar modern-day warning, President Benson explained that pride is a widely misunderstood sin and that many people are sinning in ignorance.[11] Then he defined pride using a referenced quote from Lewis saying, "Pride gets no pleasure out of having something, only out of having more of it than the next man. . . . It is the comparison that makes you proud: the pleasure of being above the rest. Once the element of competition has gone, pride has gone."[12] He specified that the central feature of pride was enmity, which means " 'hatred toward, hostility to, or a state of opposition.' "[13]

The day after President Benson's address, Russell M. Nelson continued on this theme. He stood before the congregation and reflected on his recent visit to the Holy Land with Elder Carlos Asay. While there he noticed the irony of the political contention in a land where Christ spoke the very words, "Peace I leave with you, my peace I give unto you: not as the world giveth, give I unto you" (John 14:27).[14] Elder Nelson suggested that contention does not begin between countries but in an individual's heart. From there, contention spreads until it can infect neighbors and nations like a disease. Elder Nelson referred to President Benson's talk where he said that contention is a face of pride and lamented that in today's world too often contention is becoming an accepted way of life.[15]

In discussing why contention is so serious, Elder Nelson read a scripture from the book of 3 Nephi, explaining that the devil "is the father of contention,"[16] and recounted the story of the Grand Council in Heaven, detailing Satan's fall. As President Benson had mentioned the day before, Satan fell due to his pride. How very much like Lewis's own observation, "it was through Pride that the devil became devil."[17] Elder Nelson goes on to detail the specific targets of the attack led by Satan and his followers which encompass first, the family; second, Church leaders; and finally, the divine doctrines of the Church. Elder Nelson ends by declaring that the only way we can have personal peace is to let go of our pride and become humble.[18]

PRIDE AND THE NATURAL MAN

Brother Robert Millet wrote an *Ensign* article that discusses the enmity of pride in terms of the natural man. In specifying the characteristics of one who has not been redeemed from the fall, he emphasized that the natural man is proud.[19] He repeated the words of C. S. Lewis as quoted by President Benson, "There is no pleasure in 'having something,' only in 'having more than the next man.' "[20] As an example, he explained how Samuel the Lamanite's words of excitement, good news, and joy about the coming of the Messiah fell on deaf ears. A lifetime pursuit of only pleasure eventually leads to no pleasure at all because "ye have sought all your lives for that which ye could not obtain; and ye have sought for happiness in doing iniquity, which thing is contrary to the nature of that righteousness which is in our great and Eternal Head" (Helaman 13:38).[21]

Finally, Brother Millet proposed that we do not overcome this state of pride by simply living longer or attending our meetings. The solution is found in the words of President Benson from an earlier conference address: "The world would mold men by changing their environment. Christ changes men, who then change their environment. The world would shape human behavior, but Christ can change human nature."[22] At the end of the article, Brother Millet returns to the words of Lewis, explaining that such a change "is precisely what Christianity is about. This world is a great sculptor's shop. We are the statues and there is a rumor going round the shop that some of us are some day going to come to life."[23]

PRIDE FROM THE BOTTOM LOOKING UP

In explaining the inevitable progression of pride, C. S. Lewis stated that the enmity of pride does not stop between man and man but eventually includes our feelings toward God and our perspective of who God really is.[24] President Benson specified three causes for this infestation of worldly pride in our spiritual lives. First, when we listen to the shouts of the world they become louder than the soft inspiration of the Spirit. Second, too often men let their own opinions come before the revelations of God. Third, we let go of the iron rod by not reading the scriptures or following the feelings we get from them.[25] These words on pride encouraged the sharing of several personal experiences from other Church members in conjunction with President Benson's remarks.

In a 1994 *Ensign* article, a young father told about his trips to the temple with his wife. He appreciated the relief and peace it brought from their busy lives while living in a crowded home with three young children. On the way home, they would often go on what they jokingly called "coveting expeditions" in the nicer neighborhoods and dream of having more. It seemed harmless enough until they decided to build their own home. They began with plans of building a home they could afford but then kept adding landscaping, furniture, and draperies. Finally, they stopped themselves and realized two things: first, that Satan has a way of letting us rationalize any desire as justified, and, second, that the more we seek for happiness in things of the world, the hungrier we become for more things until we are never satisfied.[26] This young father realized that he should instead count his many blessings and find joy in what he already had.

Jackie Witzel, a full-time mother of ten, described another aspect of pride. When she was suddenly divorced and left to care for her children single-handedly, she resisted going on Church assistance until she realized it was in the best interest of her children. Embarrassed by her inability to provide for her family, she related how she wanted to explain to the sister at the checkout counter at the Bishop's Storehouse that she was not just being lazy or taking advantage of the Church. Sister Witzel chronicled her journey of understanding. She struggled with a different type of pride that comes from the bottom up.[27] President Benson also touched on this principle, saying it is a far more common problem among Church members. We need to be generous givers and gracious receivers.[28]

POOR SELF-ESTEEM IS A FACE OF PRIDE

President Benson also explained that another face of pride is lack of self-esteem. Often this presents itself in "me" thinking: spending a majority of time focused on how things make "me" feel, how every event affects "me," and focusing on how people like "me" or think better of "me."[29] This was the same struggle Lewis admittedly faced as previously mentioned in his daily meditations. He was not worried about how to serve his student but was rather consumed with how his student would respond to his clever ideas.

When Abigail Morris broke up with her fiancé just days before her wedding, her first question was, "What is wrong with me?" She found herself comparing her situation to others and becoming more hostile and depressed. When she heard President Benson's talk, she realized she was holding on to pride. As C. S. Lewis said, "The first step is to realize one is proud."[30] As she attempted to serve and increase the depth of her daily worship, she found the truthfulness of President Spencer W. Kimball's words, "The more we serve our fellowmen in appropriate ways, the more substance there is to our souls. We become more significant individuals. . . . Indeed, it is easier to 'find' ourselves because there is so much more of us to find!"[31]

In the Book of Mormon, Jacob addresses both the highs and lows of this concept of pride by saying, "The one being is as precious in [God's] sight as the other. And all flesh is of the dust; and for the selfsame end hath he created them, that they should keep his commandments and glorify him forever."[32] In an *Ensign* article, Sister Barbara Lockhart discussed her struggle with self-worth. She began feeling hopeful after hearing President Benson's promise that if she would love God and obey him, fearing his opinion of us more than man's, that she would have self-esteem.[33] After putting these conditions to the test, Sister Lockhart came to the conclusion that it doesn't make sense for Latter-day Saints to suffer from poor self-esteem. As we live the gospel and love our Savior, he will change us and perfect us in his own way.[34] We simply need faith.

HUMILITY IS THE ANTIDOTE OF PRIDE

Elder Marlin K. Jensen of the Seventy spoke about President Gordon B. Hinckley's "Six Be's," in particular "be humble." He recounted the story told in *Screwtape Letters* where a good man is being recruited by the devil's assistant and the devil remarks, "Your patient has become humble; have you drawn his attention to the fact?"[35] As before mentioned, Lewis conceded that humility is the first step to rid ourselves of pride. President Benson even called humility and submissiveness the antidote of pride.

Twenty years before President Benson's address, Elder Joe J. Christenson stood before the student body of Brigham Young University and delivered a devotional on pride that was later published in part in the

Ensign.[36] He said, "C. S. Lewis wrote that in his opinion, pride is the 'parent sin'—out of it comes all others."[37]

Touching on this point, Elder Jensen stated that pride's antithesis, humility, leads us to other virtues, including modesty and teachableness.[38] Scriptural examples of true humility are included in the words of John the Baptist who said of the Savior, "He must increase, but I must decrease." Elder Jensen reminded us of the humble words of Moroni at the end of the Book of Mormon when he pleads for forgiveness of his imperfections and the astonishing words of Moses after his first meeting with deity where he exclaims, "for this cause I know that man is nothing, which thing I never had supposed."[39]

Finally, a favorite phrase of Elder Neal A. Maxwell, "Lord of the narrow gate and the needle's eye," was from a poem by C. S. Lewis that he had included in a letter to a friend. As we grapple with trying to be more humble and eliminating pride from our lives as outlined by modern-day apostles and prophets, a key is to ask our Heavenly Father for assistance. In this heartfelt plea to our Savior for humility, Lewis shares his true thoughts on pride:

The Apologist's Evening Prayer

From all my lame defeats and oh! much more
From all the victories that I seemed to score;
From cleverness shot forth on Thy behalf
At which, while angels weep, the audience laugh;
From all my proofs of Thy divinity,
Thou, who wouldst give no sign, deliver me.
Thoughts are but coins. Let me not trust, instead
of Thee, their thin-worn image of Thy head.
From all my thoughts, even from my thoughts of Thee,
O thou fair Silence, fall, and set me free.
Lord of the narrow gate and needle's eye,
Take from me all my trumpery lest I die.[40]

NOTES

1. Green and Hooper, *C. S. Lewis: A Biography,* 105 (per *Narnian,* 133).
2. Lewis, *Mere Christianity,* 109.
3. Benson, "Beware of Pride," *Ensign,* May 1989, 4.
4. Moroni 8:27 (per Benson, "Beware of Pride").
5. D&C 38:39 (per Benson, "Beware of Pride").
6. Benson, "Beware of Pride," *Ensign,* May 1989, 4.

7. See Appendix A for specific references to *Ensign* articles and general conference talks referencing pride.

8. See Appendix C for specific references of lessons with excerpts from Benson's address.

9. Lewis, *Mere Christianity,* 112.

10. Ibid., 114.

11. Benson, "Beware of Pride," *Ensign,* May 1989, 4.

12. Ibid., 5; see also Lewis, *Mere Christianity,* 109–10.

13. Ibid., 5.

14. Nelson, "The Canker of Contention," *Ensign,* May 1989, 68.

15. Ibid., 68.

16. Ibid., 69; see also 3 Nephi 11:29–30.

17. Lewis, *Mere Christianity,* 109.

18. Nelson, "The Canker of Contention," *Ensign,* May 1989, 72.

19. Millet, "Putting Off the Natural Man: An Enemy to God," *Ensign,* June 1992, 7–9.

20. Benson, "Beware of Pride," *Ensign,* May 1989, 4. See also Lewis, *Mere Christianity,* 109.

21. Millet, "Putting Off the Natural Man: An Enemy to God," *Ensign,* June 1992, 9.

22. Ibid. See also Ezra Taft Benson, "Born of God," *Ensign,* November 1985, 6.

23. Lewis, *Mere Christianity,* 140.

24. See Lewis, *Mere Christianity,* 111–12.

25. Benson, "Beware of Pride," *Ensign,* May 1989, 6.

26. Brent L. Top, "Thou Shalt Not Covet," *Ensign,* Dec. 1994, 22.

27. Jackie Witzel, "Lessons Learned at the Bishop's Storehouse," *Ensign,* Dec. 2001, 53–55.

28. Benson, "Beware of Pride," *Ensign,* May 1989, 6.

29. Ibid.

30. Lewis, *Mere Christianity,* 114.

31. Spencer W. Kimball, "The Abundant Life," *Ensign,* July 1978, 3.

32. See Jacob 2:21 as quoted by Barbara Day Lockhart, "Our Divinely Based Worth," *Ensign,* June 1995, 51.

33. Benson, "Beware of Pride," *Ensign,* May 1989, 6.

34. Barbara Day Lockhart, "Our Divinely Based Worth," *Ensign,* June 1995, 51.

35. Lewis, *Screwtape Letters,* 62–63 as quoted in Marlin K. Jensen, " 'To Walk Humbly with Thy God,' " *Ensign,* May 2001, 9.

36. Joe J. Christensen, "Pride—The 'Parent Sin,' " *Ensign,* June 1974, 24.

37. Lewis, *Mere Christianity,* 109–10, per Joe J. Christensen, "Pride—The 'Parent Sin.' "

38. Marlin K. Jensen, " 'To Walk Humbly with Thy God,' " *Ensign,* May 2001, 9.

39. See John 3:30; Ether 12:23–27; Moses 1:10.

40. Lewis, *Poems* (San Diego: Harcourt Brace & Company, 1992).

CHAPTER TWENTY

Temptation and Repentance

In the winter of 1916, a young "Jack" Lewis jumped off the train and stepped onto the streets of Oxford for the first time. He had come to take his entrance exams and had been offered a scholarship if he passed. His tutor, William T. Kirkpatrick, had told his father in a letter that he could make a writer or a scholar out of him, but that was in essence all he was capable of.[1] Jack believed this of himself, and it terrified him. He felt he was playing a game in which hundreds lose and very few win. His first set of exams were based on the classics and although Lewis was nervous about how he had performed, by Christmas Eve he was relieved to hear he had been accepted to University College with very high scores.

The process was not over. He could begin school, but he still had to pass the "Responsions," a basic skills test which included elementary math. This was a huge problem since Lewis had always struggled with mathematics. Undaunted, he poured over his algebra books for the next few months but the more he studied the more mistakes he made.[2] Not surprisingly, Lewis failed the exam, but was immediately called into military service. After a short war career, Lewis was able to return to the university, because an exception had been made for veterans.[3] If it had not been for this window of opportunity, Lewis believed he never would have been accepted at Oxford because of his deficiency in math.

THE UPSIDE OF PROBLEMS WITH MATHEMATICS

Lewis loved reasoning and enjoyed geometry which was concept-based, but the moment he had to do calculations, he froze. He believed he understood the principles of math but despite his best efforts, he just couldn't get the answers right.[4] At the age of twenty-three he wrote in his diary that he had spent a good portion of the night trying to figure out his accounts, but came up with a different total every time he tried to recheck it. Years later, he wrote to a young girl named Lucy about his problem with simple calculations, especially when it came to figuring out his change in shops.[5]

As is often the case with personal challenges, Lewis learned a great principle through this trial. He saw how coming to the correct calculation was a symbol of obedience, and to wrong answers, a symbol of sin. Unlike the arts, which are subjective, the black and white, right or wrong nature of mathematics was an ideal illustration of moral truth.

THERE IS A RIGHT AND WRONG

Lewis's book *Mere Christianity* began as a series of radio broadcasts during World War II to explain what Christianity meant to the British people at a time when their faith was waning. Given such a great responsibility, it was surprising that Lewis did not begin his lectures touching on the life of Christ, the commandments, or the organization of a specific denomination. Instead, the first principle he presented was the concept of basic truth—that right and wrong actually exist and are not merely an arbitrary standard created by a certain culture.

To prove this, Lewis illustrated that within each of us there seems to be a pre-programmed concept of what is fair or good, similar to what we might call "the Light of Christ." He termed this phenomenon the "Law of Human Nature." Unlike some laws which cannot be broken like gravity or heredity, man alone has the power to choose whether to follow or disobey the voice within him.

There is a higher law, which follows the same pattern as the "Law of Nature" called the "Moral Law," and it dictates what really is right or wrong. If you set your clock to a different time, that act will not change the reality of what the actual time is. Moral mistakes or sin are not subjective, but occur whenever we are not in compliance with what is right. In our journey through life, if a man is on a wrong road, the greatest decision he can make is to turn around as fast as he can and fix it.

Comparing this idea to mathematics, Lewis states, "When I have started a sum the wrong way, the sooner I admit this and go back and start again, the faster I shall get on. There is nothing progressive about being pigheaded and refusing to admit a mistake."[6] Lewis understood that unless you believe in right and wrong—that there is a single right answer—the value of the Atonement would be meaningless. Until people grasp that there is only one road that will bring them greater happiness, they cannot begin to understand the profound gift of repentance offered through our Savior's loving sacrifice.

Later, in his preface to *The Great Divorce,* Lewis mirrored the same sentiment, expanding his views to their inevitable conclusion. He begins with the analogy of life being more like a tree than a river. As we make personal choices, we branch out into different directions. With each new branch, we either draw closer to God or away from him. For those who have gotten themselves way off track or "out on a limb," so to speak, Lewis explains the solution, "I do not think that all who choose the wrong roads perish; but their rescue consists in being put back on the right road. A sum can be put right; but only by going back till you find the error and working it afresh from that point, never by simply going on. Evil can be undone, but it cannot 'develop' into good." Then he adds this clever insight, "If we accept Heaven we shall not be able to retain even the smallest and most intimate souvenirs of Hell."[7]

The Lost Wallet and the Perfect Picture

In a July 1976 *New Era* article, Ardeth Kapp used the above quote to clarify the power of repentance and illustrated it with the following story. One day, Sister Kapp received a letter from someone she did not know, in regards to some unfinished business at Brigham Young University. It had been nine years since her graduation and she had no idea what it could be about. Sister Kapp looked up the telephone number, dialed it, and a young woman began to explain. The woman had been attending nursing school nine years earlier and had worked hard to pay her own way. When tuition had come due, she was ten dollars short. After exhausting every other venue, she begged her boyfriend for a loan but he was also tight. He reluctantly agreed, under the condition she would pay him back by Friday. On that Friday morning she was distraught, despite her prayers, no answer had come. Without a reason she wandered into the telephone booth in the Joseph Smith building and there she found a wallet. It had no ID that she could find and ten dollars. It seemed an answer to her prayers.

Since then, she had felt differently. Her faithful conscience continually pricked her through graduation from nursing college, raising a wonderful family, and various moves. All that time, she had kept the wallet in her top drawer, not knowing how to right the wrong she had done. She knew that Satan had tempted her when she was most vulnerable. Years later while cleaning out her top drawer, she saw the wallet again and happened to find a small compartment she had overlooked, which had an orange card with a health clinic's address and a name on it. She sent them a note, asking if they knew the whereabouts of the wallet's owner, which was forwarded to her parents and finally to Sister Kapp. The woman and Sister Kapp arranged a time to meet and the young mother returned the wallet and ten dollars, grateful to be forgiven. By putting the sum right, she could move forward, free of guilt and sin.[8]

Almost ten years later, Sister Kapp told the same story in a *New Era* article,[9] repeating the C. S. Lewis' math analogy, but here she preceded it with a foil, illustrating the flip-side of temptation. Recounting a story from *Reader's Digest,* she spoke of a young journalist who had been sent on an assignment to the home of a grandfather who had accidentally run over his young granddaughter. When the reporter arrived, the man was explaining to police officers that he didn't even know the child was outside and was backing up the pickup just a few feet to put new dirt in a flower bed.

Later, the young journalist headed inside the house to look in on the body of the deceased little girl. As he approached the doorway, he stopped and saw the grandfather alone with his head bowed over the young child, filled with grief and despair. The light was perfect and the journalist knew in that moment he had a prize-winning photo. He adjusted the lens and then stopped. Something in him also knew that such an invasion of privacy was wrong. He ended the story stating that even today he knew what he did was the right thing.[10]

Freedom from guilt and peace are the natural consequences of resisting temptation and sin. Sister Kapp used a line from Chaim Potok's book *The Chosen* to clarify this feeling. The main character, speaking of his valiant father, explains, "He taught me to look into myself, to find my own strength, to walk around inside myself in company with my soul."[11] Then Sister Kapp asked if each of us could live in the company of our own souls and feel at peace. Finally, she told of her own father's gentle passing, facing death without fear or remorse.

SCREWTAPE LETTERS

Most people find different challenges or weaknesses they need to work on. This was precisely the case with C. S. Lewis and the basis for his work *Screwtape Letters.* In his original introduction to the book, Lewis confessed, "Some have paid me an undeserved compliment by supposing that my Letters were the ripe fruit of many years' study in moral and ascetic theology. They forgot that there is an equally reliable, though less creditable, way of learning how temptation works. My heart—I need no other's—showeth me the wickedness of the ungodly."[12]

Perhaps this is why Lewis's little newspaper articles hit such a resonance with the public, being republished as a book and becoming his first international success. In addition to poking fun at society through these letters, Lewis reaches into our own hearts, exposing common temptations, weakness, and sin with incredible accuracy. He said of the work, "Though I have never written anything more easily, I had never wrote with less enjoyment."[13] He went on to say that the idea of diabolical letters "exploits itself spontaneously," the act of focusing on evil created a type of "spiritual cramp" in him that "almost smothered [him] before [he] was done."[14] But the fruits of Lewis's brooding have produced an introspective work filled with clear examples of pitfalls we should be wary of.

SMALL SINS

One case in point is illustrated when Screwtape writes Wormwood, proposing suggestions for ways to trap his patient, "You will say that these are very small sins; and doubtless, like all young tempters, you are anxious to be able to report spectacular wickedness. . . . It does not matter how small the sins are, provided that their cumulative effect is to edge the man away from the Light and out into the Nothing. . . . Indeed the safest road to Hell is the gradual one—the gentle slope, soft underfoot, without sudden turnings, without milestones, without signposts."[15]

At the 1987 October general conference, Elder James E. Faust, then an apostle, used this quote to warn us of the wiles of Satan.[16] About ten years later he presented a similar message.[17] Then in a January 2007 *Ensign* article, President James E. Faust, as a member of the First Presidency, went into far greater depth, discussing the reasons for resisting even the smallest temptations. Obviously, this was a subject President Faust felt should be repeated.

In his most recent address just prior to quoting Lewis, President Faust repeated something he heard the president of the Guatemala City Temple say, that the devil is not smart because he is the devil, but the reason he is so smart is because he is old.[18] Despite all he knows, Satan's powers are limited. President Faust explained that Satan has no power over us unless we permit it.[19] This was also a concept clearly taught by Joseph Smith.[20]

President Faust warned us about Satan's success with this gullible generation. As a result, sometimes it can be difficult to recognize the small sins Lewis was referring to. Again, President Faust gives a solution. He reminded us that the spirit of discernment comes through the gift of the Holy Ghost. We can know what is right and if we do it, we will thwart

the power of Satan.[21] Then, President Faust enumerated the forces we have
been given to assist us in this battle, namely, temple attendance, observing
the Sabbath Day, taking the Sacrament worthily, paying tithes and offer-
ings, saying regular contrite prayers, serving in the Church, and supporting those who preside over us.

Even with these great helps, Joseph Smith warned that the more
righteous we become, the more the adversary will try to prevent us from
accomplishing God's purposes in our lives.[22] In explaining this idea, President Faust used another statement from Lewis, "A silly idea is current
that good people do not know what temptation means. This is an obvious
lie. Only those who try to resist temptation know how strong it is . . . You
find out the strength of a wind by trying to walk against it, not by lying
down."[23]

President Faust concluded by reminding members that their personal
victory over sin is not simply manifest in their own lives, but affects the
world as a whole. In speaking of the magnanimous gifts of the priesthood
and the forces mentioned above that assist us in our efforts to remain
pure, President Faust reminded members of the Church that they are the
custodians of these commanding powers for not just all the earth but for
those who have died before and for those yet to come.[24] This is the curse
that will affect the whole earth if we as the Saints of these latter days do
not do our part.

THE SMALL SIN OF GAMBLING

At a devotional at Ricks College[25] (later printed as an *Ensign* article[26]), Elder Dallin H. Oaks talked specifically about one of the small sins
that allows Satan to have power over us. He warned against the popular
attitudes toward gambling as an effective fund raiser and form of entertainment. Past prophets, including Heber J. Grant, Joseph F. Smith, and
Gordon B. Hinckley have released specific statements clarifying that,
as President Joseph F. Smith phrased it, the Church looks on gambling
as "morally wrong" and "disapproves of any of its members engaging
therein."[27]

Ironically, Screwtape specifically mentions this vice to Wormwood.
After explaining that "small sins" can be just as effective as large ones if
they pull one away from the light, Screwtape goes on to say, "Murder is
no better than cards if cards can do the trick."[28] The concept that small
sins can be as spiritually devastating as larger sins is totally opposite to
what the world would teach. Nephi foresaw this in the latter days: "There
shall also be many which shall say, Eat, drink and be merry; nevertheless,

fear God—he will justify in committing a little sin . . . there is no harm in this."[29]

The greatest harm we face, taught Elder Oaks, is the harm we don't notice. It can overtake us before we are even aware of it. In the case of gambling, the harm consists in both individual attitudes and its effect on society as a whole. Not only is an individual who participates in gambling exposing themselves to possible addiction, he is also feeding the evils of "greed and covetousness," while undermining the virtues of work, industry, thrift, and service to others.[30]

At a community level Elder Oaks taught that state-sponsored lotteries are often sold as supporting some good cause, but that is a phony claim. A statement from the First Presidency goes on to explain that "lotteries only add to the problems of the financially disadvantaged by taking money from them and giving nothing of value in return."[31]

In conclusion, Elder Oaks ended his remarks asking, "If members do not oppose immoral and pernicious practices, who will? If not now, when? We can make a difference!"[32] With the words of this great apostle echoing in our ears, gambling does not seem like such a small sin anymore.

THE SMALL SIN OF HOW WE USE OUR LEISURE TIME

Another relatively small sin that has the Brethren concerned is the use of our leisure time. Elder Jeffrey R. Holland repeated this insight from C. S. Lewis: "Our leisure [time], even our play, is a matter of serious concern. [That is because] there is no neutral ground in the universe: every square inch, every split second, is claimed by God and counterclaimed by Satan."[33]

To illustrate this point, he told the story of a Little League football game played on September 30, 1998, in Inkom, Idaho. They had just finished warm-ups and were starting to practice plays when clouds gathered and it started to sprinkle lightly. But the boys were not concerned. Suddenly, lightning struck A. J. Edwards, and he lay motionless on the ground. Two men came forward, could find no pulse, and began CPR while a young assistant coach, Bryce Reynolds, held A. J.'s head. Elder Reynolds was preparing for a mission and had received the Melchizedek Priesthood just thirty-nine days before. Watching the scene, he remembered a blessing his grandfather had received after an equally tragic accident and felt impressed to give him a blessing. As Reynolds ended the brief but fervent prayer, A. J. drew his first breath. When Elder Holland recounted this story at the October 2000 general conference priesthood session, he was pleased to announce that a very healthy A. J. Edwards and his family were sitting in the audience.[34]

In conjunction with this story, Elder Holland quoted this scripture, given to the men of Israel who were assigned the task of recapturing the Holy Land: "Sanctify yourselves: for tomorrow the Lord will do wonders among you."[35] Elder Holland went on to discuss the importance of personal purity, amid the Internet, TV, personal computers, and movies, which have become amusements fraught with danger.[36]

In a time of discouraging warfare, Winston Churchill said to the people of England, "To every man there comes . . . that special moment when he is figuratively tapped on the shoulder and offered the chance to do a special thing unique to him and fitted to his talent. What a tragedy if that moment finds him unprepared or unqualified for the work which would be his finest hour."[37] Then Elder Holland spoke of the more serious kind of spiritual warfare, he is certain will come and of the critical need for each of us to be ready and to be clean.

WORDS OF THE PROPHETS ABOUT OUR LEISURE TIME

Prophets have been warning us for years of the importance of safeguarding our leisure time and especially of parents protecting their children from destructive influences that can enter our homes in the form of entertainment. In 1979, President Spencer W. Kimball wrote a sweet letter to the children of the Church which was printed in the *Friend* where he warned children to choose wisely what they read, listened to, and watched on television because they would affect how they both thought and acted.[38]

About thirteen years later, President Ezra Taft Benson echoed these same sentiments to parents, emphasizing that increased family activities, especially well-planned family home evenings were an effective solution, which he called "iron links" in a chain that would bind our families together with love, tradition, loyalty, and righteousness.[39]

In the 2004 October priesthood session of general conference, President Gordon B. Hinckley focused on leisure time, as he has various times before.[40] The prophet told of a woman's letter to him about her husband's fight with pornographic addictions. The he relayed the following shocking statistics:

1. Pornography has become a $57 billion industry worldwide, exceeding the combined revenues of all professional football, baseball and basketball franchises or the combined revenues of ABC, CBS and NBC.[41]

2. Twenty percent of men and 13 percent of women admit to

accessing pornography at work and 10 percent of adults admit to having Internet sexual addictions.[42]

3. One in five children ages ten to seventeen have received a sexual solicitation over the internet and three million of the visitors to adult websites were under seventeen.[43]

4. Sex is the number one topic searched on the Internet.[44]

President Hinckley admitted that bad influences are all around us on the Internet, television, DVDs, and magazines, but we do not need to watch or read it: "Suppose a storm is raging and the winds howl and the snow swirls about you. You find yourself unable to stop it. But you can dress properly and seek shelter, and the storm will have no effect upon you." He goes on to remind those who have fallen prey to these pernicious evils that unless they repent, when they become immortal, "they will be filthy still" (2 Nephi 9:16). But for those who stay clean, they can walk with an "unblemished brow in the sunlight of virtue and strength."[45]

NOTES

1. Lewis, *Surprised by Joy,* 184.

2. Ibid., 186–87.

3. Ibid., 137.

4. Lewis, *All My Roads Before Me,* 18.

5. Lewis, *Letters to Children,* 75.

6. Lewis, *Mere Christianity,* 29.

7. Lewis, *The Great Divorce,* viii–ix.

8. Kapp, "Will You Please Forgive Me? I Want to Be Forgiven," *New Era,* July 1976, 7.

9. Kapp, "What Have You to Declare?" *New Era,* Sept. 1985, 9.

10. Thom, "The Perfect Picture," *Reader's Digest,* Aug. 1976, 114.

11. Chaim Potok, *The Chosen,* 264–65.

12. Lewis, *Screwtape Letters,* xiii.

13. Ibid., 183.

14. Ibid., 183.

15. Ibid., 60–61.

16. Faust, "The Great Imitator," *Ensign,* Nov. 1987.

17. Faust, "Serving the Lord and Resisting the Devil," *Ensign,* Sept. 1995, 2.

18. Quote attributed to Ernest LeRoy Hatch. See Faust, "The Forces that Will Save Us," *Ensign,* Jan. 2007, 5.

19. Ibid., 6.

20. Andrew F. Ehat and Lyndon W. Cook, eds. *The Words of Joseph Smith,* (1980), 60, as quoted in above 2007 *Ensign* article.

21. Ibid., 8.

22. In Orson F. Whitney, *Life of Heber C. Kimball* (1945), 132, as quoted in the above 2007 *Ensign* article.

23. C. S. Lewis, *Mere Christianity*, 143.

24. Faust, "The Forces that Will Save Us," *Ensign*, Jan. 2007, 7.

25. Now Brigham Young University—Idaho.

26. Oaks, "Gambling—Morally Wrong and Politically Unwise," *Ensign*, June 1987, 69.

27. Ibid., 69.

28. Lewis, *Screwtape Letters*, 61.

29. 2 Nephi 2:28, as quoted by Elder Oaks.

30. Oaks, "Gambling—Morally Wrong and Politically Unwise," *Ensign*, June 1987, 70.

31. Letter of the First Presidency of The Church of Jesus Christ of Latter-day Saints, 26 Sept. 1986, as quoted in the above address.

32. Oaks, "Gambling—Morally Wrong and Politically Unwise," 70.

33. Lewis, *Christian Reflections*, 1967, 33.

34. Holland, "Sanctify Yourselves," *Ensign*, Nov. 2000, 39.

35. Joshua 3:5, as quoted by Elder Holland.

36. Holland, "Sanctify Yourselves," *Ensign*, Nov. 2000, 42.

37. Churchill in Covey, *The 8th Habit: From Effectiveness to Greatness*, 813.

38. Kimball, "The Savior Loves You," *Friend*, Aug. 1979, 6.

39. Benson, "Salvation—A Family Affair," *Ensign*, July 1992, 2.

40. Hinckley, "A Tragic Evil among Us," *Ensign*, Nov. 2004, 59; See also "I am Clean," *Ensign*, May 2007; "Gambling," *Ensign*, May 2005; "True to the Faith," *Ensign*, June 1996; "Overpowering the Goliaths in Our Lives," *Ensign*, Jan. 2002; "Inspirational Thoughts," *Ensign*, July 1998; "A Prophet's Counsel and Prayer for the Youth," *Ensign*, Jan. 2001 (The prophet introduces the Six Be's; See "Be Clean"); "To Men of the Priesthood," *Ensign*, Nov. 2002; "An Ensign to the Nations, a Light to the World," *Ensign*, Nov. 2003; "Come Listen to a Prophet's Voice: God's Power Within You," *Friend*, Jan. 2002. (This is not an exhaustive list.)

41. Internet Pornography Statistics: 203, Internet, http://www.healthymind.com/5-port-stats.html, as quoted in "A Tragic Evil among Us."

42. Ibid.

43. From the National Coalition for the Protection of Children and Families, as quoted in "A Tragic Evil among Us."

44. NCPCE Online, "Current Statistics," Internet, http://www.nationalcoalition.org/stat.html, as quoted in "A Tragic Evil among Us."

45. Hinckley, "A Tragic Evil among Us," *Ensign*, Nov. 2004, 62.

CHAPTER TWENTY-ONE

Loving My Neighbor and the Ultimate Joy

or Lewis, the most powerful part of the gospel of Jesus Christ was the joy it would bring not just in the eternities but day by day as followers of Christ stayed on its path. In his spiritual autobiography, *Surprised by Joy,* Lewis describes the hoped for joy which may come along life's journey as "an unsatisfied desire which itself [is] more desirable than any other satisfaction." He said that *joy* was neither happiness nor pleasure and the only thing they had in common is that once you have felt joy, happiness, or pleasure, you want to feel them again. Lewis warns that is where their commonality ends. Those who have felt true joy would not exchange it for all the pleasures in the world.[1]

DRINKING JOY FROM THE FOUNTAIN OF JOY

At the end of "The Weight of Glory," Lewis describes our ultimate reward of returning to Christ in these terms, "The whole man is to drink joy from the fountain of joy." This is the potential of man, the foundation of faith that carries us through trials, the great joy for which we hope and the opportunity available to every man and woman on earth. We should remember our neighbor "may one day be a creature which, if you saw it now, you would be strongly tempted to worship" and "the holiest object presented to your senses." There is a flipside to this grand potential because man may also become "a horror and a corruption such as you now meet, if at all, only in a nightmare." Lewis describes every person taking one step toward one destination or the other each day, either toward eternal joy or "immortal horrors."[2]

I KNOW WHO YOU ARE

Sister Susan W. Tanner spoke of the divine nature within each of us at a Young Women general meeting in 2007. She told of a day soon after being called to serve as the president when her daughter received a parking ticket for having an expired registration sticker. Knowing the papers were in the mail, Sister Tanner marched down to the courthouse to plead her case when someone said, "I know who you are." It caught her off guard and made her remember to act in accordance not only with her calling but with her divine potential.

Sister Tanner spoke of a girl's camp in Chile that encouraged the girls to keep a journal of the positive qualities of the girls they met while interacting with their new friends. At the end of the week, each girl shared what she had written in her journal. The leaders were amazed because not only were the girls happier but both contention and competition seemed to disappear and the tone of the entire week was one of joy as the girls appreciated each other's divine qualities.[3]

Hoping that we might all catch this divine vision, Sister Tanner then quoted C. S. Lewis: "It is a serious thing to live in a society of possible gods and goddesses, to remember that the dullest and most uninteresting person you can talk to may one day be a creature which, if you saw it now, you would be strongly tempted to worship. . . . There are no *ordinary* people. . . . Your neighbor is the holiest object presented to your senses."[4]

Sister Tanner taught that when we see our neighbors for what they can become—the way our Father in Heaven sees all of us—it changes our own hearts.

She ended her remarks with the personal experience of her own feelings of inadequacy when she was called to be General Young Women President. She would lie in her bed awake for many nights crying, worrying and repenting. Then she started thinking about the young women she knew. Her thoughts continued outwards to the young women throughout the world and she was filled with love for all of them. As soon as she remembered and felt Heavenly Father's love for all the young women and as she felt her own love increase, she felt peace for the first time since being called.[5]

Sister Tanner's words are reminiscent of Lewis's phrase, "drinking joy from the fountain of joy."[6] As we feel our Savior's love for his children, we are "filled with this love, which he hath bestowed upon all who are true followers of his Son, Jesus Christ" (Moroni 7:48). Perhaps, another term for the "joy" spoken of by Lewis is, indeed, the pure love of Christ.

Infinite Joy or Existential Despair

Prophets speak of the joy brought by the gospel and the many scriptural accounts of hope and gladness. Elder Neal A. Maxwell looked at the philosophies of the world in stark contrast, lamenting at the increasing amount of despair, and hopelessness present in literature, film, and music. He quoted one scientist who said that one of the key problems in modern life is that man has lost his belief that life has significance, and it is spreading to all types of people throughout society.[7]

In defiance of this statement, Elder Maxwell taught that when we see life through an eternal perspective, we can see the entire purpose of difficulties and not get trapped in momentary trials. Comparing this life to a play, he warned that it too will have a final act. Using the words of C. S. Lewis, Elder Maxwell stated that when Christ "comes on the stage, the play is over."[8]

The followers of Christ have hope as an anchor for their souls[9] to "make them sure and steadfast, always abounding in good works."[10] Elder Maxwell explained that although the righteous may live quieter and less dramatic lives than those who follow the extreme acts of the world swirling around them, theirs is a joyful drama.[11] The joyful drama Elder Maxwell discusses is not due to circumstance, but to character. He rehearsed story after story of valiant people in difficult situations: a mission president called on short notice to replace one who had died and the willing sacrifice of the wives who each had to cope with their overwhelming challenges; a young mission president living with his family of five in primitive conditions and deciding to adopt children of another culture; a paralyzed woman gymnast who spends her time strengthening others; and various widows and widowers who continue to serve faithfully as they wait for the time they will be united with their loved ones again. Of these people and others who meet their challenges with faith, Elder Maxwell says that the joy brought by the gospel in their lives dispels any darkness the world can bring.[12]

At another time Elder Maxwell taught that this infusion of joy occurs when we focus on eternity.[13] The key is to look beyond the passing mortal situation to the immense possibilities of each individual. To illustrate this idea Elder Maxwell uses a unique portion of the "Gods and Goddesses" quote discussed previously: "It is in the light of these overwhelming possibilities, it is with the awe and the circumspection proper to them, that we should conduct all our dealings with one another, all friendships, all loves, all play, all politics. There are no ordinary people. You have never talked to a mere mortal. Nations, cultures, arts, civilisations—these are mortal, and their life is to ours as the life of a gnat. But it is immortals whom we joke with, work with, marry, snub, and exploit."[14] Only by seeing the world in its eternal perspective can we see things "as they really are" and as "they really will be" (Jacob 4:13).

Elder Maxwell warns that even with this understanding we still need time and the wise use of agency to become the "sturdy, all-weather souls" that God wants us to be.[15] There is also a way we can know if we are on the path to joy and a way to know if we are obeying and pleasing God. Elder Maxwell notes that Brigham Young explained that it is only by the spirit of revelation that we can know it, by which we also will feel his love.[16] This knowledge of God's love can be certain in an uncertain world so that like Nephi we may be able to say "I know that [God] loveth his children; nevertheless, I do not know the meaning of all things" (1 Nephi 11:17). That assurance will give us hope, strength, and joy.

With this perspective, Elder Maxwell explains, we will begin to look at the "thou shalt not" commandments as "misery prevention" and the "thou shalt" commandments as those that bring happiness. These become our major focus. Through this active engagement in righteousness, we can come to know true joy, for as the scriptures say, man is that he might have joy (see 2 Nephi 2:25).

A Thousand Miles from Joy

As C. S. Lewis stated, with each decision we choose to move either closer to joy or away from it. Like children playing the game "Mother, May I?" some mistakes are merely baby steps in the wrong direction while others are giant leaps. One such leap away from our goal of joy is the attitude of flippancy, which Lewis says is "a thousand miles away from joy."[17]

In our current culture saturated in entertainment, Elder Peter B. Rawlins takes "A Serious Look at Humor" in his 1974 New Era article.[18] The scriptures say "a merry heart doeth good like a medicine" (Proverbs 17:22), and Elder Rawlins admits that mirth can ease tense situations, strengthen bonds of friendship, lift the discouraged, and teach important life lessons. Unfortunately, as with many gifts, humor can be used inappropriately, especially when people refuse to be serious about spiritual things. This attitude of flippancy, referred to by Brigham Young as empty levity,[19] was the subject of C. S. Lewis's sage advice: "If prolonged, the habit of flippancy builds up around a man the finest armour plating against [God] that I know . . . It is a thousand miles away from joy; it deadens instead of sharpening the intellect; and it excites no affection between those who practice it."[20]

Elder Rawlins encouraged members to avoid using humor as a "dangerous weapon," and to always be mindful of and compassionate to those who are weak and all that is sacred. He ended by reminding us that although it may be tempting to have a warped sense of humor, at the judgment day you may not find it funny.[21]

THE ONLY WAY OUT OF THE DUNGEON OF SELF

There is another way we block joy in our lives and treat our fellowmen inappropriately. The writings of George MacDonald touched C. S. Lewis and were partially responsible for his serious consideration of Christianity. After his conversion, C. S. Lewis condensed his sermons, taking out the best gems and putting them into an anthology. Neal A. Maxwell quotes on such nuggets of truth: "Love of one's neighbor is 'the only door out of the dungeon of self.' "[22] This point has been previously touched on, but there are a few more subtle roads that draw us away from our neighbors and ultimate joy.

THE INNER RING

Sometimes we exclude our neighbor unwittingly by creating what C. S. Lewis referred to as "The Inner Ring." In a lecture he gave at King's College at the University in London in 1944, Lewis stood before a roomful of students and said he knew they had probably guessed he would speak on one of three things—the world, the flesh, or the devil. The devil he vowed to leave strictly alone, and the flesh he believed the young students knew more about than he did, so he turned his remarks to the world.

In the world, Lewis teaches, there are two modes of behavior. The first may be printed in books and subject to laws. The second is not written anywhere and is usually discovered when you have broken it and find yourself looked down upon by those who know it. What Lewis is referring to is the "the Inner Ring," which can also be called the "gang," "so-and-so and his set," or perhaps today, "the in-crowd."[23] By belonging to this group, we may not see how insensitive and snobbish we have become to those outside of our little circle; the philosophy is that no one else really matters. As Lewis put it, "An invitation from a duchess would be very cold comfort to a man smarting under the sense of exclusion from some artistic or communist coterie. Poor man—it is not large, lighted rooms, or champagne, or even scandals about peers . . . that he wants: it is the sacred little attic or studio . . . and the delicious knowledge that we—we four or five all huddled beside this stove—are the people who know."[24]

Brother Gary L. Bunker discussed this subject in an *Ensign* article where he referenced the preceding quote in talking of the tragedy of a sixteen-year-old boy who jumped off the Golden Gate Bridge out of despondency related to the rejection of his peers. Brother Bunker added that the cost of exclusive behavior carries vast consequences both in this world and in the world to come.[25] The greatest consequence is that as we turn our hearts away from our neighbors, we drift away from the love and the joy we could have had. Brother Bunker ends his comments with the words of Dietrich Bonhoeffer, the Protestant martyr, who wrote from prison, "There is a very real danger of our drifting into an attitude of contempt for humanity . . . the man who despises others can never hope to do anything with them."[26] Perhaps this is why the love of a neighbor is a necessary condition of discipleship.

IMAGINARY BENEVOLENCE

Another example of exclusion of love and withdrawal of joy is when we employ a form of selective kindness, that is, showing charity toward a particularly needy group of people while being frustrated with those nearest to us. In the 2007 general conference, Elder Michael Teh quoted Screwtape describing just such a condition: "Do what you will, there is going to be some benevolence, as well as some malice, in your patient's soul. The great thing is to direct the malice to his immediate neighbours whom he meets every day and to thrust his benevolence out to the remote circumference, to the people he does not know. The malice thus becomes wholly real and the benevolence largely imaginary."[27]

Ten years earlier Sister Anna Reynolds wrote an article for the *New Era* also quoting a similar sentiment from *Screwtape Letters*, "Let him think if he ever meets a German he will be kind to him; but his neighbors, the people he associates with every day, let the little things about them annoy him."[28]

In today's world, it is easy to think of examples of people who express great compassion for groups outside their community, yet feel anger, disgust, or frustration with the people within their communities. They may picket for the release of murderers or drive farmers from their livelihood over the preservation of some little known species of fish, but often these same proponents of tolerance hold feelings of anger and even hatred for those around them. The words of Nephi come to mind when he enumerated the steps we need to take after we have entered in at the gate: "Wherefore, ye must press forward with a steadfastness in Christ, having a perfect brightness of hope, and a love of God and of all men" (2 Nephi 31:20). To become like Christ, our love must increase until it encompasses all of humanity, not just a select few.

LEARNING OF JOY FROM THE FOUNTAIN OF JOY

As we develop the attributes of Christ we become closer to him in two ways. First, we are more spiritually open to receive revelation and his love. Second, we understand him better from the inside out. One way we draw closer to Christ and get to know him better is through forgiveness. C. S. Lewis brought this George McDonald quote to life: "No man who will not forgive his neighbor, can believe that God is willing, yea wanting, to forgive him. . . . No doubt God takes what wrong there is, and what provocation there is, into the account: but the more provocation, the more excuse that can be urged for the hate, the more reason . . . that the hater should [forgive, and] be delivered from the hell of his [anger]."[29]

In an address to Salt Lake City Temple workers, Elder Holland spoke of the Savior and of the great example he set in every aspect of his life, but he felt the most amazement at his words to those who had mocked, beaten, and scoured him, "Father, forgive them; for they know not what they do."[30] Elder Holland then reminds us of not only the great gift that Christ himself gave through the Atonement, but also of the equal heartache of our Father in Heaven watching his beloved son's suffering.[31]

Elder Holland asked how we can best show our gratitude for this great gift. The answer lies in those words of forgiveness uttered on the cross, for we do so by joining in the work of forgiveness.[32] In response to Paul's words, "Bear ye one another's burdens, and so fulfill the law of Christ" (Galatians 6:2), an early Christian martyr once said, "My brother's burden which I must bear is not only his outward lot [and circumstance] . . . but quite literally his sin. And the only way to bear that sin is by forgiving it in the power of the cross of Christ in which [we] now share. Thus the call to follow Christ always means a call to share [in] the work of forgiving men their sins."[33] Then Elder Holland shared the quote by George MacDonald that emphasizes Christ's deep love for us because he allows us to forgive others so we are "delivered from the hell of [our] anger."[34]

Every commandment, every direction is merely a reflection of our Savior's divine love for us, a love we can hardly fathom. C. S. Lewis wrote, "He has infinite attention to spare for each one of us. He does not have to deal with us in the mass. You are as much alone with Him as if you were the only being He had ever created. When Christ died, He died for you individually just as much as if you had been the only man [or woman] in the world."[35]

To illustrate this love, Elder Holland told of his experience with the family of a young missionary anticipating the return of their son at an airport.

Elder Holland had just stepped off a plane and noticed them waiting and decided to stay to watch the event unfold. Looking at the family, he tried to figure out which person would be the first to break from the group and run up to welcome the missionary home. There was the mother whose handkerchief was wet and worn, the girlfriend, little siblings running around in excitement, and a serious looking father.

When people started to exit from the plane, Elder Holland could easily tell who the missionary son was because there were squeals of joy from the family as soon as they could see him. Surprisingly, it was not the mother, the girlfriend, or the little brothers and sisters, but the father who could bear it no longer. The large man, who looked weathered from work, pushed through the crowd and full-out ran forward, sweeping his son into his arms. "This big bear of a father grabbed him, took him clear off his feet, and held him for a long, long time. . . . It seemed like all eternity stood still, and for a precious moment the Salt Lake City Airport was the center of the entire universe."[36]

Lewis once wrote "Our Father [in Heaven] refreshes us on the journey [through life] with some pleasant inns, but [he] will not encourage us to mistake them for home."[37] These pleasant inns may be found in moments of joy, but they are nothing compared with the time we shall be welcomed home and bathed in the complete joy and love of our Lord.

Lewis wrote about his expectation of this day in *The Silver Chair*. King Caspian dies of old age. While his heartbroken friends are mourning his death in Narnia, King Caspian is reunited with Aslan. He has awakened to a joyful new life in Aslan's country. After his death, Caspian realizes that he does not belong in Narnia. He is now part of a new world where he "cannot want wrong things any more." He "gave Aslan the strong kisses of a king, and Aslan gave him the wild kisses of a Lion."[38]

Lewis's death could not end his search for joy. During his life, he understood that there was a far-off country where he would find everlasting joy. There, as the scriptures promise, he will have the opportunity to receive a "fulness of joy" (D&C 93:33). He will also be "eternally encircled in the arms of [Christ's] love" (2 Nephi 1:15). May we all look forward to that joyous homecoming with the same enthusiasm, faith, and clarity as C. S. Lewis, knowing with all our hearts that only with Christ can we truly be home.

NOTES

1. Lewis, *Surprised by Joy*, 17–18.
2. Lewis, *Weight of Glory*, 45.
3. Susan W. Tanner, "Daughters of Heavenly Father," *Ensign*, May 2007, 106–9.
4. Lewis, *Weight of Glory* , 45.
5. Susan W. Tanner, "Daughters of Heavenly Father," 106–9.
6. Lewis, *Weight of Glory*, 44.
7. Maxwell, "Shine As Lights in the World," *Ensign*, May 1983, 9, quoting Rene Dubos, *So Human an Animal* (New York: Scribners, 1968), 14–15.
8. Ibid., 11, quoting Lewis, *Weight of Glory*.
9. See Hebrews 6:19.
10. See Ether 12:4; Colossians 1:23; Mosiah 5:15.
11. Maxwell, "Shine As Lights in the World," 12.
12. Ibid., 13.
13. Neal A. Maxwell, "The Pathway of Discipleship," *Ensign*, Sept. 1998, 7.
14. Ibid., quoting Lewis, *The Weight of Glory*.
15. Ibid., see Jacob 4:13.
16. Ibid., quoting *Deseret News Semi-Weekly*, 26 Nov. 1867, n.p.
17. Lewis, *Screwtape Letters*, 56.
18. Peter B. Rawlins, "A Serious Look at Humor," *New Era*, Aug. 1974, 48.
19. Ibid., quoting Brigham Young (no reference).
20. Ibid., quoting Lewis, *Screwtape Letters*, 56.
21. Ibid., 49.
22. Maxwell, "The Prohibitive Costs of a Value-free Society," *Ensign*, Oct. 1978, 52–55; Lewis, *George MacDonald: An Anthology*, 27.
23. Lewis, *Weight of Glory*, 141.
24. Ibid., 142.
25. Gary L. Bunker, "Mocking Our Brother," *Ensign*, Apr. 1975, 36.
26. *Letters and Papers from Prison*, SCM Press LTD, London, 1967, as quoted by Bunker.
27. *Screwtape Letters*, as quoted by Michael J. Teh, "Out of Small Things," *Ensign*, Nov. 2007, 35–37.
28. *Screwtape Letters*, as quoted by Anna K. Reynolds, "Always Nice," *New Era*, Jan. 1997, 11.
29. C. S. Lewis, ed., *George MacDonald, An Anthology*, 6–7.
30. Jeffrey R. Holland, "I Stand All Amazed," *Ensign*, Aug. 1986, 68; See also Luke 23:34.
31. Ibid., 68. See also Melvin J. Ballard, *Crusader of Righteousness*, Salt Lake City: Bookcraft, 1966, 136–38.
32. Ibid., 74.
33. Dietrich Bonhoeffer, *The Cost of Discipleship*, as quoted by Holland, "I Stand All Amazed," *Ensign*, Aug. 1986.

34. Lewis, *George MacDonald, An Anthology,* 6–7, as quoted by Holland.

35. Lewis, *Mere Christianity,* 168; also quoted in Dale E. Miller, "Bringing Peace and Healing to Your Soul," *Ensign,* Nov. 2004, 12–14.

36. Jeffrey R. Holland, "I Stand All Amazed," *Ensign,* August 1986, 75–76.

37. C.S. Lewis, *The Problem of Pain,* 116.

38. Lewis, *Narnia,* 661.

Appendix A

ATTITUDE

If prolonged, the habit of Flippancy builds up around a man the finest armour-plating against [God] that I know. . . . It is a thousand miles from joy: it deadens, instead of sharpening, the intellect; and it excites no affection between those who practise it. (*Screwtape Letters*, 56)

Peter B. Rawlins, "A Serious Look at Humor," *New Era,* Aug. 1974, 48

We have trained them to think of the future as a promised land which favoured heroes attain—not as something which everyone reaches at the rate of sixty minutes an hour, whatever he does. (*Screwtape Letters*, 139)

"FYI: For Your Information," *New Era,* Nov. 1979, 38–41
"FYI: For Your Information," *New Era,* Mar. 1984, 40–43

Health is a great blessing, but the moment you make health one of your main, direct objects you start becoming a crank and imagining there is something wrong with you. You are only likely to get health provided you want other things more—food, games, work, fun open air. (*Mere Christianity*, 134)

John K. Carmack, "To My Single Friends," *Ensign,* Mar. 1989, 27

Take care. It is so easy to break eggs without making omelettes." (*Richard Evans' Quote Book,* 169)

Paul H. Dunn, "We Have Been There All the Time," *Ensign,* Nov. 1977, 24

DIVINITY OF MAN

You say the materialist universe is "ugly." I wonder how you discerned that? If you are really a product of a materialistic universe, how is it you don't feel at home there? Do fish complain of the sea for being wet . . . Notice how we are perpetually surprised by time. (How time flies! Fancy John being grown up and married? I can hardly believe it!') In heaven's name why? Unless, indeed, there is something in us which is not temporal. (*Collected Letters of C. S. Lewis*, vol. III, 76)

Neal A. Maxwell, "The Prohibitive Costs of a Value-free Society," *Ensign*, Oct. 1978, 52–55

EXALTATION

Christ says, "Give me All. I don't want so much of your time and so much of your money and so much of your work: I want You. I have not come to torment your natural self, but to kill it. No half-measures are any good. I don't want to cut off a branch here and a branch there, I want to have the whole tree down. . . . Hand over the whole natural self, all the desires which you think innocent as well as the ones you think wicked—the whole outfit. I will give you a new self instead. In fact, I will give you Myself: my own will shall become yours. (*Mere Christianity*, 196–97)

Robert L. Backman, "Jesus the Christ," *Ensign*, Nov. 1991, 8

Imagine yourself as a living house. God comes in to rebuild that house. At first, perhaps, you can understand what He is doing. He is getting the drains right and stopping the leaks in the roof and so on: you knew those jobs needed doing and so you are not surprised. But presently he starts knocking the house about in a way that hurts abominably and does not seem to make sense. What on earth is He up to? The explanation is that He is building quite a different house from the one you thought of—throwing out a new wing here, putting on an extra floor there, running up towers, making courtyards. You thought you were going to be made into a decent little cottage: but He is building a palace. (*Mere Christianity*, 205)

Marvin J. Ashton, "Progress through Change," *Ensign*, Nov. 1979, 61

John K. Carmack, "Upheld by the Prayers of the Church," *Ensign*, May 1984, 75

Neal A. Maxwell, "The Value of Home Life," *Ensign*, Feb. 1972, 4

It is a serious thing to live in a society of possible gods and goddesses, to remember that the dullest and most uninteresting person you can talk to may one day be a creature which, if you saw it now, you would be strongly tempted to worship. It is in the light of these overwhelming possibilities, it is with the awe and the circumspection proper to them, that we should conduct all our dealings with one another, all friendships, all loves, all play, all politics. There are no ordinary people. You have never talked to a mere mortal. Nations, cultures, arts, civilisations—these are mortal, and their life is to ours as the life of a gnat. But it is immortals whom we joke with, work with, marry, snub, and exploit. . . . Your neighbor is the holiest object presented to your senses. (*The Weight of Glory,* 45)

Ruth H. Funk, " 'Come, Listen to a Prophet's Voice,' " *Ensign,* Nov. 1978, 106

"FYI: For Your Information," *New Era,* Sept. 1981, 41–44

James S. and Jeanne N. Jardine, "Avoiding Unrighteous Dominion," *Ensign,* Sept. 1990, 62

Neal A. Maxwell, "The Pathway of Discipleship," *Ensign,* Sept. 1998, 7

Susan W. Tanner, "Daughters of Heavenly Father," *Ensign,* May 2007, 106–9

The command Be ye perfect is not idealistic gas. Nor is it a command to do the impossible. He [Christ] is going to make us creatures that can obey that command. He said (in the Bible) that we were "Gods" and He is going to make good His words. If we let Him—for we can prevent Him, if we choose—He will make the feeblest and filthiest of us into a god or goddess, a dazzling, radiant, immortal creature, pulsating all through with such energy and joy and wisdom and love as we cannot now imagine . . . The process will be long and in parts very painful; but that is what we are in for. Nothing less. He meant what He said. (*Mere Christianity,* 205–6)

Alexander B. Morrison, " 'I Am the Resurrection and the Life,' " *Ensign,* Apr. 1995, 36

There are only two kinds of people in the end: those who say to God, "Thy will be done," and those to whom God says, in the end, "Thy will be done." All that are in Hell, choose it. Without that self-choice there could be no Hell. No soul that seriously and constantly desires joy will ever miss it. Those who seek find. To those who knock it is opened. (*The Great Divorce,* 75)

W. Jeffrey Marsh, " 'Remember How Merciful the Lord Hath Been,' " *Ensign,* Apr. 2000, 18

This world is a great sculptor's shop. We are the statues and there is a rumour going round the shop that some of us are some day going to come to life. (*Mere Christianity,* 159)

Robert L. Millet, "Putting off the Natural Man," *Ensign,* Aug. 2000, 7

Robert L. Millet, "Putting Off the Natural Man: 'An Enemy to God,' " *Ensign,* Jun. 1992, 7–9

We are bidden to 'put on Christ,' to become like God. That is, whether we like it or not, God intends to give us what we need, not what we now think we want. (*The Problem of Pain*, 46–47)

> Neal A. Maxwell, "Insights from My Life," *Ensign,* Aug. 2000, 7.
> From a talk given on 12 January 1999 at Brigham Young University.

FAITH

[C. S. Lewis, compared grace and works to the blades of a pair of scissors.] I have no right really to speak on such a difficult question, but it does seem to me like asking which blade in a pair of scissors is the most necessary. (*Mere Christianity*, 148)

> Dallin H. Oaks, Tough Topics: Are You Saved by Grace or Works?" *New Era,*
> Mar. 2005, 38 (reprint)

Faith may mean (a) A settled intellectual assent. In that sense faith (or "belief") in God hardly differs from faith in the uniformity of Nature or in the consciousness of other people. This is what, I think, has some-times been called . . . "rational" or "intellectual" or "carnal" faith. It may also mean (b) A trust, or confidence, in the God whose existence is thus assented to. This involves an attitude of the will. It is more like our confidence in a friend. (*A Mind Awake*, 137)

> Mollie Hobaugh Sorensen, "Learning Faith," *Ensign,* Mar 1985, 24

FORGIVING

No man who will not forgive his neighbor, can believe that God is willing, yea wanting, to forgive him. . . . If God said, "I forgive you" to a man who hated his brother, and if (as impossible) that voice of forgiveness should reach the man, what would it mean to him? How would the man interpret it? Would it not mean to him, "You may go on hating. I do not mind it. You have had great provocation and are justified in your hate"?

No doubt God takes what wrong there is, and what provocation there is, into the account: but the more provocation, the more excuse that can be urged for the hate, the more reason . . . that the hater should [forgive, and] be delivered from the hell of his [anger]. (*Anthology of George MacDonald*)

> Jeffrey R. Holland, "'I Stand All Amazed,'" *Ensign,* Aug. 1986, 68

JESUS CHRIST

He has infinite attention to spare for each one of us. He does not have to deal with us in the mass. You are as much alone with Him as if you were the only being He had ever created. When Christ died, He died for you individually just as much as if you had been the only man [or woman] in the world." (*Mere Christianity*, 168)

> Dale E. Miller, "Bringing Peace and Healing to Your Soul," *Ensign*,
> Nov. 2004, 12–14

I am trying here to prevent anyone saying the really foolish thing that people often say about Him: [that is,] "I'm ready to accept Jesus as a great moral teacher, but I don't accept His claim to be God." That is the one thing we must not say. (*Mere Christianity*, 52)

> Jeffrey R. Holland, "True or False," *New Era*, June 1995, 64

What Satan put into the heads of our remote ancestors was the idea that they could . . . invent some sort of happiness for themselves outside God, apart from God. And out of that hopeless attempt has come nearly all that we call human history—money, poverty, ambition, war, prostitution, classes, empires, slavery—the long terrible story of man trying to find something other than God which will make him happy.

It seems to start up all right and runs a few years, and then it breaks down. They are trying to run it on the wrong juice. (*Mere Christianity*, 49–50)

> Neal A. Maxwell, "Eternalism vs. Secularism," *Ensign*, Oct. 1974, 69

JUSTICE

But the Humanitarian theory wants simply to abolish Justice and substitute Mercy for it. . . . Mercy, detached from Justice, grows unmerciful. That is the important paradox. As there are plants which will flourish only in mountain soil, so it appears that Mercy will flower only when it grows in the crannies of the rock of Justice: transplanted to the marshlands of mere Humanitarianism, it becomes a man-eating weed, all the more dangerous because it is still called by the same name as the mountain variety. (*God in the Docks*, 294)

> Neal A. Maxwell, "Jesus, the Perfect Mentor," *Ensign*, Feb. 2001, 8
> From a talk given at a CES fireside at Brigham Young University on
> 6 February 2000

LEISURE TIME

Our leisure, even our play, is a matter of serious concern. [That is because] there is no neutral ground in the universe: every square inch, every split second, is claimed by God and counterclaimed by Satan. (*Reflections*, 33)

> Jeffrey R. Holland, "'Sanctify Yourselves,'" *Ensign*, Nov. 2000, 38
> Jeffrey R. Holland, "Be Ready and Worthy," *New Era*, May 2006, 2–5

LOVE AND SERVICE

Do what you will, there is going to be some benevolence, as well as some malice, in your patient's soul. The great thing is to direct the malice to his immediate neighbours whom he meets every day and to thrust his benevolence out to the remote circumference, to people he does not know. The malice thus becomes wholly real and the benevolence largely imaginary. (*Screwtape Letters*, 28)

Anna K. Reynolds, "Always Nice," *New Era*, Jan. 1997, 11
Michael J. Teh, "Out of Small Things," *Ensign*, Nov. 2007, 35–37

[Homemaking] is surely in reality the most important work in the world. What do ships, railways, mines, cars, and governments, etc. exist for except that people may be fed, warmed, and safe in their own homes? . . . We wage war in order to have peace, we work in order to have leisure, we produce food in order to eat it. So your job is the one for which all others exist. (*The Collected Letters of CSL*, vol. III, 62)

Marvin J. Ashton, "A Yearning for Home," *Ensign*, Nov. 1992, 21
James E. Faust, "How Near to the Angels," *Ensign*, May 1998, 95
James E. Faust, "A Message to My Granddaughters: Becoming 'Great Women,' " *Ensign*, Sept. 1986, 16
Barbara B. Smith, "Women for the Latter Day," *Ensign*, Nov. 1979, 107

I am afraid the only safe rule is to give more than we can spare. . . . If our charities do not at all pinch or hamper us . . . they are too small. There ought to be things we should like to do and cannot do because our charitable expenditure excludes them. (*Mere Christianity*, 86)

Joe J. Christensen, "Greed, Selfishness, and Overindulgence," *Ensign*, May 1999, 9
Visiting Teaching Message "Living within Our Means," *Ensign*, Feb. 2001, 69

The love of our neighbor is the only door out of the dungeon of self. (*Anthology of George MacDonald*, 27)

Neal A. Maxwell, "The Prohibitive Costs of a Value-free Society," *Ensign*, Oct. 1978, 52–55

The more often he feels without acting, the less he will be able ever to act, and, in the long run, the less he will be able to feel. (*Screwtape Letters*, 67)

Jack H. Goaslind, " 'Yagottawanna,' " *Ensign*, May 1991, 45
Jack H. Goaslind, " 'Yagottawanna,' " *New Era*, Feb. 1992, 4
Ardeth G. Kapp, "Taking Upon Us His Name," *New Era*, Apr. 1982, 38

PERSPECTIVE

I believe in Christianity as I believe the sun has risen, not only because I see it, but because, by it, I see everything else. (*The Weight of Glory*, "Is Theology Poetry?")

> Neal A. Maxwell, "Talk of the Month," *New Era*, May 1971, 28

The great thing, if one can, is to stop regarding all the unpleasant things as interruptions of one's "own," or "real" life. The truth is of course that what one calls the interruptions are precisely one's real life—the life God is sending one day by day. (*Arther Greeves*, 499)

> Rex D. Pinegar, "Faith—The Force of Life," *Ensign*, Nov. 1982, 24

You've begun to suspect that those moments, of which the memory is now so ravishing, weren't at the time quite so wonderful as they now seem. You're right. They weren't. Each great experience is "a whisper Which Memory will warehouse as a shout." (From an unpublished poem by Owen Barfield; *The Quotable C. S. Lewis*, 425)

> Neal A. Maxwell, " 'Settle This in Your Hearts,' " *Ensign*, Nov. 1992, 65

PRIDE

A proud man is always looking down on things and people; and, of course, as long as you are looking down, you cannot see something that is above you. (*Mere Christianity*, 124)

> Gary L. Bunker, "Mocking Our Brother," *Ensign*, Apr. 1975, 36

The Apologist's Evening Prayer
From all my lame defeats and oh! much more
From all the victories that I seemed to score;
From cleverness shot forth on Thy behalf
At which, while angels weep, the audience laugh;
From all my proofs of Thy divinity,
Thou, who wouldst give no sign, deliver me.
Thoughts are but coins. Let me not trust, instead
of Thee, their thin-worn image of Thy head.
From all my thoughts, even from my thoughts of Thee,
O thou fair Silence, fall, and set me free.
Lord of the narrow gate and needle's eye,
Take from me all my trumpery lest I die.
(*Poems*, 129)

> Neal A. Maxwell, "Premortality, a Glorious Reality," *Ensign*, Nov. 1985, 15

It is the comparison that makes you proud: the pleasure of being above the rest. (*Mere Christianity*, 122)

> Pam Wilson Vandenaker, " 'Stripped of Envy,' " *Ensign,* Mar. 1999, 19

People who believe themselves to be free, and indeed are free, from snobbery, and who read satires on snobbery with tranquil superiority, may be devoured by the desire in another form. It may be the very intensity of their desire to enter some quite different Ring which renders them immune from the allurements of high life. An invitation from a duchess would be very cold comfort to a man smarting under the sense of exclusion from some artistic or communist coterie. Poor man—it is not large, lighted rooms, or champagne, or even scandals about peers and Cabinet Ministers that he wants: it is the sacred little attic or studio, the heads bent together, the fog of tobacco smoke, and the delicious knowledge that we—we four or five all huddled beside this stove—are the people who know." (*Inner Ring*)

> Gary L. Bunker, "Mocking Our Brother," *Ensign,* Apr. 1975, 36

Pride gets no pleasure out of having something, only out of having more of it than the next man. . . . It is the comparison that makes you proud: the pleasure of being above the rest. Once the element of competition has gone, pride has gone. (*Mere Christianity*, 122)

> Ezra Taft Benson, "Beware of Pride," *Ensign,* May 1989, 4
> Ezra Taft Benson, "The Faces of Pride," *New Era,* Oct. 2003, 40 (reprint)

Pride leads to every other vice: it is the complete anti-God state of mind. (*Mere Christianity*, 122)

> Joe J. Christensen, "Pride—The 'Parent Sin,' " *Ensign,* June 1974, 24

Your patient has become humble; have you drawn his attention to the fact? (*Screwtape Letters*, 69)

> Marlin K. Jensen, " 'To Walk Humbly with Thy God,' " *Ensign,* May 2001, 9

PROCRASTINATION

Oh Adam's sons, how cleverly you defend yourselves against all that might do you good! (*The Magician's Nephew*, 185)

> Jan D. Andersen, "Financial Freedom on Any Income," *Ensign,* Aug. 2006, 27–31
> Robert S. Wood, "The Quest for Spiritual Knowledge," *Ensign,* June 2007, 30–35

Reading Lists

Reading Lists including C. S. Lewis, *The Lion, the Witch and the Wardrobe:*
Carolyn McDonald, "The Textbook Was a Revelation," *Ensign,* Mar. 1989, 10
Elliott D. Landau, "Of Books, Children, and Parents," *Ensign,* May 1971, 31
John S. Gholdston, "Words of Darkness, Words of Light," *Ensign,* Jan. 1992, 57
"Windows on Wonder: An Interview with James C. Christensen," New Era,
Aug. 1989, 44
Melvin Leavitt, "Robert Van Dam of New Orleans, Louisiana," *Friend,*
Aug. 1993, 20

Repentance

I do not think that all who choose wrong roads perish; but their rescue
consists in being put back on the right road. A wrong sum can be put
right: but only by going back till you find the error and working it afresh
from that point, never by simply going on. If we insist on keeping Hell (or
even earth) we shall not see Heaven: If we accept Heaven we shall not be
able to retain even the smallest and most intimate souvenirs of Hell. (*The
Great Divorce,* viii–ix)
Steve Gilliland, "The Psychological Case for Chastity," *Ensign,* July 1975, 54–58
Ardeth G. Kapp, "What Have You to Declare?" *New Era,* Sept. 1985, 9
Ardeth G. Kapp, " 'Will You Please Forgive Me? I Want to Be Honest,' " *New
Era,* July 1976, 7

If I am a field that contains nothing but grass-seed, I cannot produce
wheat. Cutting the grass may keep it short: but I shall still produce grass
and no wheat. If I want to produce wheat, the change must go deeper than
the surface. I must be ploughed up and re-sown. (*Mere Christianity,* 198)
Colin B. Douglas, "What I've Learned about Grace Since Coming Down from
the Sycamore Tree," *Ensign,* Apr. 1989, 13

No amount of falls will really undo us if we keep picking ourselves up each
time. We shall of course be very muddy and tattered children by the time
we reach home. But the bathrooms are all ready, the towels put out, and
the clean clothes in the airing cupboard. (*Collected Letters of CSL,* vol. II,
507)
Neal A. Maxwell, "On the Straight and Narrow Way," *New Era,* Aug. 1971, 42

This Helper who will, in the long run, be satisfied with nothing less than
absolute perfection, will also be delighted by the first feeble, stumbling
effort you make tomorrow to do the simplest duty. As a great Christian
writer (George MacDonald) pointed out, every father is pleased at the

baby's first attempt to walk: no father would be satisfied with anything less than a firm free, manly walk in a grown-up son. In the same way he said, "God is easy to please, but hard to satisfy." (*Mere Christianity*, 202)

Heidi Holfeltz Parker, "Am I What I Appear to Be?" *Ensign*, Oct. 1991, 28

SECOND COMING

But I wonder whether people who ask God to interfere openly and directly in our world quite realise what it will be like when He does. When that happens, it is the end of the world. When the author comes on to the stage the play is over. (*Mere Christianity*, 65)

Homer S. Ellsworth, "The Love That Never Ceases to Be," *New Era*,
June 1975, 14

We cannot mingle with the splendours we see. But all the leaves of the New Testament are rustling with the rumour that it will not always be so. (*The Weight of Glory*, 33)

Neal A. Maxwell, "Premortality, a Glorious Reality," *Ensign*, Nov. 1985, 15

SIN AND TEMPTATION

A Christian would be wise to avoid, where he decently can, any meeting with people who are bullies, lascivious, cruel, dishonest, spiteful and so forth. Not because we are "too good" for them. In a sense because we are not good enough. We are not good enough to cope with all the temptations, not clever enough to cope with all the problems, which an evening spent in such society produces. The temptation is to condone, to connive at; by our words, looks and laughter, to "consent." (*Reflections on the Psalms*, 71.)

Neal A. Maxwell, "What Is Real Love and Happiness?" *New Era*, June 1992, 4
Neal A. Maxwell, "The Stern but Sweet Seventh Commandment," *New Era*,
June 1979, 36

A silly idea is current that good people do not know what temptation means. This is an obvious lie. Only those who try to resist temptation know how strong it is. . . . You find out the strength of a wind by trying to walk against it, not by lying down. (*Mere Christianity*, 143)

James E. Faust, "The Forces That Will Save Us," *Ensign*, Jan. 2007, 4–9
James E. Faust, " 'The Great Imitator,' " *Ensign*, Nov. 1987
Sharon G. Larsen, "Agency—A Blessing and a Burden," *Ensign*, Nov. 1999, 11
Neal A. Maxwell, "Enduring Well," *Ensign*, Apr 1997, 7

Hence nearly all vices are rooted in the Future. Gratitude looks to the past and love to the present; fear, avarice, lust, and ambition look ahead.

(*Screwtape Letters*, 76)
>   F. Burton Howard, "On Giving and Getting," *New Era*, Oct. 1985, 44

If it becomes irresistible . . . [t]he time for plucking out the right eye has arrived. (*The Weight of Glory*, 43–54)
>   Carolyn G. Owen, "Book Learning," *Ensign*, Sept. 1983, 9

We are half-hearted creatures, fooling about with drink and sex and ambition when infinite joy is offered us, like an ignorant child who wants to go on making mud pies in a slum because he cannot imagine what is meant by the offer of a holiday at the sea. . . . We are far too easily pleased. (*The Weight of Glory*, 29)
>   Marvin J. Ashton, "A Yearning for Home," *Ensign*, Nov. 1992, 21

When I was a youngster, all the progressive people were saying, "Why all this prudery? Let us treat sex just as we treat all other impulses." I was simple-minded enough to believe they meant what they said. I have since discovered that they meant exactly the opposite. They meant that sex was to be treated as no other impulse in our nature has ever been treated by civilized people. All others, we admit, have to be bridled . . . it is like having a morality in which stealing fruit is considered wrong—unless you steal nectarines. (*God in the Docks*, 319–20)
>   Neal A. Maxwell, "The Stern but Sweet Seventh Commandment," *New Era*,
>   June 1979, 36

You will say that these are very small sins; and doubtless, like all young tempters, you are anxious to be able to report spectacular wickedness. . . . It does not matter how small the sins are provided that their cumulative effect is to edge the man away from the Light and out into the Nothing. . . . Indeed, the safest road to Hell is the gradual one—the gentle slope, soft underfoot, without sudden turnings, without milestones, without signposts. (*Screwtape Letters*, 61)
>   James E. Faust, "The Forces That Will Save Us," *Ensign*, Jan. 2007, 4–9
>   James E. Faust, "Serving the Lord and Resisting the Devil," *Ensign*,
>   Sept. 1995, 2
>   James E. Faust, " 'The Great Imitator,' " *Ensign*, Nov. 1987
>   "FYI: For Your Information," *New Era*, Apr. 1983, 40
>   Dallin H. Oaks, "Gambling—Morally Wrong and Politically Unwise," *Ensign*,
>   June 1987, 69

TRIALS

I have seen great beauty of spirit in some who were great sufferers. I have seen men, for the most part, grow better not worse with advancing years, and I have seen the last illness produce treasures of fortitude and meekness from most unpromising subjects. (*The Problem of Pain*, 108–9)

Marvin J. Ashton, "Adversity and You," *Ensign*, Nov. 1980, 54

Our Father [in Heaven] refreshes us on the journey [through life] with some pleasant inns, but [he] will not encourage us to mistake them for home. (*The Problem of Pain*, 116)

Neal A. Maxwell, "Thanks Be to God," *Ensign*, July 1982, 51

The cross comes before the crown and tomorrow is a Monday morning! (*The Weight of Glory*, 14)

Neal A. Maxwell, " 'Shine As Lights in the World,' " *Ensign*, May 1983, 9

I must have some drug, and reading isn't a strong enough drug now. By writing it all down (all?—no: one thought in a hundred) I believe I get a little outside it. . . . In so far as this record was a defence against total collapse, a safety-valve, it has done some good. (*A Grief Observed*, 9–10)

Janet Brigham, "Discover Yourself: Keep a Journal," *Ensign*, Dec. 1980, 57

WORLDLINESS

A moderated religion is as good . . . as no religion at all. (*Screwtape Letters*, 46)

Elizabeth VanDenBerghe, "Religion and the Abundant Life," *Ensign*, Oct. 1994, 32

As St. Augustine says somewhere, "God wants to give us something, but cannot, because our hands are full—there's nowhere for Him to put it." Or as a friend of mine said, "We regard God as an airman regards his parachute; it's there for emergencies but he hopes he'll never have to use it." (*The Problem of Pain*, 95)

Valerie Holladay "Walk in the Wilderness," *Ensign*, July 1998, 46

Let him begin by treating the Patriotism or the Pacifism as a part of his religion. Then let him, under the influence of partisan spirit, come to regard it as the most important part. Then quietly and gradually nurse him on to the stage at which the religion becomes merely part of the "cause," in which Christianity is valued chiefly because of the excellent arguments it can produce in favour of the British war effort or of Pacifism. . . . Once you have made the World an end, and faith a means, you have almost won your man, and it makes very little difference what kind of worldly end he is pursuing. (*Screwtape Letters*, 34)

Dallin H. Oaks, "Powerful Ideas," *Ensign,* Nov. 1995, 25

The game is to have them all running about with fire extinguishers whenever there is a flood, and all crowding to that side of the boat which is already nearly gunwale under. (*Screwtape Letters,* 138)

Neal A. Maxwell, "Spiritual Ecology," *New Era,* Feb. 1975, 35
Neal A. Maxwell, "Remember How Merciful the Lord Hath Been," *Ensign,*
May 2004, 44

They wanted some corner in the universe of which they could say to God, "This is our business, not yours." But there is no such corner. (*The Problem of Pain,* 75)

Karl T. Haglund, "To Know Christ in This World," *New Era,* Apr. 1974, 7

Appendix B

ANDERSEN (1)

Jan D. Andersen, "Financial Freedom on Any Income," *Ensign,* Aug. 2006, 27–31

> Oh Adam's sons, how cleverly you defend yourselves against all that might do you good!
> *The Magician's Nephew,* 185

ASHTON (4)

Marvin J. Ashton, "Adversity and You," *Ensign,* Nov. 1980, 54

> I have seen great beauty of spirit in some who were great sufferers. I have seen men, for the most part, grow better not worse with advancing years, and I have seen the last illness produce treasures of fortitude and meekness from most unpromising subjects.
> *The Problem of Pain,* 108–9

Marvin J. Ashton, "Progress through Change," *Ensign,* Nov. 1979, 61

> Imagine yourself as a living house. God comes in to rebuild that house. At first, perhaps, you can understand what He is doing. He is getting the drains right and stopping the leaks in the roof and so on: you knew those jobs needed doing and so you are not surprised. But presently he starts knocking the house about in a way that hurts abominably and does not seem to make sense. What on earth is He up to? The explanation is that He is building quite a different house from the one you thought of—throwing out a new wing here, putting on an extra floor there, running up towers, making courtyards. You thought you were going to be made into a decent little cottage: but He is building a palace."
> *Mere Christianity,* 205

Marvin J. Ashton, "A Yearning for Home," *Ensign,* Nov 1992, 21

[Homemaking] is surely in reality the most important work in the world. What do ships, railways, mines, cars, and governments, etc. exist for except that people may be fed, warmed, and safe in their own homes? . . . We wage war in order to have peace, we work in order to have leisure, we produce food in order to eat it. So your job is the one for which all others exist.

The Collected Letters of CSL, vol. III, 62

Marvin J. Ashton, "A Yearning for Home," *Ensign,* Nov 1992, 21

We are half-hearted creatures, fooling about with drink and sex and ambition when infinite joy is offered us, like an ignorant child who wants to go on making mud pies in a slum because he cannot imagine what is meant by the offer of a holiday at the sea. . . . We are far too easily pleased.

The Weight of Glory, 29

BACKMAN (1)

Robert L. Backman, "Jesus the Christ," *Ensign,* Nov. 1991, 8

Christ says, "Give me All. I don't want so much of your time and so much of your money and so much of your work: I want You. I have not come to torment your natural self, but to kill it. No half-measures are any good. I don't want to cut off a branch here and a branch there, I want to have the whole tree down. . . Hand over the whole natural self, all the desires which you think innocent as well as the ones you think wicked—the whole outfit. I will give you a new self instead. In fact, I will give you Myself: my own will shall become yours."

Mere Christianity, 196–97

BENSON (2)

Ezra Taft Benson, "Beware of Pride," *Ensign,* May 1989, 4
Ezra Taft Benson, "The Faces of Pride," *New Era,* Oct. 2003, 40

Pride gets no pleasure out of having something, only out of having more of it than the next man . . . It is the comparison that makes you proud: the pleasure of being above the rest. Once the element of competition has gone, pride has gone.

Mere Christianity, 122

BRIGHAM (1)

Janet Brigham, "Discover Yourself: Keep a Journal," *Ensign,* Dec. 1980, 57

"What would H. herself think of this terrible little notebook to which I come back and back? Are these jottings morbid? . . . I not only live each endless day in grief, but live each day thinking about living each day in grief. Do these notes merely aggravate that side of it? Merely confirm the monotonous, tread-mill march of the mind round one subject? But what am I to do? I must have some drug, and reading isn't a strong enough drug now. By writing it all down (all?—no: one thought in a hundred) I believe I get a little outside it. . . . In so far as this record was a defence against total collapse, a safety-valve, it has done some good.

A Grief Observed, 9–10

BUNKER (2)

Gary L. Bunker, "Mocking Our Brother," *Ensign,* Apr. 1975, 36

A proud man is always looking down on things and people; and, of course, as long as you are looking down, you cannot see something that is above you.

Mere Christianity, 124

Gary L. Bunker, "Mocking Our Brother," *Ensign,* Apr. 1975, 36

People who believe themselves to be free, and indeed are free, from snobbery, and who read satires on snobbery with tranquil superiority, may be devoured by the desire in another form. It may be the very intensity of their desire to enter some quite different Ring which renders them immune from the allurements of high life. An invitation from a duchess would be very cold comfort to a man smarting under the sense of exclusion from some artistic or communist coterie. Poor man—it is not large, lighted rooms, or champagne, or even scandals about peers and Cabinet Ministers that he wants: it is the sacred little attic or studio, the heads bent together, the fog of tobacco smoke, and the delicious knowledge that we—we four or five all huddled beside this stove—are the people who know.

The Memorial Lecture at King's College, University of London, 1944

CARMACK (2)

John K. Carmack, "To My Single Friends," *Ensign,* March 1989, 27

Health is a great blessing, but the moment you make health one of your main, direct objects you start becoming a crank and imagining there is something wrong with you. You are only likely to get health provided you want other things more—food, games, work, fun open air.

Mere Christianity, 134

John K. Carmack, "Upheld by the Prayers of the Church," *Ensign,* May 1984, 75

> Imagine yourself as a living house. God comes in to rebuild that house. At first, perhaps, you can understand what He is doing. He is getting the drains right and stopping the leaks in the roof and so on: you knew those jobs needed doing and so you are not surprised. But presently he starts knocking the house about in a way that hurts abominably and does not seem to make sense. What on earth is He up to? The explanation is that He is building quite a different house from the one you thought of—throwing out a new wing here, putting on an extra floor there, running up towers, making courtyards. You thought you were going to be made into a decent little cottage: but He is building a palace.
>
> *Mere Christianity,* 205

CHRISTENSEN (2)

Joe J. Christensen, "Greed, Selfishness, and Overindulgence," *Ensign,* May 1999, 9

> I am afraid the only safe rule is to give more than we can spare . . . If our charities do not at all pinch or hamper us . . . they are too small. There ought to be things we should like to do and cannot do because our charitable expenditure excludes them.
>
> *Mere Christianity,* 86

Joe J. Christensen, "Pride—The 'Parent Sin,' " *Ensign,* June 1974, 24

> Pride leads to every other vice: it is the complete anti-God state of mind.
>
> *Mere Christianity,* 122

DOUGLAS (1)

Colin B. Douglas, "What I've Learned about Grace Since Coming Down from the Sycamore Tree," *Ensign,* Apr. 1989, 13

> If I am a field that contains nothing but grass-seed, I cannot produce wheat. Cutting the grass may keep it short: but I shall still produce grass and no wheat. If I want to produce wheat, the change must go deeper than the surface. I must be ploughed up and re-sown.
>
> *Mere Christianity,* 198

DUNN (1)

Paul H. Dunn, "We Have Been There All the Time," *Ensign,* Nov. 1977, 24

> Take care. It is so easy to break eggs without making omelettes.
>
> *Richard L. Evans' Quote Book,* 169

ELLSWORTH (1)

Homer S. Ellsworth, "The Love That Never Ceases to Be," *New Era,* June 1975, 14

> But I wonder whether people who ask God to interfere openly and directly in our world quite realise what it will be like when He does. When that happens, it is the end of the world. When the author comes on to the stage the play is over.
>
> *Mere Christianity,* 65

FAUST (7)

James E. Faust, "A Message to My Granddaughters: Becoming 'Great Women,'" *Ensign,* Sept. 1986, 16

James E. Faust, "How Near to the Angels," *Ensign,* May 1998, 95

> [Homemaking] is surely in reality the most important work in the world. What do ships, railways, mines, cars, and governments, etc. exist for except that people may be fed, warmed, and safe in their own homes? . . . We wage war in order to have peace, we work in order to have leisure, we produce food in order to eat it. So your job is the one for which all others exist.
>
> *The Collected Letters of CSL,* vol. III, 62

James E. Faust, "'The Great Imitator,'" *Ensign,* Nov. 1987, 33

James E. Faust, "Serving the Lord and Resisting the Devil," *Ensign,* Sept. 1995, 2

James E. Faust, "The Forces That Will Save Us," *Ensign,* Jan. 2007, 4–9

> You will say that these are very small sins; and doubtless, like all young tempters, you are anxious to be able to report spectacular wickedness. . . It does not matter how small the sins are provided that their cumulative effect is to edge the man away from the Light and out into the Nothing. . . Indeed, the safest road to Hell is the gradual one—the gentle slope, soft underfoot, without sudden turnings, without milestones, without signposts.
>
> *Screwtape Letters,* 61

James E. Faust, "'The Great Imitator,'" *Ensign,* Nov. 1987, 33

James E. Faust, "The Forces That Will Save Us," *Ensign,* Jan. 2007, 4–9

> A silly idea is current that good people do not know what temptation means. This is an obvious lie. Only those who try to resist temptation know how strong it is. . . . You find out the strength of a wind by trying to walk against it, not by lying down.
>
> *Mere Christianity,* 143

Funk (1)

Ruth H. Funk, " 'Come, Listen to a Prophet's Voice,' " *Ensign,* Nov. 1978, 106

> It is a serious thing to live in a society of possible gods and god-desses, to remember that the dullest and most uninteresting person you can talk to may one day be a creature which, if you saw it now, you would be strongly tempted to worship. It is in the light of these overwhelming possibilities, it is with the awe and the circumspec-tion proper to them, that we should conduct all our dealings with one another, all friendships, all loves, all play, all politics. There are no ordinary people. You have never talked to a mere mortal. Nations, cultures, arts, civilisations—these are mortal, and their life is to ours as the life of a gnat. But it is immortals whom we joke with, work with, marry, snub, and exploit . . . Your neighbor is the holiest object presented to your senses.
>
> *The Weight of Glory,* 45

FYI (4)

"FYI: For Your Information," *New Era,* Apr. 1983, 40

> You will say that these are very small sins; and doubtless, like all young tempters, you are anxious to be able to report spectacular wickedness . . . It does not matter how small the sins are provided that their cumulative effect is to edge the man away from the Light and out into the Nothing . . . Indeed, the safest road to Hell is the gradual one—the gentle slope, soft underfoot, without sudden turnings, without milestones, without signposts.
>
> *Screwtape Letters,* 61

"FYI: For Your Information," *New Era,* Nov. 1979, 38–41
"FYI: For Your Information," *New Era,* Mar. 1984, 40–43

> We have trained them to think of the Future as a promised land which favoured heroes attain—not as something which everyone reaches at the rate of sixty minutes an hour, whatever he does, who-ever he is.
>
> *Screwtape Letters,* 139

"FYI: For Your Information," *New Era,* Sept. 1981, 41–44

> It is a serious thing to live in a society of possible gods and goddesses, to remember that the dullest and most uninteresting person you can talk to may one day be a creature which, if you saw it now, you would be strongly tempted to worship. It is in the light of these overwhelming possibilities, it is with the awe and

the circumspection proper to them, that we should conduct all our dealings with one another, all friendships, all loves, all play, all politics. There are no ordinary people. You have never talked to a mere mortal. Nations, cultures, arts, civilisations—these are mortal, and their life is to ours as the life of a gnat. But it is immortals whom we joke with, work with, marry, snub, and exploit . . . Your neighbor is the holiest object presented to your senses.

The Weight of Glory, 45

GILLILAND (1)

Steve Gilliland, "The Psychological Case for Chastity," *Ensign,* July 1975, 54–58

I do not think that all who choose wrong roads perish; but their rescue consists in being put back on the right road. A wrong sum can be put right: but only by going back till you find the error and working it afresh from that point, never by simply going on. If we insist on keeping Hell (or even earth) we shall not see Heaven: If we accept Heaven we shall not be able to retain even the smallest and most intimate souvenirs of Hell."

The Great Divorce, viii-ix

GOASLIND (1)

Jack H. Goaslind, " 'Yagottawanna,' " *Ensign,* May 1991, 45
Jack H. Goaslind, " 'Yagottawanna,' " *New Era,* Feb. 1992, 4

The more often he feels without acting, the less he will be able ever to act, and, in the long run, the less he will be able to feel.

Screwtape Letters, 67

HAGLUND (1)

Karl T. Haglund, "To Know Christ in This World," *New Era,* Apr. 1974, 7

They wanted some corner in the universe of which they could say to God, "This is our business, not yours." But there is no such corner.

The Problem of Pain, 75

HOLLADAY (1)

Valerie Holladay, "Walk in the Wilderness," *Ensign,* July 1998, 46

As St. Augustine says somewhere, "God wants to give us something, but cannot, because our hands are full—there's nowhere for Him to put it." Or as a friend of mine said, "We regard God as an airman regards his parachute; it's there for emergencies but he hopes he'll never have to use it."

The Problem of Pain, 95

HOLFELTZ (1)

Heidi Holfeltz Parker, "Am I What I Appear to Be?" *Ensign,* Oct. 1991, 28

This Helper who will, in the long run, be satisfied with nothing less than absolute perfection, will also be delighted by the first feeble, stumbling effort you make tomorrow to do the simplest duty. As a great Christian writer (George MacDonald) pointed out, every father is pleased at the baby's first attempt to walk: no father would be satisfied with anything less than a firm free, manly walk in a grown-up son. In the same way he said, "God is easy to please, but hard to satisfy."

Mere Christianity, 202

HOLLAND (4)

Jeffrey R. Holland, " 'Sanctify Yourselves,' " *Ensign,* Nov. 2000, 38
Jeffrey R. Holland, "Be Ready and Worthy," *New Era,* May 2006, 2–5

Our leisure, even our play, is a matter of serious concern. [That is because] there is no neutral ground in the universe: every square inch, every split second, is claimed by God and counterclaimed by Satan.

Christian Reflections, 33

Jeffrey R. Holland, "'I Stand All Amazed,' " *Ensign,* Aug. 1986, 68

No man who will not forgive his neighbor, can believe that God is willing, yea wanting, to forgive him. . . . If God said, "I forgive you" to a man who hated his brother, and if (as impossible) that voice of forgiveness should reach the man, what would it mean to him? How would the man interpret it? Would it not mean to him, "You may go on hating. I do not mind it. You have had great provocation and are justified in your hate"?

No doubt God takes what wrong there is, and what provocation there is, into the account: but the more provocation, the more excuse that can be urged for the hate, the more reason . . . that the hater should [forgive, and] be delivered from the hell of his anger.

George MacDonald: An Anthology #13

Jeffrey R. Holland, "True or False," *New Era,* June 1995, 64

I am trying here to prevent anyone saying the really foolish thing that people often say about Him: [that is,] 'I'm ready to accept Jesus as a great moral teacher, but I don't accept His claim to be God.' That is the one thing we must not say.

Mere Christianity, 52

Howard (1)

F. Burton Howard, "On Giving and Getting," *New Era,* Oct. 1985, 44

> Hence nearly all vices are rooted in the Future. Gratitude looks to the past and love to the present; fear, avarice, lust and ambition look ahead.
>
> *Screwtape Letters,* 76

Jardine (1)

James S. and Jeanne N. Jardine, "Avoiding Unrighteous Dominion," *Ensign,* Sept. 1990, 62

> It is a serious thing to live in a society of possible gods and goddesses, to remember that the dullest and most uninteresting person you can talk to may one day be a creature which, if you saw it now, you would be strongly tempted to worship. It is in the light of these overwhelming possibilities, it is with the awe and the circumspection proper to them, that we should conduct all our dealings with one another, all friendships, all loves, all play, all politics.
>
> There are no ordinary people. You have never talked to a mere mortal. Nations, cultures, arts, civilisations—these are mortal, and their life is to ours as the life of a gnat. But it is immortals whom we joke with, work with, marry, snub, and exploit . . . Your neighbor is the holiest object presented to your senses.
>
> *The Weight of Glory,* 45

Jensen (1)

Marlin K. Jensen, " 'To Walk Humbly with Thy God,' " *Ensign,* May 2001, 9

> Your patient has become humble; have you drawn his attention to the fact?
>
> *Screwtape Letters,* 69

Kapp (3)

Ardeth G. Kapp, "Taking Upon Us His Name," *New Era,* Apr. 1982, 38

> The more often he feels without acting, the less he will be able ever to act, and, in the long run, the less he will be able to feel.
>
> *Screwtape Letters,* 67

Ardeth G. Kapp, " 'Will You Please Forgive Me? I Want to Be Honest,' " *New Era,* July 1976, 7

Ardeth G. Kapp, "What Have You to Declare?" *New Era,* Sept. 1985, 9

> I do not think that all who choose wrong roads perish; but their rescue consists in being put back on the right road. A wrong sum can be put right: but only by going back till you find the error and

working it afresh from that point, never by simply going on. If we insist on keeping Hell (or even earth) we shall not see Heaven: If we accept Heaven we shall not be able to retain even the smallest and most intimate souvenirs of Hell.

The Great Divorce, viii-ix

LARSEN (1)

Sharon G. Larsen, "Agency—A Blessing and a Burden," *Ensign,* Nov. 1999, 11

A silly idea is current that good people do not know what temptation means. This is an obvious lie. Only those who try to resist temptation know how strong it is. . . . You find out the strength of a wind by trying to walk against it, not by lying down.

Mere Christianity, 14

MARSH (1)

W. Jeffrey Marsh, " 'Remember How Merciful the Lord Hath Been,' " *Ensign,* Apr. 2000, 18

There are only two kinds of people in the end: those who say to God, 'Thy will be done,' and those to whom God says, in the end, 'Thy will be done.' All that are in Hell, choose it. Without that self-choice there could be no Hell. No soul that seriously and constantly desires joy will ever miss it. Those who seek find. To those who knock it is opened.

The Great Divorce, 75

MAXWELL (19)

Neal A. Maxwell, "The Pathway of Discipleship," *Ensign,* Sept. 1998, 7

It is a serious thing to live in a society of possible gods and goddesses, to remember that the dullest and most uninteresting person you can talk to may one day be a creature which, if you saw it now, you would be strongly tempted to worship. It is in the light of these overwhelming possibilities, it is with the awe and the circumspection proper to them, that we should conduct all our dealings with one another, all friendships, all loves, all play, all politics. There are no ordinary people. You have never talked to a mere mortal. Nations, cultures, arts, civilisations—these are mortal, and their life is to ours as the life of a gnat. But it is immortals whom we joke with, work with, marry, snub, and exploit. . . Your neighbor is the holiest object presented to your senses.

The Weight of Glory, 45

Neal A. Maxwell, "The Stern but Sweet Seventh Commandment," *New Era*, June 1979, 36

Neal A. Maxwell, "What Is Real Love and Happiness?" *New Era,* June 1992, 4

A Christian would be wise to avoid, where he decently can, any meeting with people who are bullies, lascivious, cruel, dishonest, spiteful and so forth. Not because we are "too good" for them. In a sense because we are not good enough. We are not good enough to cope with all the temptations, not clever enough to cope with all the problems, which an evening spent in such society produces. The temptation is to condone, to connive at; by our words, looks and laughter, "to consent."

Reflections on the Psalms, 71

Neal A. Maxwell, " 'Settle This in Your Hearts,' " *Ensign,* Nov. 1992, 65

You've begun to suspect that those moments, of which the memory is now so ravishing, weren't at the time quite so wonderful as they now seem. You're right. The weren't. Each great experience is "a whisper Which Memory will warehouse as a shout." (From an unpublished poem by Owen Barfield.)

The Quotable Lewis, 425

Neal A. Maxwell, "Insights from My Life," *Ensign,* Aug. 2000, 7. From a talk given on 12 January 1999 at BYU.

We are bidden to "put on Christ," to become like God. That is, whether we like it or not, God intends to give us what we need, not what we now think we want.

The Problem of Pain, 46–47
The Weight of Glory, 45

Neal A. Maxwell, "The Stern but Sweet Seventh Commandment," *New Era,* June 1979, 36

When I was a youngster, all the progressive people were saying, "Why all this prudery? Let us treat sex just as we treat all other impulses." I was simple-minded enough to believe they meant what they said. I have since discovered that they meant exactly the opposite. They meant that sex was to be treated as no other impulse in our nature has ever been treated by civilized people. All others, we admit, have to be bridled . . . it is like having a morality in which stealing fruit is considered wrong—unless you steal nectarines.

God in the Dock, 319–20

Neal A. Maxwell, "Jesus, the Perfect Mentor," *Ensign,* Feb. 2001, 8. From a talk given at a CES fireside at BYU on 6 February 2000.

> But the Humanitarian theory wants simply to abolish Justice and substitute Mercy for it. . . . Mercy, detached from Justice, grows unmerciful. That is the important paradox. As there are plants which will flourish only in mountain soil, so it appears that Mercy will flower only when it grows in the crannies of the rock of Justice: transplanted to the marshlands of mere Humanitarianism, it becomes a man-eating weed, all the more dangerous because it is still called by the same name as the mountain variety.
>
> *God in the Dock,* 294

Neal A. Maxwell, "Spiritual Ecology," *New Era,* Feb. 1975, 35
Neal A. Maxwell, "Remember How Merciful the Lord Hath Been," *Ensign,* May 2004, 44

> The game is to have them all running about with fire extinguishers whenever there is a flood, and all crowding to that side of the boat which is already nearly gunwale under.
>
> *Screwtape Letters,* 38

Neal A. Maxwell, "On the Straight and Narrow Way," *New Era,* Aug. 1971, 42

> No amount of falls will really undo us if we keep picking ourselves up each time. We shall of course be very muddy and tattered children by the time we reach home. But the bathrooms are all ready, the towels put out, and the clean clothes in the airing cupboard.
>
> *Collected Letters of CSL,* vol. II, 507

Neal A. Maxwell, "The Prohibitive Costs of a Value-free Society," *Ensign,* Oct 1978, 52–55

> The love of our neighbor is the only door out of the dungeon of self.
>
> *George MacDonald: An Anthology,* 27

> You say the materialist universe is "ugly." I wonder how you discerned that? If you are really a product of a materialistic universe, how is it you don't feel at home there? Do fish complain of the sea for being wet? . . . Notice how we are perpetually surprised by time. (How time flies! Fancy John being grown up and married? I can hardly believe it!') In heaven's name why? Unless, indeed, there is something in us which is not temporal.
>
> *Collected Letters of CSL,* vol. III, 76

Neal A. Maxwell, "The Value of Home Life," *Ensign,* Feb. 1972, 4

> Imagine yourself as a living house. God comes in to rebuild that house. At first, perhaps, you can understand what He is doing. He is getting the drains right and stopping the leaks in the roof and so on: you knew those jobs needed doing and so you are not surprised. But presently he starts knocking the house about in a way that hurts abominably and does not seem to make sense. What on earth is He up to? The explanation is that He is building quite a different house from the one you thought of—throwing out a new wing here, putting on an extra floor there, running up towers, making courtyards. You thought you were going to be made into a decent little cottage: but He is building a palace.
>
> *Mere Christianity,* 205

Neal A. Maxwell, "Talk of the Month," *New Era,* May 1971, 28

> I believe in Christianity as I believe the sun has risen, not only because I see it, but because, by it, I see everything else.
>
> *The Weight of Glory,* "Is Theology Poetry?"

Neal A. Maxwell, "Thanks Be to God," *Ensign,* July 1982, 51

> Our Father [in Heaven] refreshes us on the journey [through life] with some pleasant inns, but [he] will not encourage us to mistake them for home.
>
> *The Problem of Pain,* 116

Neal A. Maxwell, " 'Shine As Lights in the World,' " *Ensign,* May 1983, 9

> The cross comes before the crown and tomorrow is a Monday morning!
>
> *The Weight of Glory,* 14

Neal A. Maxwell, "Enduring Well," *Ensign,* Apr. 1997, 7

> A silly idea is current that good people do not know what temptation means. This is an obvious lie. Only those who try to resist temptation know how strong it is. . . . You find out the strength of a wind by trying to walk against it, not by lying down.
>
> *Mere Christianity,* 143

Neal A. Maxwell, "Eternalism vs. Secularism," *Ensign,* Oct. 1974, 69

> What Satan put into the heads of our remote ancestors was the idea that they could . . . invent some sort of happiness for themselves outside God, apart from God. And out of that hopeless attempt has come nearly all that we call human history—money, poverty, ambition, war, prostitution, classes, empires, slavery—the long

terrible story of man trying to find something other than God
which will make him happy.

It seems to start up all right and runs a few years, and then it
breaks down. They are trying to run it on the wrong juice. That is
what Satan has done to us humans.

Mere Christianity, 49–50

Neal A. Maxwell, "Premortality, a Glorious Reality," *Ensign*, Nov. 1985, 5

We cannot mingle with the splendours we see. But all the leaves
of the New Testament are rustling with the rumour that it will not
always be so.

The Weight of Glory, 33

"Lord of the narrow gate and the needle's eye"
(Complete Poem)

The Apologist's Evening Prayer

From all my lame defeats and oh! much more
From all the victories that I seemed to score;
From cleverness shot forth on Thy behalf
At which, while angels weep, the audience laugh;
From all my proofs of Thy divinity,
Thou, who wouldst give no sign, deliver me.
Thoughts are but coins. Let me not trust, instead
of Thee, their thin-worn image of Thy head.
From all my thoughts, even from my thoughts of Thee,
O thou fair Silence, fall, and set me free.
Lord of the narrow gate and needle's eye,
Take from me all my trumpery lest I die.

Poems, 129

MILLER (1)

Dale E. Miller, "Bringing Peace and Healing to Your Soul," *Ensign*, Nov.
2004, 12–14

He has infinite attention to spare for each one of us. He does not
have to deal with us in the mass. You are as much alone with Him
as if you were the only being He had ever created. When Christ
died, He died for you individually just as much as if you had been
the only man [or woman] in the world.

Mere Christianity, 205–6

MILLET (2)

Robert L. Millet, "Putting off the Natural Man," *Ensign,* Jun. 1992, 7–9 and reprinted in *Ensign,* Aug. 2000, 7–9

> This world is a great sculptor's shop. We are the statues and there is a rumour going round the shop that some of us are some day going to come to life.
>
> *Mere Christianity,* 159

MORRISON (1)

Alexander B. Morrison, "'I Am the Resurrection and the Life,' " *Ensign,* Apr. 1995, 36

> The command Be ye perfect is not idealistic gas. Nor is it a command to do the impossible. He [Christ] is going to make us creatures that can obey that command. He said (in the Bible) that we were 'Gods' and He is going to make good His words. If we let Him—for we can prevent Him, if we choose—He will make the feeblest and filthiest of us into a god or goddess, a dazzling, radiant, immortal creature, pulsating all through with such energy and joy and wisdom and love as we cannot now imagine . . . The process will be long and in parts very painful; but that is what we are in for. Nothing less. He meant what He said.
>
> *Mere Christianity,* 205–6

OAKS (3)

Dallin H. Oaks, Tough Topics: Are You Saved by Grace or Works?" *New Era,* March 2005, 38

> [C. S. Lewis, compared grace and works to the blades of a pair of scissors.] I have no right really to speak on such a difficult question, but it does seem to me like asking which blade in a pair of scissors is the most necessary.
>
> *Mere Christianity,* 148

Dallin H. Oaks, "Gambling—Morally Wrong and Politically Unwise," *Ensign,* June 1987, 69

> You will say that these are very small sins; and doubtless, like all young tempters, you are anxious to be able to report spectacular wickedness. . . It does not matter how small the sins are provided that their cumulative effect is to edge the man away from the Light and out into the Nothing . . . Indeed, the safest road to Hell is the gradual one—the gentle slope, soft underfoot, without sudden turnings, without milestones, without signposts.
>
> *Screwtape Letters,* 61

Dallin H. Oaks, "Powerful Ideas," *Ensign*, Nov. 1995, 25

Let him begin by treating the Patriotism or the Pacifism as a part of his religion. Then let him, under the influence of partisan spirit, come to regard it as the most important part. Then quietly and gradually nurse him on to the stage at which the religion becomes merely part of the 'cause,' in which Christianity is valued chiefly because of the excellent arguments it can produce in favour of the British war effort or of Pacifism. . . . Once you have made the World an end, and faith a means, you have almost won your man, and it makes very little difference what kind of worldly end he is pursuing.

Screwtape Letters, 34

Owen (1)

Carolyn G. Owen, "Book Learning," *Ensign*, Sept. 1983, 9

If it becomes irresistible . . . [t]he time for plucking out the right eye has arrived.

The Weight of Glory, 43

Pinegar (1)

Rex D. Pinegar, "Faith—The Force of Life," *Ensign,* Nov. 1982, 24

The great thing, if one can, is to stop regarding all the unpleasant things as interruptions of one's "own," or "real" life. The truth is of course that what one calls the interruptions are precisely one's real life— the life God is sending one day by day.

They Stand Together, 499

Rawlins (1)

Peter B. Rawlins, "A Serious Look at Humor," *New Era,* Aug. 1974, 48

If prolonged, the habit of Flippancy builds up around a man the finest armour-plating against [God] that I know . . . It is a thousand miles from joy: it deadens, instead of sharpening, the intellect; and it excites no affection between those who practise it.

Screwtape Letters, 56

Reynolds (1)

Anna K. Reynolds, "Always Nice," *New Era,* Jan. 1997, 11

"Do what you will, there is going to be some benevolence, as well as some malice, in your patient's soul. The great thing is to direct the malice to his immediate neighbours whom he meets every day and to thrust his benevolence out to the remote circumference, to

people he does not know. The malice thus becomes wholly real and the benevolence largely imaginary."
Screwtape Letters, 28

SMITH (1)

Barbara B. Smith, "Women for the Latter Day," *Ensign,* Nov. 1979, 107

[Homemaking] is surely in reality the most important work in the world. What do ships, railways, mines, cars, and governments, etc. exist for except that people may be fed, warmed, and safe in their own homes? . . . We wage war in order to have peace, we work in order to have leisure, we produce food in order to eat it. So your job is the one for which all others exist.
Collected Letters of CSL, vol. III, 62

SORENSEN (1)

Mollie Hobaugh Sorensen, "Learning Faith," *Ensign,* March 1985, 24

Faith may mean (a) A settled intellectual assent. In that sense faith (or "belief") in God hardly differs from faith in the uniformity of Nature or in the consciousness of other people. This is what, I think, has sometimes been called . . . "rational" or "intellectual" or "carnal" faith. It may also mean (b) A trust, or confidence, in the God whose existence is thus assented to. This involves an attitude of the will. It is more like our confidence in a friend.
A Mind Awake, 137

TANNER (1)

Susan W. Tanner, "Daughters of Heavenly Father," *Ensign,* May 2007, 106–9

It is a serious thing to live in a society of possible gods and goddesses, to remember that the dullest and most uninteresting person you can talk to may one day be a creature which, if you saw it now, you would be strongly tempted to worship. It is in the light of these overwhelming possibilities, it is with the awe and the circumspection proper to them, that we should conduct all our dealings with one another, all friendships, all loves, all play, all politics. There are no ordinary people. You have never talked to a mere mortal. Nations, cultures, arts, civilisations—these are mortal, and their life is to ours as the life of a gnat. But it is immortals whom we joke with, work with, marry, snub, and exploit . . . Your neighbor is the holiest object presented to your senses.
The Weight of Glory, 45

Teh (1)

Michael J. Teh, "Out of Small Things," *Ensign,* Nov. 2007, 35–37

> Do what you will, there is going to be some benevolence, as well as some malice, in your patient's soul. The great thing is to direct the malice to his immediate neighbours whom he meets every day and to thrust his benevolence out to the remote circumference, to people he does not know. The malice thus becomes wholly real and the benevolence largely imaginary.
> *Screwtape Letters,* 28

Vandenaker (1)

Pam Wilson Vandenaker, " 'Stripped of Envy,' " *Ensign,* March 1999, 19

> It is the comparison that makes you proud: the pleasure of being above the rest.
> *Mere Christianity,* 122

VanDenBerghe (1)

Elizabeth VanDenBerghe, "Religion and the Abundant Life," *Ensign,* Oct. 1994, 32

> A moderated religion is as good . . . as no religion at all.
> *Screwtape Letters,* 46

Visiting Teaching Message (1)

"Living within Our Means," *Ensign,* Feb. 2001, 69

> I am afraid the only safe rule is to give more than we can spare. . . . If our charities do not at all pinch or hamper us, . . . they are too small. There ought to be things we should like to do and cannot do because our charitable expenditure excludes them.
> *Mere Christianity,* 86

Wood (1)

Robert S. Wood, "The Quest for Spiritual Knowledge," *Ensign,* June 2007, 30–35

> Oh Adam's sons, how cleverly you defend yourselves against all that might do you good!
> *The Magician's Nephew,* 185

Appendix C

GOSPEL DOCTRINE MANUALS

Book of Mormon
> Lesson 22: "Have Ye Received His Image in Your Countenances?" *Book of Mormon Gospel Doctrine Teacher's Manual*, 98

Doctrine & Covenants
> Lesson 7: "The First Principles and Ordinances of the Gospel," *Doctrine and Covenants and Church History Gospel Doctrine Teacher's Manual*, 35
> Lesson 10: "This Is My Voice unto All," *Doctrine and Covenants and Church History Gospel Doctrine Teacher's Manual*, 53

Old Testament
> Lesson 23: "The Lord Be Between Thee and Me For Ever," *Old Testament Gospel Doctrine Teacher's Manual*, 107
> Lesson 26: "King Solomon: Man of Wisdom, Man of Foolishness," *Old Testament Gospel Doctrine Teacher's Manual*, 123
> Lesson 31: "Happy Is the Man That Findeth Wisdom," *Old Testament Gospel Doctrine Teacher's Manual*, 151

Aaronic Priesthood
> Lesson 42: Being Humble and Teachable," *Aaronic Priesthood Manual 3*, 170
> Lesson 48: Preparing to Serve through Education," *Aaronic Priesthood Manual 3*, 192

Primary

Lesson 38: Peace among the Nephites," *Primary 4: Book of Mormon*, 135

OTHER RESOURCES

Our Heritage: A Brief History of The Church of Jesus Christ of Latter-day Saints, Chapter Eleven: "The Present-day Church," 133

Gospel Art Picture 518: Ezra Taft Benson, President of the Church 1985-1994

Appendix D

EARLY POETRY

Spirits in Bondage: A Cycle of Lyrics (1919, under the pseudonym Clive Hamilton)

Dymer (1926, published under the pseudonym Clive Hamilton)

FICTION WORKS

The Pilgrim's Regress (1933)
Out of the Silent Planet (1938)
Screwtape Letters (1942)
Perelandra (1943)
That Hideous Strength (1945)
The Great Divorce (1945)
The Lion, the Witch and the Wardrobe (1950)
Prince Caspian (1951)
The Voyage of the *Dawn Treader* (1952)
The Silver Chair (1953)
The Horse and His Boy (1954)
The Magician's Nephew (1955)
The Last Battle (1956)
Till We Have Faces (1956)

CHRISTIAN NONFICTION WORKS

The Problem of Pain (1940)
The Abolition of Man (1943)
Miracles (1947)
Mere Christianity (1952)
Reflections on the Psalms (1958)

The Four Loves (1960)
The World's Last Night and Other Essays (1960)
Letters to Malcolm: Chiefly on Prayer (1964)
The Weight of Glory (1949, and an expanded version in 1980)

LITERARY CRITICISM AND ACADEMIC WORKS
The Allegory of Love (1936)
Rehabilitations and other Essays (1939)
The Personal Heresy (1939)
A Preface to Paradise Lost (1942)
English Literature in the Sixteenth Century Excluding Drama (1954)
Studies in Words (1960)
An Experiment in Criticism (1961)
Autobiographical Works
Surprised by Joy (1955)
A Grief Observed (1961, published under the pseudonym N.W. Clerk)

WORKS PUBLISHED POSTHUMOUSLY
Poems (1964)
The Discarded Image: An Introduction to Medieval and Renaissance Literature (1964)
Of Other Worlds: Essays and Stories (1966)
On Stories: And Other Essays on Literature (1966)
Studies in Medieval and Renaissance Literature (1966)
Letters to an American Lady (1967)
God in the Dock: Essays on Theology and Ethics (1970)
The Dark Tower and Other Stories (1977)
They Stand Together: The Letters of C. S. Lewis to Arthur Greeves, 1914-1963 (1979)
Boxen: The Imaginary World of the Young C. S. Lewis (1985)
C. S. Lewis' Letters to Children (1985)
All My Road Before Me: The Diary of C. S. Lewis, 1922–1927 (1991)
Letters of C. S. Lewis (1994)
Collected Letters of C. S. Letters, volumes I, II, III (2000–)

It is important to keep in mind that many of Lewis's essays and poems have been assembled and re-assembled in a variety of collections or different books. Be aware that a "new" collection may have the same works that are in other books, just with a new title.

Bibliography

Baehr, Ted and James Baehr. *Narnia Beckons: C. S. Lewis's The Lion, The Witch, and the Wardrobe and Beyond.* Nashville, TN: Broadman & Holman Publishers, 2005.

Ballard, Melvin J. *Crusader of Righteousness.* Salt Lake City: Bookcraft, 1966.

Bonhoeffer, Dietrich. *The Cost of Discipleship,* London: SMC Press LTD, 1959.

Bonhoeffer, Dietrich. *Letters and Papers from Prison.* London: SCM Press LTD, 1967.

Carpenter, Humphrey (editor). *The Letters of J. R. R. Tolkien.* Boston: Houghton Mifflin, 1981.

Carpenter, Humphrey. *The Inklings: C. S. Lewis, J. R. R. Tolkien, Charles Williams, and Their Friends.* New York: Ballantine Books, 1981.

Covey, Stephen R. *The 8th Habit: From Effectiveness to Greatness.* New York: Simon & Schuster, 2005.

Covey, Stephen R. *The Seven Habits of Highly Effective People.* Free Press, 1990.

Davidman, Joy. "The Longest Way Round" in *These Found the Way: Thirteen Converts to Protestant Christianity.* David Wesley Soper, ed. Philadelphia: Westminster Press, 1951.

Dorsett, Lyle W., and Marjorie Lamp Mead, eds. *C. S. Lewis Letters to Children.* New York: Macmillan, 1985.

Duriez, Colin. *A Field Guide to Narnia*. Downers Grove, IL: InterVarsity Press, 2004.

Duriez, Colin. *Tolkien and C. S. Lewis: The Gift of Friendship*. Mahwah, NJ: HiddenSpring, 2003.

Gilbert, Douglas and Clyde S. Kilby. *C. S. Lewis: Images of His World*. Grand Rapids, MI: Wm. B. Eerdmans, 2005.

Gormley, Beatrice. *C. S. Lewis: The Man Behind Narnia*. Grand Rapids, MI: Eerdmans Books for Young Readers, 1998.

Green, Roger Lancelyn and Walter Hooper. *C. S. Lewis: A Biography* (revised edition). New York: HarperCollins, 2002.

Hafen, Bruce C. *A Disciple's Life: The Biography of Neal A. Maxwell*. Salt Lake City, UT: Deseret Book, 2002.

Jacobs, Alan. *The Narnian: The Life and Imagination of C. S. Lewis*. San Francisco, CA: HarperSanFrancisco, 2005.

Kimball, Wm. Clayton. "The Christian Commitment: C. S. Lewis and the Defense of Doctrine," *BYU Studies,* vol. 12, 1971–1972.

King, Arthur Henry. *Abundance of the Heart*. Salt Lake City, UT: Bookcraft, 1986.

Lewis, C. S., *All My Road Before Me: The Diary of C. S. Lewis, 1922–1927*. Lightning Source Inc., 2002.

———. *Boxen: The Imaginary World of Young C. S. Lewis*. Hooper, Walter ed. London: Collins, 1985.

———. *Christian Reflections*. Grand Rapids, MI: Wm. B. Eerdmans Publishing, 1994.

———. *The Chronicles of Narnia*. New York: HarperCollins, 2005.

———. *Chronicles of Narnia* (box set) including *The Magician's Nephew; The Lion, the Witch and the Wardrobe; The Horse and his Boy; Prince Caspian; The Voyage of the* Dawn Treader; *The Silver Chair;* and *The Last Battle*. New York: Harper Trophy, 1983.

———. *The Collected Letters of C. S. Lewis,* vol. 1, *Family Letters 1905–1931*. San Francisco, CA: HarperSanFrancisco, 2004.

———. *The Collected Letters of C. S. Lewis,* vol. 2, *Books, Broadcasts, and the War, 1931–1949*. Hooper, Walter ed. San Francisco: HarperSanFrancisco, 2004.

———. *The Collected Letters of C. S. Lewis,* vol. 3. Hooper, Walter, ed. San Francisco: HarperSanFrancisco, 2007.

———. *The Four Loves.* New York: Harcourt Brace, Inc., 1960

———. *The Great Divorce.* New York: Touchstone Book, 1996.

———. *George MacDonald: An Anthology.* New York: HarperCollins, 2001.

———. *God in the Dock,* Grand Rapids, MI: Eerdmans Publishing, 1994.

———. *Letters of C. S. Lewis.* Warren Lewis, ed. London: Geoffrey Bles Ltd., 1952.

———. *Letters to Malcolm: Chiefly on Prayer.* New York: Harcourt, Brace & Javanovich. 1964.

———. *Mere Christianity.* New York: HarperCollins, 2001.

———. *A Mind Awake: An Anthology of C. S. Lewis.* New York: Harcourt, 2001.

———. *The Pilgrim's Regress: An Allegorical Apology for Christianity Reason and Romanticism.* New York: Bantam Books, 1981.

———. *Poems.* Orlando, FL: Harcourt, 1992

———. *Preface to Paradise Lost* [1942]. Oxford: Oxford University Press, 1979.

———. *The Problem of Pain.* New York: HarperCollins, 2001.

———. *Reflections on the Psalms.* Orlando, FL: Harcourt Brace, 1986.

———. *Screwtape Letters.* New York: HarperCollins, 2001.

———. *Surprised by Joy: The Shape of My Early Life.* London: HarperCollins, 2002.

———. *They Stand Together: The Letters of C. S. Lewis to Arthur Greeves.* ed. Walter Hooper, London: Collins, 1979.

———. *Till We Have Faces: A Myth Retold.* New York: Harcourt, Brace and Co., 1957.

———. *The Weight of Glory: And Other Addresses.* New York: HarperCollins, 2001.

MacDonald, George. *The Princess and the Goblin* [1872], London: Puffin, 1996.

Martindale, Wayne and Jerry Root, eds. *The Quotable Lewis*. Tyndale House Publishers, 1989.

Millet, Robert L. and Andrew C. Skinner, ed. *C. S. Lewis: The Man and His Message*. Salt Lake City, UT: Bookcraft, 1999.

Milton, John. *English Minor Poems; Paradise Lost; Samson Agonistes; Areopagitica*. Chicago: Encyclopaedia Britannica, Inc., 1952.

Peck, Dr. Scott M. *The Road Less Traveled*. New York: Simon Schuster, 1978.

Potok, Chaim. *The Chosen*. Ballantine Books, 1982.

Sanders, N. K. ed. *The Epic of Gilgamesh: An English Version with an Introduction*. New York, New York: Penguin Books, 1972.

Sayer, George. *Jack: A Life of C. S. Lewis*. Wheaton, IL: Crossway Books, 1994.

Schultz, Jeffrey D. and John G. West, Jr., (editors). *The C. S. Lewis Readers' Encyclopedia*. Grand Rapids, MI: Zondervan Publishing House, 1998.

Tolstoy, Leo. *How I Came to Believe*. Christchurch, New Zealand: The Free Age Press, 1901.

Wagner, Richard. *C. S. Lewis and Narnia for Dummies*. Hoboken, NJ: Wiley Publishing, Inc., 2005.

Wilcox, S. Michael. *Of Lions, Dragons and Turkish Delight: C. S. Lewis for Latter-Day Saints*. Salt Lake City, UT: Deseret Book, 2008

Williams, Charles. *The Place of the Lion*. London: Pellegrini & Cudahy, 1933.

Wilson, A. N. *C. S. Lewis: A Biography*. New York: Norton, 1990.

Woodger, Mary Jane. "The Words of C. S. Lewis as used by the Leadership of the LDS Church." The Cumberland River Lamppost (website dedicated to insights into C. S. Lewis.) http://www.crlamppost.org/woodger.htm.

Wordsworth, William. "Desideria," *The Oxford Book of Verse*, 1919.

Wordsworth, William. *William Wordsworth's The Prelude with a Selection from the Shorter Poems, the Sonnets, The Recluse, and The Excursion and Three Essays on The Art of Poetry*. Edited with an introduction by Carlos Baker. New York: Holt, Rinehart and Winston, Inc. 1954.

About the Authors

Marianna Edwards Richardson enjoys studying and reading about a variety of topics. She received a bachelor of arts degree from Brigham Young University in English literature, with a minor in art history. She also earned a master's degree from Johns Hopkins University in special education and a doctorate in education from Seattle Pacific University in curriculum and development. She has been the assistant to the editor for the past three years of the American Counseling Association journal, Counseling and Values. But the most important work she does is caring for her large family. She has been married to Stephen D. Richardson for over thirty years, and they have twelve wonderful children and eight grandchildren (with more to come). Marianna and Steve have recently been called to preside over the Sao Paulo South, Brazil Mission for The Church of Jesus Christ of Latter-day Saints.

After receiving her bachelor of arts degree in English from Brigham Young University, Christine married Greg Thackeray. She has seven beautiful children—five boys and two girls. Christine has had a diverse career. She has developed a phonics program used in private schools, authored several brochures and articles, worked as a technical writer, and completed many studies as a professional marketing analyst. She has also served as the Relief Society president, Young Women president, activities chairman, stake librarian, nursery coordinator, seminary teacher, and a zillion other callings.

During that time, she always maintained a love of writing. She assisted her sister Dr. Marianna Richardson with editing and research on *Alfred Edersheim: Jewish Scholar for the Mormon Prophets* in the *Spiritual Context—LDS Perspectives* series. Christine is also the author of *The Crayon Messages.*

0 26575 51937 2

236